'*Partition Voices* is probably the clos memorial ... Heartfelt and beautifu *Literary Review*

'An original and moving collection of testimonies from Sikhs, Muslims and Hindus about the transformative era of India's partition' *Guardian*, 50 Best Books of the Summer

'*Partition Voices* is important because Puri does not flinch as she dissects the tumultuous event, never shying away from the trauma' Nikesh Shukla, *Observer*

'This collection reveals how families are still impacted generations down the line and is a crucial read for understanding South Asian history' *Cosmopolitan*

'Confronts the difficult truths at the heart of Britain's shared – and often ignored – shared history with South Asia' *Stylist*, Best non-fiction books of 2019

'A poignant account of unbearable journeys and unimaginable loss' *Elle* (India)

'A powerful and timely work. Kavita Puri coaxes often unspeakable and unspoken memories from a time of unimaginable trauma. A must-read for those interested in the fault lines in today's geopolitics' Anita Anand

'An important book ... Changed the way I see the world' Jeremy Vine

'This is moving, thought-provoking stuff' *BBC History Magazine*, Book of the Month

'Puri's excellent book is a welcome antidote to British amnesia over its colonial legacy. Partition is not just an Indian story, it is a British one too' *All About History*

'*Partition Voices* is a unique and powerful work, combining a depth of oral history with the most sensitive storytelling. It is one of a kind in a burgeoning field of partition studies because it places Britain so squarely as a site in which partition has continued to unfurl since 1947, prising it loose from its subcontinental moorings. This was an inspired move and one that inspired many to engage with the past' Professor Joya Chatterji, Centre of South Asia Studies, Cambridge University

'*Partition Voices* is remarkable in its reach and power – a book of witness and testimony that should have the widest readership possible' Edmund de Waal

'*Partition Voices* takes its place alongside other valuable books on partition such as Khushwant Singh's *Train to Pakistan* and Urvashi Butalia's *The Other Side of Silence*' Amit Roy, *Eastern Eye*

'With a masterful mix of history, biography and contemporary reportage, Puri crafts a fascinating account of the living memory of South Asia in modern Britain. This book brings together a rich and disparate chronicle of lives ripped apart and remade by the trauma of partition, and deftly traces how the diaspora of post-colonial India and Pakistan helped to reshape the UK' Tristram Hunt

'The most extraordinary book. The prologue already had me in tears. The book of 2019 that opened my eyes more than anything else. Seminal work, beautifully told' Emily Maitlis

'Powerful, compelling and heartbreaking – these are stories of division and conflict rescued from the past that offer valuable lessons for the present' Sarfraz Manzoor

'An intimate, moving and important book by a daughter of partition. Kavita Puri reveals untold stories of those who lived through one of the most violent political earthquakes of the twentieth century. These are stories we need to hear' Kirsty Wark

'Through *Partition Voices*, Puri discusses the human cost of division and brings to the forefront the unheard voices of South Asia that are imperative in understanding the national British history' Priyanka Mehta, *Asian Voice*

'An amazing, deeply moving book' Dan Snow

'An important document of those turbulent times – raw and unbiased' Bishwanath Ghosh, *The Hindu*

'An important milestone in the partition project because it ascribes importance to the British-South Asian dynamic and talks about the shared history of these two nations without villainising or glorifying either side ... and looks at their accounts as human experiences, wrapped in love, hate, betrayal, revenge, loss and longing' Anodya Mishra, *Scroll*

'An evocative book that leaves you breathless with its human predicament and gives voice to stories long held prisoner to silence ... Nobody has ever brought out the stories of South Asians now settled in the United Kingdom ... Kudos to Kavita Puri for documenting partition's lasting legacy in Britain, an irony in itself. It is a unique book, one that lives with you long after the stories end' Ziya Us Salam, *Frontline Magazine*

'A valuable collection ... Puri's book makes us aware of the necessity of social histories ... and its (Britain's) unfinished

business of adding the partition chapter to school syllabi'
Rumina Sethi, *Tribune* (India)

'This is an important, interesting and elegantly written book ... Their voices are not just a part of South Asian history, but also British history' Ramesh Thakur, *Australian Journal of International Affairs*

KAVITA PURI is an award-winning BBC journalist, executive producer and broadcaster. She presents documentaries on Radio 4 and the World Service including *The Inquiry*. She devised, wrote and presented the landmark three-part series *Partition Voices* for Radio 4, which won the Royal Historical Society's Radio and Podcast Award and its overall Public History Prize. It is currently being adapted for the stage by the Donmar Warehouse in London with Tara Theatre. She is the creator and presenter of the critically acclaimed Radio 4 series *Three Pounds in My Pocket*, which charts the social history of British South Asians from the post-war years. It is on its fifth series. While editor of *Our World*, its foreign documentaries were recognised with awards including the Royal Television Society and the Foreign Press Association. She worked for many years at *Newsnight* and studied Law at Cambridge University.

PARTITION VOICES

Untold British Stories

KAVITA PURI

BLOOMSBURY PUBLISHING

LONDON · OXFORD · NEW YORK · NEW DELHI · SYDNEY

BLOOMSBURY PUBLISHING
Bloomsbury Publishing Plc
50 Bedford Square, London, WC1B 3DP, UK
29 Earlsfort Terrace, Dublin 2, Ireland

BLOOMSBURY, BLOOMSBURY PUBLISHING and the Diana logo are trademarks of
Bloomsbury Publishing Plc

First published in Great Britain 2019
This edition published 2022

A catalogue record for this book is available from the British Library

Library of Congress Cataloguing-in-Publication data has been applied for

ISBN: HB: 978-1-4088-9907-6; TPB: 978-1-4088-9908-3; PB: 978-1-4088-9898-7;
ANNIVERSARY EDITION PB: 978-1-5266-3840-3; EBOOK: 978-1-4088-9906-9

2 4 6 8 10 9 7 5 3

Typeset by Newgen KnowledgeWorks Pvt. Ltd., Chennai, India
Printed and bound in Great Britain by CPI Group (UK) Ltd, Croydon CR0 4YY

MIX
Paper | Supporting
responsible forestry
FSC
www.sc.org FSC® C171272

To find out more about our authors and books visit www.bloomsbury.com
and sign up for our newsletters

For my father
and my girls

Contents

CONTENTS

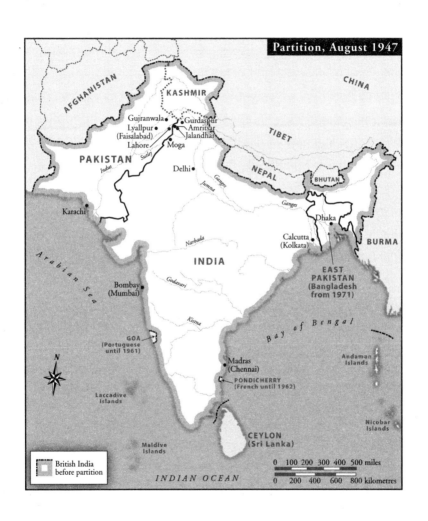

Partition, August 1947

Prologue

The place where heaven meets earth is the River Ganges. Ma Ganges.

It is the place we carried my father on his final journey.

He requested his ashes to be taken to the sacred place of Haridwar, where his siblings, parents and ancestors before him had been scattered. It is where the Ganges enters North India for the first time, and is one of the holiest places in Hinduism.

We took him to a peaceful corner of the river, our small group settling together on the ghat, a flight of steps leading down to the waters. A priest was found. A shaven-headed man in his saffron robes laid down a blue embroidered carpet for us to sit cross-legged on and in practised fashion took my father's ashes out of the urn onto a stainless-steel plate. To be confronted with your parent in such a stark way – face to face with their remains – is difficult and surreal. It is what the physical life is reduced to for observant Hindus like my father. Before me, it was not the texture of ashes as I expected but small grey granules of what must have been his bones.

My father had been cremated near his home in Kent in his favourite suit and shoes, along with fresh rose petals, camphor, ghee and tulsi leaves, which we had sprinkled on his body during the final rites. The last thing we had done before we closed the casket was to place a picture in it, drawn days earlier by my younger daughter. I wondered where that drawing – covered in hearts – was in my father's remains in front of me, on that cold stainless-steel plate.

The priest began his Sanskrit prayers. Following his instructions, at intervals, we threw marigolds and rose petals on the ashes, while the priest sprinkled holy Ganges water. When the time came, my sister and I took the plate and ashes, which were now almost covered by flowers, to the river's edge, where the waters lapped our bare feet, as we held our father for the last time.

The priest gave the final prayer as we stood:

> Om Asatho Maa Sad Gamaya.
> Thamaso Maa Jyotir Gamaya.
> Mrithyur Maa Amritham Gamaya.
> Om Shanti, Shanti, Shanti.
>
> From untruth lead us to Truth.
> From darkness lead us to Light.
> From death lead us to Immortality.
> Om Peace, Peace, Peace.

Holding each side of the plate, my sister and I gently tipped it towards the river, allowing my father's ashes to slowly descend into the waters, the waters which had carried his forefathers' ashes. We watched as his remains swirled in the Ganges, drifting away from us.

Gradually, our small group returned to the steps. As we sat down it was still possible to differentiate his ashes from the waters. My aunt sang an Indian bhajan, a devotional song, 'Tare Nahi Tare'. 'What Has to Happen Has to Happen'.

We sat in silence as the sun began to set. The light was starting to grow hazy and the first pink of the sky was emerging. Another family next to us were committing a loved one to the waters. On the opposite bank an elderly woman in a fuchsia-coloured sari had been sitting statue-like, watching the waters all the time we had been there. I looked carefully to check she was real. A young boy, his trousers hitched to his waist, was knee-deep in the river, panning for metals, hoping no doubt to make some quick money. And my father, his remains now disappeared from view, finally in the place he wanted to be, where sins are cleansed and Hindus believe immortality is to be found.

Born in Lahore, Pakistan, an adult life lived in England, he now rests somewhere along the most sacred and blessed river in India.

Introduction

My father broke his silence after nearly seventy years to speak about what happened to him during the partition of British India. Seventy years. A lifetime. He never returned to the place of his birth, the place he was forced to leave, the place he always hoped to see again.

Ravi Datt Puri was born in 1935 in Lahore, Punjab, in British Colonial India. When he finally told me about the things he had witnessed as a twelve-year-old boy, I understood why he had kept his silence.

The division of British India in August 1947 along religious lines into the independent states of Hindu-majority India and Muslim-majority Pakistan sparked the largest mass migration – outside war and famine – the world has ever seen. In the months around partition, at least 10 million people were on the move: Muslims to West and East Pakistan (now Bangladesh), and Hindus and Sikhs in the opposite direction. It was accompanied by unimaginable violence on all sides.

The human cost of dividing British India was staggering. Up to a million people were killed in communal fighting and tens of thousands of women raped and abducted. The statistics are hard to comprehend, and yet behind every single number is a story. It is one of centuries of coexistence shattered, homes left hurriedly, painful goodbyes, epic journeys and traumatic loss. Not just loss of a house or possessions but a loss more profound. Loss of a homeland. This grief is still tangible seventy years on.

For centuries, across the Indian subcontinent, Muslims, Hindus and Sikhs had lived together largely peacefully with shared traditions and culture, observing each other's religious festivals. Ties to land could be stronger than ties to religion. Of course there were differences: there was no intermarriage; most Hindus did not eat at the homes of Muslims; there were socio-economic disparities and cases of localised outbreaks of communal trouble. But mostly, these people of different faiths had lived together, side by side, for generations.

However, religious identity in the decades leading up to partition was becoming stronger. Many argue that it was stoked by the British policies of divide and rule. There were two visions of independence emerging and they were becoming politicised along religious lines. The Congress Party led by Jawaharlal Nehru wanted India to remain united after the British left. By 1940, the leader of the Muslim League, Mohammed Ali Jinnah (formerly a member of the Congress Party) was bitterly at odds with Nehru. He felt India's almost 100 million Muslims, a quarter of the population, would be marginalised by the Hindu majority in an independent India. He demanded safeguards – even a separate homeland for India's Muslims.

Once partition became an inevitability, the situation deteriorated: incidents of communal violence increased and it was no longer safe to be a minority in the newly independent states. But there were acts of humanity amidst the horror too. The one partition story that my father did share while I was growing up was of how his Hindu family had been protected by Muslim neighbours; how they had warned my grandfather to leave, as they could no longer shield them from the mobs. My father's family left for India, and Lahore is now part of a country which is India's enemy. Yet it is also the birthplace of my Hindu father.

This is not a story from lands far away. It has direct relevance to British citizens, once subjects of the British Raj. Dotted across homes in Britain are some of those who, like my father, witnessed the traumatic birth of two nations and who subsequently migrated to post-war Britain. Yet their partition story is barely known.

South Asians have a long history in Britain pre-dating partition. There had been a flow of princes, students, lawyers, ayahs, servants and seamen stretching back to the seventeenth century and earlier. But post-war migration assumed a volume and scale not seen before. And there is a link between partition and migration to Britain. The areas of India and Pakistan which were most disrupted by partition were major contributors to the emigrant flow to Britain. 'As the British tide retreated from India,' writes the Oxford academic Ceri Peach, 'the Indian, Pakistani and then Bangladeshi waters disturbed by partition lapped into Britain.'[1]

Crucially these were also groups of people who, prior to partition, had networks and connections to particular parts of Britain, such as the Sylhetis, who were merchant seamen, or Punjabis in the Indian Army. Some had direct links via chain migration, where family members or neighbours had already settled. For others, without direct contacts, Britain was, as Professor Joya Chatterji describes, 'the imaginative world they could go to in times of trouble', where they sensed possibilities. Whether it was as a lascar (sailor) who had once sailed into London, or a sepoy, an Indian soldier who had served under British command, they would rely on 'that resource of memory'[2] to find their way to Britain. In the years after independence, they came in their thousands to build a new life.

South Asian migration started seriously in the 1950s. The British Nationality Act of 1948 conferred British citizenship on all who lived in the Empire and Commonwealth: a citizen of India or Pakistan was a citizen of the United Kingdom. Legal limitations only began to be placed on this principle in 1962. Their migration was essentially related to British post-war labour shortages in the mills, factories, foundries and public services. People came in search of a better life and settled in towns and cities across Britain.

So the end of Empire caused huge migration flows not only on the Indian subcontinent but it also explains the presence of many of the main groups of South Asians in Britain. Our histories – those of the Indian subcontinent and Britain – are profoundly interconnected. We need to understand this past. It is impossible to grasp the make-up of contemporary Britain without understanding Britain's place in India leading up to 1947, and how it extracted itself. The children and grandchildren of partition are touched by the legacy today, here in the UK, in their thousands.

And yet, like my father, so many of the survivors who now live in Britain have kept quiet for decades about their experiences. They are only beginning to speak about what they witnessed seventy years ago. Why now? Journalists love a peg on which to hook a story, and an anniversary is always a popular one. But the seventieth anniversary of the partition of India was genuinely a watershed moment. The coverage was more extensive, thorough and sensitive than before. There were prime-time programmes explaining the history;

debates about the legacy; and young British South Asians tracing their past.

During the summer of 2017, I presented a series on BBC Radio 4 called *Partition Voices*, talking to survivors. There was a sense when I was interviewing them that this could be the last big anniversary for many. It was their final chance to speak about that time. I think the South Asian diaspora are curious about their history and how it informs their identity, some of whom are now powerful commissioners in TV, radio and the newspapers. They understood what this anniversary meant. And, as Brexit looms, and the country questions its international standing, I do wonder if there is some increased curiosity too about why and how Britain's retreat from Empire happened.

I also think that finally and perhaps most importantly we are asking and listening in a way we have not done before. And it's about time. A public space has been finally created where British people can discuss their partition stories. Oral history projects are now taking place across Britain in local areas, and there is a hunger to record these stories. It's a race against time.

I was giving a public lecture at Cambridge University recently about the Radio 4 series, and a member of the audience, a retired professor at the university, came up to me afterwards. He told me that he had escaped from Delhi to Lahore when he was six years old, and how he still remembers seeing heads floating down the river. 'I can never forget that,' he told me. The deputy master from the same college, who had been standing nearby and overheard the conversation, was dumbfounded. The two men had known each other professionally for thirty years, and yet he had no idea of the childhood experiences of his colleague. 'I shall never look at him in the same way, knowing what he has been through,' he said. It is only when the space is created for people to speak that their stories will be told and heard, their experiences understood.

There has been silence not only here, but also in India and Pakistan. But there are different reasons for the silence in Britain. Many who came to the UK in the years after partition were just getting on with their lives, fighting different battles to be accepted in this country. There was no time to dwell on the past. And, unlike back home, they were fighting together, whether it was within the Indian Workers' Association to improve their working lives, or in the fight against racism. Here they were all lumped together as 'Asians' – no one saw the differences so exposed on the Indian subcontinent. And their children and grandchildren knew little of life back home, so why speak of it?

There was an institutional silence too – no one talks of partition. There are no memorials or museums in Britain. Few people talk about the end of Empire, or even Empire, so there was no open, safe arena to discuss it. And for my father, it was simple: why would you want to burden your children?

But there is another reason too, as Dr Anindya Raychaudhuri of the University of St Andrews says: 'For all the unimaginable horrors of the Holocaust, in most cases it was easy to distinguish between bad from good. In partition it just isn't.' How do families cope with partition, he goes on to ask, when your father, your uncle, may well have killed their neighbour? Therefore no one discusses it. Many partition memories are bound up in shame and honour, 'and it becomes difficult to disentangle all of that and think about what made us do what we did'. In partition there were perpetrators on all sides, and obviously within families. How do you begin to talk about that? So, for all these many reasons, there was silence.[3]

Yet even silence can be noisy. There were signs: the political unity between different South Asian groups in Britain, already fragile, started to dissipate from the early 1980s. Prejudices persisted: 'Don't marry a Muslim; don't marry a Hindu.' But there were other, different clues too. When old friends got together they would discuss and reminisce about 'home', but 'home' may not be the country their extended family now lived in on the Indian subcontinent. 'Home' could be the so-called 'enemy' state. For the subsequent generations in Britain, where identity is complex, they wanted to know and understand. And it was during the marking of the seventieth anniversary that many of these conversations began. The silence was breaking.

In Britain these stories matter – for second- and third-generation British South Asians it explains their history: who they are, and, in the context of Empire, why they are here in Britain. Those who contacted the production team or commented after the *Partition Voices* series was broadcast said they had no idea of the details of partition, and it prompted many questions and discussions amongst family members. One woman got in touch to say her eighty-nine-year-old father, upon hearing the radio programmes, shared his 'awful' story for the first time. They had been a catalyst for him to talk about his own painful experiences. She added 'how he kept quiet for seventy years I do not know'.

The range of accounts serve another crucial function. It is important that not just the stories of violence by one particular side or one religious group are heard, which could foster further division within the South Asian community today. As one woman who wrote to the BBC said, she had no idea that all sides suffered.

British audiences of the seventieth anniversary coverage, writing on social media, said they were shocked they did not know about this piece of twentieth-century history which involved their country. They were shocked too at the scale and fervour of the violence, as well as the shambolic nature of the British departure. The British population needs to understand their British South Asian compatriots, why they are here, and the connection with Empire. This is part of British history – not niche British South Asian history. It is just as important to study Empire, and how it ended, as learning about the Tudors and the Norman Conquest in school. It explains why Britain looks the way it does today. How our histories are connected.

Some partition survivors who made Britain their home have already died, and so there is a very real sense of chasing shadows; an urgency in collecting these memories. The production team started looking for testimonies in late 2016, contacting organisations and local papers across the country, academics and faith leaders; we did call-outs for contributors on the BBC Asian Network and on independent Indian language radio. Once we started looking we realised the stories were all around us. I felt like I had been walking among ghosts my whole life.

On meeting potential interviewees so many of them would say: Why would you want to hear my story? I am not Nehru, Jinnah or Gandhi. And yet what would emerge would be the most epic story, fit for a Hollywood movie. Many survivors were voicing what had happened to them, seven decades earlier, for the very first time. A pause, a facial expression, even the way words were spoken, it was as if the contributors were those young people again, seeing, living through that moment in time. Children and grandchildren may have known fragments of stories; some would sit in the corner of the room during the interviews, silently crying, unaware of the true extent of their relative's experiences.

Nick was one. His dad, Iftkahr, made an extraordinary journey from Delhi to Lahore. Iftkahr's memories were buried so deep he still had nightmares that he was being killed. Nick, who is only just learning of Iftkahr's experiences, compared his father's generation to those who lived through the First World War and how they found it difficult to speak of the enormity of what they went through. 'They just bottle everything up. I think it's hard to offload that.'[4] The partition anniversary was months apart from the centenary of the battle of Passchendaele. Many relatives commemorating this moment told how the former soldiers never spoke of what happened, and what they saw. Now that generation has passed it is too late. At least we still have time to speak to partition survivors.

I hope those I interviewed felt better for talking and documenting their experiences for posterity, though I cannot be sure. So many had lost their homes and their homeland, but they were at least able to take some small comfort in the knowledge that their stories would not be lost too. As they approached the end of their days, they choose to speak out. They recounted their experiences without reticence. They wanted them heard and recorded and respected. But their tales were often told with profound sadness, and at times I could see the telling of it took its toll. For many, however, the sharing of memories of pre-partition British India was their way of ensuring that future generations will never be able to deny that Hindus and Sikhs once lived alongside Muslims in places as diverse as Lahore, Karachi and Amritsar in relatively peaceful coexistence.

There are others among us who remember that time too; the British who lived under the Raj, who can still speak broken Urdu and Hindi, and who remember the dying days of Empire and still have deep sentiments for India. One of the great revelations for me was the affection held by those who remember the time of British India. Of course their experiences were very different from those of South Asians but no less important to acknowledge and record. Some were brought up learning Hindi from their ayah or nanny, and felt like foreigners when their families came back to Britain after independence. Colleagues and friends began to mention that their parents or grandparents were born and lived in India. Maybe they too felt they finally had permission to speak.

This generation of Brits and those South Asians who migrated here are our connection to a time which we will soon only know about from history books. Some will say how can we, seventy years on, trust these accounts. Urvashi Butalia, whose groundbreaking work on oral history in India in the 1990s, raised this question at the beginning of her seminal book *The Other Side of Silence*. 'I have come to believe that there is no way we can begin to understand what partition was about unless we look at how people remember it,' she says. 'I do not wish here to carry out a literal exercise of partition and then attempt to penetrate their narrative for its underlying facts to arrive at an approximation of some kind of "truth". Instead I wish to look at the memories themselves – even if they are shifting, changing, unreliable.'⁵ She quotes James Young, a Holocaust historian, who says, 'whatever "fictions" emerge from the survivors' accounts are not deviations from the truth but are part of truth in that particular version'. Dr Anindya Raychaudhuri, who has gathered an impressive number of testimonies for his academic study in the UK and in India, Pakistan and Bangladesh agrees, saying: 'I'm not that interested in veracity. I'm more interested in finding out what work it [memory] is doing in the present.'[6]

We would and should never attempt to understand the Holocaust, for example, without hearing testimony from survivors. These first-hand accounts are just one important facet of the partition story. And seventy years on, memories may have changed or shifted over time. Precise dates are unremembered. Yet all the contributors spoke with surprising clarity about events from so many decades ago – at times speaking so vividly that I felt transported back in time. Not every detail can be completely verified; however *how* these experiences are remembered today is also relevant.

Their stories also show the connections, not just the differences between people, which can be missing from other more formal documentary evidence on the subject, or when partition is viewed through the prism of 'high politics'. The lived story – the minutiae of it tell you so much: the loves lost; the cricket bat left behind; the longing to see – just once – the tree climbed as a child; and the search for the best friend from a land fled, decades back.

My team and I spoke to many people in the course of our research who had lived through that period, more than we were able to record. I have conducted interviews across the United Kingdom, to form a picture of life in colonial India and its aftermath. I began with my father, who finally agreed to tell me what I had long hoped he would. I also spoke to people from across British India: Muslims, Sikhs and Hindus, as well as Parsees and Anglo-Indians. I interviewed colonial Brits – from officers in the British Indian Army to the children of Scottish jute manufacturers. Kashmir and the conflict which ensued in the months after partition is beyond the scope of this work. This book gathers testimonies of British South Asians and the British under the Raj. It is far from definitive; perhaps no collection can ever be. It tells the story – through human voices – of one of the most tumultuous events of the twentieth century. It documents the individual eyewitness accounts of the dying days of Empire and the trauma of partition, as well as its continuing legacy for British South Asian descendants today.

I suppose my obsession with capturing these stories of partition was driven by my search to understand my father's past, which is my past too. Even though the drawing of the borders happened seventy years ago, in lands far away, the consequences are ever-present. I could always feel it, I just knew I could not broach it. This is a sentiment I now know I share with other children and grandchildren of survivors. Through my interviews with them I have realised that I am not the only one trying to piece together the fragments of the past through clues left in the present. It is a pursuit happening in households across Britain.

Some of the people whose homes I visited were lucky enough to have kept physical mementos from their childhood days in British India: a brick from their home, stones from the earth of long-fled lands, jars containing dust from homelands past. It was all they had left. These objects assumed the status of an ancestral home.

Partition, though filled with horror in so many ways, is also a story about love. Love of your land. A land that was lived on for centuries by a family's ancestors, where traditions and cultures, even language were shared, a time where religious differences were mostly tolerated. One Hindu interviewee, originally from Karachi who was forced to flee to India, told me that when he returned for a visit, decades later, he took dust from the ground, kissed it, and touched it to his forehead. He said he felt like he was returning to his mother, whom he had not seen for a very long time.

This is not an academic offering of partition, nor is it written to apportion blame. I could have chosen any one individual's story to write about, but I wanted to bring these voices together, in a collection, to show how wide and deep these personal experiences, and the legacy of it, are in our country. We pass people with these stories everyday on the street, sitting on the bus. They may even be our neighbours. The book is based on original interviews for the BBC Radio 4 series – many of which are now in the British Library Sound Archive and viewable online[7] – and on subsequent interviews with each contributor and independent research. I often write in the vernacular that the interviewees speak. After decades of silence *Partition Voices* will finally tell their stories, in the way that they remember them.

PART I

END OF EMPIRE

I

End of Empire

The British formally arrived in India in the 1600s, establishing trading posts under the British East India Company. The company eventually came to rule large areas of India with its own enormous private armies largely made up of Indians. In 1857 regiments of the company's army rebelled against the British authorities. After a brutal war on both sides, the following year India came under direct British rule. This began the period known as the Raj, meaning 'to rule' or 'kingdom' in Hindi.

In response to British rule and growing nationalist feeling, the Indian National Congress was founded in 1885 as an 'all-India', broadly secular political party. Just over twenty years later, the Muslim League was established as a grouping to support the interests of Indian Muslim minorities, but the party did not gain widespread support until some decades later. Identity politics began to grow stronger in the early twentieth century – exacerbated by the British decision to grant separate electorates to different religious communities, so that they were represented by their 'own' politicians.

In 1940 the Muslim League's ambitious Lahore Resolution (also known as the Pakistan Resolution) pressed for the creation of not one but several Muslim-majority states when the British left India, possibly within an Indian federation. The Indian National Congress wanted a strong, centralised and united India once the British left. Two distinct visions of independence were emerging – the calls for freedom made louder by the demands of the Second World War. India's economy was geared not towards its people but the Allied war effort. Two-and-a-half million Indian soldiers served. Over 24,000 would be killed and another 64,000 wounded.[1] While the Allies were fighting a war in the name of democracy and freedom, nationalist calls for independence for India were not being heeded by the British government, led by Winston Churchill.

Churchill had always insisted that he would not preside over the dismemberment of the British Empire. However, his successor as prime minister, Clement Attlee, concluded that in the context of the huge challenges of domestic post-war reconstruction, Britain's grip on India was too weak to be sustained.[2] Frankly, Britain could no longer afford to stay.[3] It was also a recognition of the strength of the Indian nationalist movements. Colonial policy, for the first time, came to be preoccupied with determining the best way to exit India. The pressing question in Indian politics was no longer about getting the British to leave, but what India's future would look like once the British rulers were gone.

The endgame of Empire was conducted against rising communal violence that began with the Great Calcutta Killing of August 1946 following Jinnah's call to the League's followers for Direct Action Day, in support of the demand for Pakistan. The day descended into violence, leaving thousands of Muslims and Hindus dead.[4] It was followed by the first major series of partition massacres that spanned the northern part of the Indian subcontinent in which both Muslims and Hindus were victims and perpetrators. The killing spread to Noakhali, Tippera, Bihar and the Meerut district near Garhmukteshwar, close to Delhi. By March of the following year, the Punjab quarters of most of its major cities were burning: Lahore, Amritsar, Jalandhar, Rawalpindi, Multan and Sialkot.[5]

In these places, violence was orchestrated with political purpose and organisation resulting in near civil war conditions in parts of North India, where religion stridently demanded political allegiance. This was something entirely separate from traditional communal violence: it was related to the end of Empire and sought to humiliate and even destroy those of the 'other' religion.[6] However, there were still large areas of British India, particularly the south, which remained peaceful.

Lord Louis Mountbatten, appointed Viceroy of India in March 1947, arrived with a mandate to transfer power by June 1948. All British efforts to preserve India's unity while offering safeguards for the Muslim minority failed. Amid the communal disaster unfolding, on 3 June 1947 Lord Mountbatten announced the plan for partition, which was reluctantly agreed to by Jawaharlal Nehru of the Indian National Congress. In an address to the people of India, Mountbatten said: 'There can be no question of coercing any large areas in which one community has a majority to live against their will under a Government in which another community has a majority – and the only alternative to coercion is partition.'[7] He shocked everyone by announcing that he was bringing forward the date of transition to 15 August 1947. The reason for this haste is still not clear – perhaps to inject urgency into the negotiations, maybe simply to cut and run, or a decision taken as the violence in northern India was intensifying.[8] But 'the rush was Mountbatten's, and his alone'.[9]

Partition would now be undertaken in a breathtaking ten weeks.

The provinces of Bengal and Punjab were to be divided along religious lines. There were differences between the religious communities, but these populations were intertwined through culture, language and tradition, its people having lived side by side for centuries.[10] Their unpicking, at such speed, was a virtually impossible task.

August 1947 heralded a new world order. It was the beginning of the end of the British Empire. The country's mighty rule over nearly 400 million people on the Indian subcontinent was over. But it was to close shambolically, hastily and catastrophically.

2

The Days of the Raj

Pamela Dowley-Wise is standing amidst the stables of her riding school in Surrey, pointing out her favourite filly. Aged ninety-one, she still goes out on a horse. Pamela has a youthful air, a no-nonsense walk, and perfectly coiffured white hair. Her cut-glass manner of speech is one rarely heard today. She is so formidable I am almost struck speechless as she shouts orders to the riding staff as she walks around majestically surveying her animals.

To ride is to breathe for Pamela. She tells me she was virtually brought up on a horse. The summers of her youth were spent in a missionary guest house in Kalimpong, a quiet and picturesque hill station in West Bengal on the banks of the Teesta river at the foothills of the Himalayas. It was there, in the charge of her nanny, that she learned to ride. The only way to get around was on horseback, and, even before she could walk, Pamela would travel in a basket saddle on a little pony.

Those summers in Kalimpong before the monsoons arrived were wild. Pamela describes the missionary house as being 'in the jungle'. At night she would hear the laughing hyenas and their strange howl: 'It scared the life out of us.' In the morning she would wake and see leopard footprints in the flower beds just below her bedroom window, remnants of their night prowls. But it is the view from the house that has stayed with her all those decades later. The flowered garden of the missionary house fell down thousands of feet to the plains below, 'and you could look across and see the sun setting and rising on the mountain range of the Himalayas'.[1]

The British Raj had been established since 1858, but there had been a British presence in India for centuries. The East India Company brought Pamela's forefathers to the subcontinent in the 1800s. Arthur Arnold Dowley-Wise, her father, was born in Calcutta (now Kolkata). As a young man, aged nineteen, he signed up to serve as an officer with the 92nd Prince of Wales Punjab Regiment. During the First World War he was sent to Mesopotamia and then to Palestine, where he entered Jerusalem in 1917 with General Allenby. Back in India he met his wife, Ivy, a governess, and the newly-weds embarked on life together in the princely state of Bhopal. By this time Arthur had left the army and was now in charge of the state troops for the Nawab Sultan Jehan Begum. It was a lavish but lonely life, as there were virtually no other Europeans, and the British at this stage rarely socialised with Indians. The couple soon moved to Calcutta, a thriving business centre where many of the wealthiest British families lived. In 1926 their first child, Pamela, was born.

Pamela spent little time with her parents, as was the custom. She would see her mother most evenings, all dressed up, when she came to give Pamela a goodnight kiss before heading off to their club with her father, where they socialised with other Europeans. It was Bessie Smith, her 'coloured' Anglo-Indian nanny, assisted by her ayah, Mary, who raised her. Pamela shows me her beloved Mary in a sepia photograph: a Tamil from Madras (now Chennai), with dark skin, dressed in a spotless white sari. Mary was expected to do the more menial tasks in relation to her charge. She bathed and dressed young Pamela, and would sit by her cot humming her to sleep while gently patting her back.

Pamela still recalls her favourite activity with a youthful twinkle in her eye – trips to the gardens of Calcutta's Victoria Memorial. Holding Bessie and Mary's hands she would walk the few minutes from the Dowley-Wises' residence to the memorial which stood on the Maidan, a big open space by the banks of the Hooghly river. At the gardens they would meet her little friends. Pamela would bring one of her 'exotic' dolls, pushing it in an extravagant pram, a gift from her father from his time in New York. Pamela always had a large taffeta bow in her hair, just as her mother requested. The nannies, dressed in starched white uniforms, white stockings and white shoes, would sit together and gossip – the glow of the memorial's white Makrana marble, and the shadow of the imposing design, so reminiscent of the Taj Mahal in the background.

Pamela's life was completely separate from the local population. 'We had nothing to do with any Indians. They never visited our home.' As was usual in the British Raj, the only interaction for a female of her class was with their Indian servants. Pamela's parents had eight, including a butler, a watchman, a sweeper, a bearer who served the table, and a mali, the gardener who maintained the grounds. Those that worked in the house wore white jackets and trousers, with broad red-and-gold webbing cummerbunds round their waists and white turbans. 'I do remember the table always being beautifully laid with silver service and crystal finger bowls with flowers floating in them. And it was very elegant dining. But that was just the way of life during the days of the Raj.'

There were Muslim and Hindu servants who lived happily enough together at the bottom of the Dowley-Wise's garden in the godowns, large brick-built rooms, with their families. 'So it was a lovely set-up really.' They were supplied with a daily ration of rice and dhal. Pamela would watch their children, who were the same age, playing together, but there was never any question she would join them.

At the age of seven, Pamela's life changed. She was sent to St Mary's Convent in Darjeeling for nine months to prepare for life in boarding school in England. It is the memory of bathtime that remains with her. Before bed, small tin tubs were laid out in a long line on the stone floor of a draughty room. Tibetan ayahs from mountain villages would carry heated water in kerosene cans slung from poles across their shoulders, which they emptied into the tubs. The schoolgirls in turn would be bathed. Pamela recalls the rough texture of the ayah's 'horny hands as they scrubbed my tender body and the strange smell they exuded ... Their long black hair was plaited and smeared with the grease obtained from the yaks.' Pamela muses that these 'simple peasant women' probably performed these tasks for a pittance, just a few annas a day. But even though they were poor they all wore heavy gold earrings, large beaten gold studs in their noses and turquoise beads and silver discs strung round their necks.

In 1935 Pamela and her younger sister were dispatched to England. Her parents left them at the platform in Malvern, Worcestershire, where the girls were briskly put in the charge of a teacher. It was to be five years until Pamela saw India or her parents again. Even school holidays were spent in the company of 'miserable' teachers. She has no pleasant memories of that time. Pamela was always getting into trouble, and having to endure cruel punishments. Her younger sister was terribly homesick and suffered at the hands of bullies. Pamela had no photos of her parents, just the memory of standing on the platform, the whistle blowing, hurriedly hugging and kissing her mother and father, and then the image of the train steaming away. Separation and parting was the norm for so many British families in India. Pamela admits that she forgot much about her parents. 'I used to write to them, my dear Mummy and Daddy, but it meant nothing whatsoever. I got no news from them. I didn't know what to tell them.'

Pamela was in England at the start of the war, during the Blitz in 1940. During a rare visit from her mother, they received a cable from her father telling them to come back to India immediately for their safety. Her mother promptly purchased tickets on a very 'prestigious' Sunderland flying boat. But it was becoming too dangerous to fly, so they changed plans and travelled to Southampton, securing one of the few first-class cabins aboard the passenger liner RMS *Orion*, which had been recently requisitioned as a troop ship. Mrs Dowley-Wise and daughters shared their travels with around 5,000 Allied soldiers. It was a hazardous voyage, where they were chased by U-boats. It took many weeks, via the Cape of Good Hope, until they finally reached India. As the ship was being tied up, a large military brass band with men resplendent in red and gold uniforms and white helmets greeted the troops with 'Land of Hope and Glory', and 'There'll Always be an England'. Pamela, overcome with emotion, sang along with the soldiers.

Arthur Wise, Pamela's father, was waiting in the crowds, but she had no idea what he looked like. It had been five years since she had seen him. Her mother told her to look out for a man with blond hair, dressed in a light suit. Pamela saw a man waving at them from the bottom of the gangplank, and, not looking where he was going, tripping over a bollard. The troops all roared with laughter, to Pamela's embarrassment. And that was Pamela's reintroduction to her father. When she arrived at their new home in Calcutta – number 9 Harrington Street – the servants lined up to welcome the women with garlands of marigolds and sweet-smelling jasmine flowers, which they placed round their necks. 'I felt totally at home when I got there. They were so polite.'

Pamela was not only re-acquainting herself with her parents, but also India, and its ways. It was so crowded, so noisy, so hot, she recalls. Life was very different from England. A cow and its calf would come to the house daily and be milked at the back door. Pamela's mother would watch the process, ensuring the milk was not topped up with water. Harrington Street was in a good part of town, but even here there was a communal rubbish heap nearby which served as a home for an Indian family – an elderly couple, their son, his wife and their children. One night the young mother gave birth on the pavement. While Pamela was walking her dog, Thatch, she saw the newborn lying on a rag as people walked by, while the family continued scavenging the detritus of the privileged, to eat their leftovers or to sell on scraps. 'We would send food out to them, although they would never ask for any. They just appeared to accept this as their way of life, which could never be changed, because they were born into the lowest caste of Indians.'

In the years after her arrival Pamela valued her independence: 'I could go anywhere in Calcutta totally on my own, totally in safety, totally respected.' She would bicycle even in heavy traffic. On seeing her approach on her Raleigh bike, the locals would part for her to come through. 'We felt honoured, actually.' As the heat in the city was stifling during the summer months, she often went to the Calcutta Swimming Club to keep cool. At home she played tennis in the garden or would flick through her mother's magazines, *Vogue* and *Needlewoman*. The women of the house would choose the latest designs which the durzi, dressmaker, would copy on a small Singer sewing machine as she sat on the veranda, using fabrics from the New Market.

By this time Pamela says she had learned enough Urdu to communicate with the local population. However, there was still no meaningful interaction, even with the servants in her own home: 'When you spoke to them you did not carry on conversations with them at all. You just asked them to bring you something or take something.'

It was not long before she was packed off to school again. This time Pamela and her sister were sent away to South India, a boarding school called Hebron in Coonoor. But her education was interrupted once again. On 5 April 1942, Easter Sunday, the Japanese task force which had attacked Pearl Harbor in December bombed Colombo in Ceylon (Sri Lanka) and threatened an attack on Madras, which could have cut off the south of India from Calcutta in the north, preventing the return home of Pamela and her sister. The girls were hastily evacuated to Dehradun in the foothills of the Himalayas in the United Provinces, where their mother had rented a large house. Pamela was eventually to complete her education at a finishing school in Simla, the summer capital of British India, known to most Britishers as the place to escape the heat of the Indian summer.

Back in Calcutta, as a young woman, Pamela would see British troops sitting on the pavements and gutters, 'waiting to be transported to some war zone'. By 1942, as the Eastern front became a crucial theatre of war, Calcutta had become a hub for Allied troops, who were stopping in the city either en route to the front or returning for rest and recuperation. Ian Stephens, the editor of *The Statesman* newspaper of Calcutta, recalled in a memoir that the city was 'a vortex of humanity into which men doing war-jobs from all over the world ... were being sucked'.[2] The Japanese conquest of Burma had prompted a large build-up of the British Indian Army, a significant portion of which was stationed in Bengal. American airmen and other service personnel began to arrive in India from 1942 to fly supply missions to China for its war against the Japanese from northeast India over the northern Burma hills.

At the age of seventeen Pamela was serving with the Women's Voluntary Service (WVS). A large building at the end of her road had been converted into an officers' hospital. Pamela visited the wounded soldiers there and worked in the canteen. The British soldiers were always grumbling that the American GIs who had arrived in Calcutta had pushed up prices for them, as they did not realise they were meant to bargain with the locals in the markets, as everyone else did. And they were paid much more than the Brits. Pamela offered to take them to the New Market and bargain on their behalf in Urdu. They would travel in convoy – two British soldiers in a rickshaw – she ahead of them in her father's Pontiac – down Chowringhee Road to the bazaar. That became a regular weekly outing.

The Dowley-Wises felt so sorry for these British soldiers that they would invite them to their home. Every evening the table was laid for around twelve people. Anybody, from the army, air force or navy – regardless of rank – could come for a 'home from home'. After dinner they could sit round the piano and sing, 'We'll Meet Again', and 'It's a Long Way to Tipperary'. Sometimes they would take the soldiers to the Calcutta Swimming Club or to the Tollygunge Golf Club on the outskirts of the city, where the British elite would meet to play sport and socialise. Other times, the soldiers would join the family to eat at 'Firpos' and enjoy the five-course set menu of European food, and watch entertainment provided by colourful cabaret acts. When there was a full moon Pamela organised picnics for the young soldiers at the nearby Dhakuria Lakes. She still remembers the scene with the reflection of the moon in the lake, 'and the sound of the cool breeze rustling the fronds of the palm trees ... and those boys stretched out on the grassy banks by the water, listening to the music we were playing on our gramophone. The scene was quite magical, and they loved it.'

It was later that year, 1942, when the Japanese began their air raids on Calcutta. There were explosions, and people naturally panicked. Pamela would hear the pariah dogs barking frantically around the city. The bombs exploded at ground level, sending shrapnel over a wide area and killing and injuring many hundreds. The Dowley-Wises had prepared for such an eventuality and had had an air-raid shelter built below ground level in their garden. With the first raid, the siren sounded and they hurried to take cover, only to find themselves knee-deep in stagnant water swarming with hordes of mosquitoes caused by the heavy rains of the monsoon season.

It was not war, however, that stands out for Pamela. In 1943, the city and much of Bengal was gripped by something far deadlier than the Japanese. Famine. On 24 September 1943, the *New Statesman* of London reported: 'The description of life in Calcutta reads like extracts from medieval chronicles of black death.'[3] Historians agree it was man-made, a combination of wartime inflation, the Allied forces halting the movement of food in the region following the Japanese occupation of Burma, hoarding and speculation by grain traders, as well as allegations of British indifference to the suffering of Indians.[4] Estimates vary, but the official commission led by Sir John Woodhead put the death toll from the famine at 1.5 million people, and unofficial estimates spoke of figures as high as 5 million. The economist Amartya Sen estimates that around 3 million people perished.

Pamela recalls the starvation vividly: 'There were crowds and crowds of starving families coming into Calcutta. They were half dead when they arrived.' Travelling from rural areas they were hoping that Calcutta would provide food relief for them. The area of the Maidan, which she had often visited as a toddler with her pram and dolls, was now occupied by desperate families and dead bodies. There was no food for them, no soup kitchens. She saw them sitting exhausted on the tree-lined Chowringhee Road, giving birth to babies there, and dying where they sat. There wasn't even water. There were two water tanks on the Maidan, but they weren't for drinking, just for maintaining the grass. To consume them would have meant certain death from typhoid. Vultures soon circled, pulling at the emaciated bodies, while the living existed nearby. It was a shocking sight. And the smell. She shudders. It felt terrible, Pamela says, eating her evening meal knowing what was happening outside. But there was nothing she feels anyone could have done to help them.

The war continued to dominate their lives, and despite the hunger just outside their door, there were still visitors to the house. In late November a young British officer serving with Orde Wingate's Chindit force, on leave from fighting behind Japanese lines in the Burmese jungle, came to 9 Harrington

Street. Pamela had met Bill Towill briefly during her stay in Dehradun. He was an officer cadet at the prestigious military academy there, India's equivalent of Sandhurst. Pamela's mother had invited him to visit them should he ever be in Calcutta. Three years later, Bill took up the offer, deciding to spend his week of leave with the Dowley-Wises. Pamela was surprised, and delighted, to see him again.

He would accompany Pamela as she walked her dogs early each morning. On the last day of his leave, in the shadow of the Victoria Memorial, as they were watching the sunrise, Bill confessed he had fallen in love with her and asked Pamela to marry him. She agreed. Her parents were concerned as Bill was about to return to the Burmese jungle, so he delayed the engagement until Pamela turned eighteen. He bought her an engagement ring, which was kept in her parents' safe, and a pearl necklace for her to wear every day while he was away, as a token of his love.

While Bill was in Burma, Pamela had joined the Intelligence Department, South East Asia Command (SEAC). She tells me with pride that her task was to decode top-secret ciphers. On 31 July 1945, she remembers reading that within a week a secret device would be used against the Japanese, which was believed would end the war in the Far East. The 'secret device' turned out to be the atomic bomb that was dropped on Hiroshima on 6 August 1945, exactly a week after decoding the message. The second atomic bomb that was dropped on Nagasaki three days later helped to end the war with Japan.

There was always one occasion per year when Pamela would formally meet Indians. Her father had 133 Indian staff at the American Veedol oil company where he worked as the Calcutta director after the war. The employees would come over at Christmas bringing gifts. 'Many lovely gifts. It was evidently the done thing to go and see the memsahib and the daughters. And so that is about the only time we knew them.'

'The done thing' towards the British was changing rapidly. Bengal now had some autonomy with its own government. The independence movement, which had gathered pace in the 1920s and '30s, culminated in 1942 with the Indian National Congress Party's 'Quit India' campaign, which demanded that the British leave India altogether. From that time on Pamela would hear chants from the streets – in English – 'British Quit India'. It was, she says, 'a very worrying time'. If Pamela heard these slogans while out, she would head in the opposite direction before any trouble started. On Park Street, just off the main Chowringhee Road, and around the Ochterlony Monument, where there were many British shops including the Hall & Anderson department store (Calcutta's Selfridges), she saw windows smashed. 'In the "old days" when you walked down Chowringhee amongst a crowd of Indians they would make way for you on the pavement out of respect, but as the Quit India movement grew in momentum it was *you* who would have to move out of *their* way or get jostled.'

In spite of the agitation, Pamela carried on as before. She didn't imagine she herself would be harmed. The British had been there for so long, and they had been so respected, she still felt safe, despite the unrest. Her father had implored her to take the chauffeur to drive her in their Pontiac around the city, but Pamela wanted to retain her independence.

One day in the summer of 1946 Pamela was cycling down Chowringhee Road when, 'out of the blue', an Indian man came level with her, put his right arm out, and pushed her off her bike into the heavy traffic. 'He said "Quit India" as he did it.' Pamela fell in the filthy road among the cars, rickshaws and crowds. 'It was extremely dangerous. I could have been killed, but I was grazed and battered and bruised.' When she returned home, she recalls, 'My mother had a fit.' Her father, on seeing his daughter cut and bruised, said that Pamela was forbidden to go outside by herself. 'If this is what is going to happen in India,' he told her, 'we are going to make plans to leave.'

The summer of 1946 and the riots of that time were no longer just directed at British interests; they had become communal, between the Muslim and Hindu populations, as arguments raged over what freedom from the British would look like – a united India, or a separate homeland for India's 100 million Muslims. 'There were terrible riots, and terrible killings,' Pamela recalls. 'You'd see dead bodies lying all over the place. I never got used to it. Perhaps after a riot I knew there'd be dead bodies, so I wouldn't go to the market. We used to go in the car to the Tollygunge Club where we would have tea and sit peacefully whilst father played golf or tennis. We still carried on our life as best we could.'

Pamela's father joined the European Group in Calcutta's House of Representatives and was chosen to be the speaker. Mahatma Gandhi formed the Central Peace Committee in order to try to alleviate tensions between Hindus and Muslims in Calcutta, and asked Arthur Dowley-Wise, the only European, to join. The two men got to know each other, and at Gandhi's request Arthur suggested a slogan of peace to be recited at their meetings and rallies on the Maidan: 'Hindu aur Musulman ek ho' – 'Hindus and Muslims Be One'.

There could be no unity, however, between Hindus and Muslims. The situation was only getting worse and violence was spreading not just in Bengal, but also across northern

India. Conditions had deteriorated so much that, by the end of 1946, Pamela and her mother and sisters were boarding a P&O liner, along with thousands of troops. A military band played 'Auld Lang Syne' as they stepped onto the ship. Once again she was waving goodbye to her father. Pamela was now leaving the land of her birth for good, as well as her beloved fiancé Bill who had still not been released from the army. Luckily this time the sea journey was via the shorter route through the Suez Canal.

Her new life was to be in Newtown, Montgomeryshire, in Wales. Her mother found the house by chance, after flicking through the *Lady* magazine. Their home was in the middle of a field full of sheep. No one spoke English: 'It was totally, totally foreign to us. And I think Mother thought, what have I done? It was a dreadful shock.' There was rationing. And the women of the house had no idea how to cook or look after themselves. The high life of a household with eight servants was just a distant memory; the social whirl of clubs and wild parties long gone. Pamela did not feel English at all and missed India, its way of life, and having staff who looked after her and brought her tea. The family were so unhappy they found a house in Felpham, Sussex, to rent, by the sea. They hired a housekeeper, and life became more bearable.

Some months later, Bill was discharged from the army and returned to England. Pamela met him at Euston station. It was a sorry homecoming. He was wearing his uniform, and carrying just one suitcase. All his other possessions had been stolen en route. Having escaped from the German bombardment on the beaches of Dunkirk and fought the Japanese in the Burmese jungle, Bill opted for a quieter life and retrained as a lawyer.

Pamela now lives with her daughter Diana, along with her horses, in rural Surrey. She and Bill travelled back to India many times before his death in 2013. Her home is adorned with Indian pictures, artefacts and photographs from their time there. Nowadays no one even remembers the British were in India, she shrugs. And she laments that people have forgotten the good things Britain did out there. There are the wonderful buildings around Chowringhee she points out, the British-built hospitals, schools, orphanages. Her own Uncle Harold, a committed Christian, established the Birkmyre Hostel for orphaned Anglo-Indian boys with the financial backing of her father. From Pamela's perspective, 'there was no strife between the Europeans and the Indians at all'. She likes to speak Urdu when she can. She practises on me. Pamela has lived in Britain since she was twenty, but she is very clear on where she is from. This is the point, she tells me. Her paternal family go back many generations in India. 'I'm British, but my roots are there.'

Pamela Justine Dowley-Wise was born in Calcutta in 1926. She returned to Britain at the end of 1946. She married Bill Towill in 1948 in Richmond. They were married for sixty-five years until Bill's death at the age of ninety-three. Their first home was in an attic above a village store in Sutton. They spent their married life together in Surrey, and had two daughters. Pamela runs a riding centre and writes books about her time in India.

3

Hurt the British!

'Hurt the British!' That was what twelve-year-old Ramen Bannerjee set out to do in 1942. He was following a crowd of around ten young people who were on their way to a godown in Armanitola in the old city of Dhaka in eastern Bengal. The storage unit contained cigarettes belonging to a British company, Imperial Tobacco. The group's aim was to loot the goods. 'I had no interest in seizing any cigarettes. The new thing was just part of the programme to ruin the industry since it was British.'[1] Ramen believed it was wrong that a few thousand British people were ruling the whole of India. He joined in with the theft of cigarettes that night, his first act of defiance against the British. Some of the group smashed windows in the building.

Watching this incident were stalwarts of the Bengal Volunteers, a small underground revolutionary group committed to fighting for independence from the British. They 'picked up' Ramen and asked: 'Do you love India?'

'Yes,' he replied with conviction.

'Then join us.'

That's how they recruited a twelve-year-old Hindu boy.

The Bengal Volunteer Corps had been formed in 1928 by the legendary leader Subhas Chandra Bose. By 1942 the organisation was banned by the British, and it was dangerous to be linked with them. Ramen told no one, not even family members of his association. He was given proscribed literature to read, such as *Pather Dabi*, a Bengali novel about a secret society whose aim was to free India from British rule. All the books and writings he was passed were handwritten in Bengali. Once he'd finished reading them, he handed them on to a trusted person.

The group's spirit was encapsulated in the Bengali song 'Vande Mataram', which had also been banned by the British authorities. The Volunteers would sing it together, to inspire one another. The first two verses of the song begin:

Mother, I praise thee!
Rich with thy hurrying streams,
Bright with orchard gleams,
Cool with thy winds of delight,
Dark fields waving Mother of might,
Mother free.

Glory of moonlight dreams,
Over thy branches and lordly streams,
Clad in thy blossoming trees,
Mother, giver of ease.
Laughing low and sweet!
Mother I kiss thy feet,
Speaker sweet and low!
Mother, to thee I bow.

Merely saying 'Vande Mataram' could land someone in prison. For decades since the turn of the century, independence activists (particularly Hindus) had been singing this song, from the Bengali poet Rabindranath Tagore at the end of the nineteenth century to Mahatma Gandhi in the early twentieth.

Ramen is singing this patriotic song to me, as he used to, decades back, though now from his bungalow in East London. He no longer needs to sing it furtively. Sandalwood incense fills the house he now shares with his wife, daughter and son-in-law. Indian hangings cover the walls. He has lived in Britain for over fifty years. Even though he took up arms against this country many decades ago, when it was his colonial ruler, he sees no contradiction in choosing it as his permanent home. His enviably smooth skin belies his eighty-eight years. He is an animated speaker, and enjoys talking of his revolutionary past, though people rarely ask him about that time – a time of adventure, belief and conviction.

Nineteen forty-two was the time of the Quit India movement, mass protests across India – strikes and processions – called by Mahatma Gandhi and the Indian Congress Party. It was in response to Britain's declaration of war against Germany on behalf of India, and the lack of progress on the full transfer of power. Gandhi took the religious principle of ahimsa (doing no harm) common to Buddhism, Hinduism and Jainism and turned it into a non-violent tool for mass action. Through peaceful demonstrations, fasting and strikes, Gandhi and his followers demanded the British withdrawal from India. The then Viceroy of India, Lord Linlithgow, described the movement in a letter to Prime Minister Churchill as 'the most serious rebellion since that of 1857'.[2]

Following the Quit India declaration, the Indian Congress Party was declared an unlawful organisation. The leadership of the party (including Gandhi and Nehru) were arrested and imprisoned for the duration of the Second World War. Ramen, however, like his comrades in the Bengal Volunteers, was not that bothered about their internment. He wanted independence but had little time for Gandhi's approach of non-violence. He believed the fight for freedom could only be won by using force.

For Ramen, a Hindu Bengali, the fight was not just against the British but against the Muslim League too. The League's leader, Mohammed Ali Jinnah, had not joined the Quit India movement, concerned that if the British left, the Congress Party would not safeguard the rights of the Muslim minority in India. The League lent some support to Britain's war effort, unlike the Congress Party, if only to gain political advantage and influence. Ramen still feels aggrieved that the British chose to 'side with the Muslims' – saying they did so to divide the country, in order to continue their rule in India.

There had been concerns about the song 'Vande Mataram' for years. Its later verses seem to deny Muslim membership of the desired nation.

Thou art Durga, Lady and Queen,
With her hands that strike and her swords of sheen,
Thou art Lakshmi lotus-throned,
And the Muse a hundred-toned,
Pure and perfect without peer,
Mother lend thine ear,
Rich with thy hurrying streams,
Bright with thy orchard gleams,
Dark of hue, O candid-fair.

This final verse equates the Hindu goddess Durga to 'the Motherland' (India). Muslims do not worship idols, and would no doubt have been uncomfortable with the polytheistic connotations of the song. As the Indian scholar A. G. Noorani writes: 'The context only makes it worse. "The land of Bengal, and by extension all of India, became identified with the female aspect of Hindu deity, and the result was a concept of divine Motherland." How secular is such a song?'[3]

From 1937 the leadership of the Congress Party, sensitive to the needs of the Muslim community but still inspired by the song, only permitted the singing of the first two verses, which they argued were not controversial. Gandhi, writing in his weekly journal *Harijan* in 1939, said: ' "Vande Mataram" had gripped me, and when I first heard it sung it had enthralled me. I associate the purest national spirit with it. It never occurred to me that it was a Hindu song or meant only for Hindus. Unfortunately, we have now fallen on evil days ...'[4]

At his meetings, however, Ramen Bannerjee, unconcerned by such sensitivities, would proudly sing the song in its entirety. The Motherland to him meant a united India, in which Hindu culture reigned proud, with the Hindu goddess Durga holding weapons of war. And this was war: against the British and what he saw as its agents, including the Muslims and the Muslim League.

Life had not always been so divisive. Ramen spent his early childhood in Kukutia near Bikrampur, ten miles south of Dhaka. He describes himself as being born into a Hindu landlord class. They lived in a large house with six rooms. He still has fresh memories of a simple country life there – the jackals, snakes and butterflies. It was a mixed village of Muslims and Hindus, though the Muslims lived apart in a different area of the village. His memories are of people getting along well, everyone 'knowing their place'. The most exciting thing he remembers happening in Kukutia was the day an aeroplane flew overhead.

By 1939, aged nine, Ramen had moved to the city of Dhaka for his father's job on the railways. He still recalls being in awe of electricity and motor cars when he first arrived. The Bannerjee family lived in a Hindu enclave in Armanitola. The south side backed onto the Buriganga river. On the other sides were Muslim enclaves. Ramen cannot remember many Muslims going to school with him; rather they were sent to the fields to work or taken to the rivers to row boats, or fish. 'There were hardly any Muslim families who were educated and the educated classes [Hindus] didn't like the Muslims to come up and be their equals. They like the Muslims to be subservient.'[5] Ramen says that Muslim as well as Hindu peasants just accepted their place in society. Agriculturalists and artisans formed the majority of the Bengali Muslim population. Hindus were often the landlords and businessmen.[6] Historians acknowledge there was a sense of relative deprivation amongst many Bengali Muslims compared to upper- and middle-caste Hindus, who were by and large more prosperous.[7] It is not hard to see how the economic imbalance could have played a part in fuelling Hindu–Muslim tensions and even calls for a Muslim homeland.

It was only when Ramen moved to the bustling city of Dhaka that he witnessed trouble between Hindus and Muslims. He recalls annual disturbances during processions when Muslims marked the festival of Eid, and when the Hindus celebrated Janmashtami, Lord Krishna's birth. The processions had a designated route, but some of those taking part would veer off-course causing mischief, or would be attacked while they were marching. Ramen recalls one incident when a Muslim friend named Barik was taking part in a procession which strayed into a Hindu enclave. Some Hindus took some hot syrup from the sweet-making shop and scalded the demonstrators, including Barik. Ramen said it was all a bit of fun, and his friend took it in that spirit and laughed it off. Ramen says people did die during these procession scuffles, which was sad, but he and his friends were young and no one took it too seriously at the time.

Having been spotted by the Bengal Volunteers after the raid on the Imperial Tobacco warehouse, Ramen soon became a firearms runner for them. Being a first-class student, serious-minded, and well presented, he says no one suspected him. He was given bullets and guns (but not together) in a tin case that resembled a book bag, to take to named persons, though they were strangers to him. On one occasion he knew he had been given a revolver and was tempted to take a peek at it – just to see what one looked like – but he never did. Meetings would be held at night under a tree in a field with six or seven other people to discuss strategy. The leader of the group always had their face covered, so Ramen had no idea who it was giving instructions.

Like many Bengalis, Ramen was a fervent admirer of Subhas Bose. Having set up the Bengal Volunteers, from 1943 Bose was in Singapore, where he announced the formation of the Azad Hind government-in-exile, and of the Indian National Army, which sided with the Axis forces. Bose urged his countrymen to rise up against the British Raj. Ramen recruited for Bose using the same language that was used on him: 'Do you love Netaji [Bose]? How do you show your love for him, and your country? Join us!' They would all then recite the regimental quick march of the Indian National Army, 'Qadam Qadam Badaye Ja', where the soldiers sang of not being afraid of death and 'blowing away' the enemy's head 'to raise the spirit of the nation'.

Die for your beliefs. Defeat your enemy. From 1945 Ramen was adhering to these principles. He had now progressed to making bombs, including some containing splinters of broken glass and steel. One day he and some other revolutionaries stole sulphur from Jagannath College and used it to make explosives. They also made Molotov cocktails using soda bottles and cotton doused in petrol. He and his friends would make them at an abandoned house or 'den', where no one would suspect their activities. They had wanted to use these against the British, but there was no chance. So, he says, they used them against the Muslims instead, who were an easier target, and were perceived to be the 'agents of the British'.

Ramen recalls that in his enclave there were around seven to eight attacks by Muslims on Hindus during the period 1945–46. Handmade weapons, bows, arrows and fireballs were used against them in these raids. Ramen says the police helped the Muslims at the request of the British. So it was up to people like him to defend the enclave. He used his home-made petrol bombs to disperse the crowds. Ramen gestures, showing me how he used to throw them. He would also hurl nail bombs wrapped in newspaper with explosives inside. One time during an attack he recalls using around seventeen of them. He watched them hit the crowd, and how they succeeded in pushing the invaders back. He would also throw bricks from a first-floor building. Ramen says he feels remorse now at what he did, but at the time he had no choice but to protect the enclave. It was purely for self-defence. He never instigated the aggression, he says. He admits a number of times to me that it was unfortunate that he was involved in this way.

Around the time of one of these riots, a good friend of Ramen's, a Muslim called Shamsuddin, visited him in the Hindu enclave, mistakenly believing that the trouble had subsided. Ramen's mother had to shield Shamsuddin to protect him from the raids and told him it was no longer safe for a Muslim to be in a Hindu enclave. Ramen escorted him back home and said it was probably better they did not meet from then onwards. They didn't see each other again, something that continues to fill Ramen with sadness. His daughter later told me that he still thinks of his friend, Shamsuddin.

Ramen came to realise that his mother had been a supporter of the armed struggle, and had been aware of his work all along – though perhaps not the gun-running. Once, the British police ransacked their enclave and Ramen could not work out how the home-made bombs he had been storing there had not been discovered. He later found out that his mother, seeing the police approach, had hidden them. Another time, during one of the raids by Muslims, while he was in the middle of a counter-attack, Ramen's mother brought him some of the bombs he had made and kept hidden in the tea chest in their home. She must have been watching him all that time, he thinks. Though they never once talked about it.

The situation was now so tense between the communities that a small incident could spark riots. One day Ramen was playing hockey, as he often did with friends. During

45

the match his Hindu friend was accidentally hit by another friend, a Muslim boy called Ishmael. In retaliation, Ramen hit back, and that was the end of the matter, he says, and the game continued. But Ramen says the political situation at that time was so incendiary that this minor altercation precipitated riots outside the hockey field.

By late 1946 the British announced they would be leaving India by June 1948. The aim of the Bengal Volunteers had been met. It was the best time, Ramen recalls, as India was to gain its freedom and the British were on their way out – though he still couldn't have imagined, at that point, any division of the country. They had heard of partition plans, but dismissed them as unlikely. The leaders of the Bengal Volunteers no longer had to hide their identity from their foot soldiers. One man Ramen had always suspected of being a spy and had been avoiding was in fact one of the group's leaders, whom he had unknowingly met during one of the secret night-time meetings by the tree in the field.

On Independence Day, 15 August 1947, Ramen was in his enclave in Dhaka, where he presided over the raising of the Indian flag on his building at 9 Ananda Chandra Ray Road. As the flag was hoisted up, a Muslim group approached and threatened them, swearing and ordering the flag be brought down. Ramen raises his voice repeating their insults, gesturing as they did to him that day seventy years ago: 'If you don't take the flag down you will be killed.' Ramen was shocked. He never thought that the Muslims would threaten to murder them if they did not bring down the Indian flag. 'We used to say Jai Hind,' Ramen says. No, he was told, by the Muslim group – 'this is Jai Pakistan, Victory to Pakistan'. Pakistan Zindabad not Hindustan Zindabad. Long Live Pakistan not Long Live India. Dhaka was now in East Pakistan, no longer part of India. Ramen lost all courage and took the flag down. It was then that Ramen realised: 'We are no longer the masters. Muslims were the masters and they were going to dictate to us ... we knew our time was over.'

He soon felt a foreigner in his own home. Hindus were no longer welcome. Even Muslim friends would always ask: 'When are you going to Hindustan?' Yet, even then, he still thought partition would not last. He believed, like the 1905 partition of Bengal,[8] that it would eventually be reversed. He thought the Muslims would not be able to run their own country, and the Hindus would take over.

Today, Ramen feels nothing but contempt for Mahatma Gandhi, and lays some of the blame of partition on him: 'I wish Gandhi was not born.' He still believes it was necessary to use arms to win independence, and if this approach had been used earlier, independence would have been gained quicker, and the division of the country would not have happened. 'He (Gandhi) was not a freedom fighter.'

Ramen believed passionately in independence for India. But not for a moment did he dream that freedom from the British would mean leaving the place of his birth. He left Dhaka in 1948 for West Bengal, India, when he realised partition was irreversible. He gave up his place at medical college and started life again 'as a pauper'. Dhaka and East Bengal, the place of his birth and where he spent the first seventeen years of his life, mean nothing to him now. 'Partition shattered my life,' he says. He lost everything, even his country: 'The thing is, India is never going to be India again.'

Ramen Bannerjee was born in 1930 in Bikrampur, British India. He left for Ranaghat, India in 1948. He came to Britain

47

in 1966 to study for his Bar exams. He worked in health and social security and as a human rights worker for the British South Asian community. He lives in east London with his wife, daughter and son-in-law.

4

I Became Convinced of the Muslim League

Bashir Maan began life in Glasgow selling clothes from a heavy suitcase, door to door, in 1953. Just imagine that.[1] A man who attended Punjab University, whose English was not bad, but no match for the Glaswegian accent, stifling his ambitions and accepting no doubt countless humiliations. How many doors must have closed in his face? As a young boy he used to laugh with his friends at the Pathans (Pashtuns) from Afghanistan who would come as labourers to Punjab. Now the same was happening to him. Local kids would follow and pester this exotic figure in the streets and alleys as he tried to sell his wares. 'There is a darkie, Johnnie the darkie, hello Mister Darkie, here comes a darkie, darkie, blarkie.'[2] But Bashir is not one to dwell on adversities. People were kind too, especially on the outskirts of Glasgow – 'Sorry, Johnnie,' they would say, if they didn't want to buy anything. In those days every Indian or Pakistani was called Johnnie.

Today on his study wall at his home hangs a letter from the queen. It is addressed to Bashir, almost fifty years after he arrived in Scotland. It awards the man who was born in a Punjabi village in British India, and came to Scotland after independence, who first worked as a pedlar, the honour of Commander of the Order of the British Empire for his work in public life in Glasgow. Bashir went on to become the first Muslim city councillor, a district court judge and was heavily involved in race relations and Scottish politics. He had been active in politics since he was a young man, when he was a subject, rather than Commander, of the British Empire. In fact, he had fought against the principle of empire, demanding independence and even a homeland for India's Muslims. Yet it was the Empire that brought him here to Scotland.

Bashir was born in the province of Punjab, in the west of British India, into a village his forefathers had lived in for generations. His family name and that of his village were synonymous: Maan. Over a thousand people resided there – the majority, like Bashir, were Muslim. The village was mixed; there was a Hindu temple, a gurdwara and a number of mosques nearby. It was the childhood of storybooks. His favourite pastime was gulli-danda – an ancient Indian sport where a large stick (danda) hits a small stick (gulli), as well as playing marbles on the ground. A mischievous boy, he and a friend once bolted all the villagers' outside doors so no one could get out the next morning. But his mother and father never disciplined him with their hand, as many of the other parents would have done. At five he was sent to the village school, and then on to DB High School in Qila Didar Singh, four miles away. His friends were mostly Sikhs and Hindus, as 'educating the children was not very common for Muslims. But it was very common for Hindus and Sikhs. There were only one or two who were Muslims.' His family were landowners owning the surrounding wheat and rice fields, and lived comfortably off the rent. It was a peaceful, privileged life.

From 1943 Bashir studied economics, history and English at the nearby city of Gujranwala at a branch of Punjab University. It was the time of Quit India – and he was involved in the Congress Party. 'I liked Gandhi and I thought he was the right person to lead the country.' But early on at university a friend introduced him to the Muslim League. He hadn't heard much of it while living in the countryside. But once he understood its aims – a country where Muslims could live according to their own faith and culture, and not subjugated by a Hindu majority – he was convinced and joined up. 'I did feel it would be a very good idea,' he says. 'A Muslim country where we could live according to our religion. Because in a democracy, which India was going to be, we couldn't have imposed our religion, our village values. In Pakistan we could – it was a Muslim country, a separate independent country. And that was the idea of the Muslim League. I thought that Pakistan would be created and everyone would be living here peacefully. The others would be living in India peacefully. We never thought how it would end up.'

British policies had resulted in encouraging co-religionists to bond tightly together. In *The Great Partition*, historian Yasmin Khan says the most important of these moves was the decision to give separate electorates to different religious communities from 1909 so that they were represented by their 'own' politicians. A voter could only cast a vote for the candidate in their own category.[3] In 1935 the Government of India Act was passed, giving a substantial measure of representative government through provincial autonomy (while the British reserved power for themselves at the centre). The Act, as Ian Talbot and Gurharpal Singh argue in *The*

Partition of India, 'constituted an important landmark in the democratisation of colonial rule ... [but] heightened Muslim-minority anxieties and fears of Hindu dominion'.[4] Provincial elections for Indian representatives were due to take place in early 1946 against this background. The powerful province of Punjab had a slight Muslim majority. Local politics there had been dominated by the secular Unionist Party, which had built a formidable power base through policies of patronage, allowing them to retain the loyalty of landlords who exerted significant local influence. For the Muslim League to claim to represent the Muslim vote, they would need to win over the majority of the seats held by the Unionists.

In the run-up to the crucial 1946 provincial elections, Bashir travelled with his fellow students around Gujranwala to convince Muslims to vote for the Muslim League. They would go from village to village and a group of people would huddle around them as they explained the League's aims. Many people they encountered knew little of the Muslim League. Bashir said he used the same arguments on the villagers that his friend had used to persuade him of the significance of the League. He could see that, like him, they were convinced.

On polling day Bashir was in Qila Didar Singh, just a few miles from his village. He was manning the booths in his old school, and was also tasked with bringing people out, and physically taking them to the polling station to vote. He said they never persuaded people how to vote inside the polling station, only outside. He already sensed that Muslim support for the Unionist Party was dwindling.

The Muslim League won the overwhelming majority of Muslim seats in Punjab. Across India the party secured 439 of the 494 seats reserved for Muslims in the provincial assemblies. It was, as Talbot and Singh argue, 'a decisive verdict in favour of Pakistan'.[5] On hearing this news Bashir felt proud and elated. He knew then the Muslim League had the upper hand and could now legitimately demand an independent homeland. But the elections would also foreshadow something much more sinister. In the aftermath of the 1946 provincial elections, 'the consolidation of political allegiances around religious community both reflected and contributed to the communal polarisation ... the polls paved the way for Pakistan but also formed a prelude to the violence which accompanied partition'.[6]

Bashir reflects on how the atmosphere in the months leading to partition was poisoned to demonise the 'other'. 'All my friends were Hindu, they went to school with me, they went to university with me. You had established such good relationships with them. Then suddenly you see them as enemies, as a people who have to be killed. It was a terrible situation.' He then describes a moment he too felt this way in the run-up to partition. 'It was tit for tat. It was definitely tit for tat.' One day Bashir travelled to Lahore train station to pick up a family friend; when he got there he heard that a train was coming through India with dead bodies on board – he saw blood in the train. He thought to himself: is this what is happening to Muslims? He was with a friend and told him: '"The first thing I am going to do is kill all the Hindus in my village." That's how I came home.' He says the situation then was so bad that when people left their village everyone was concerned for their safety. Everyone was anxious that day as a group of people had been killed near to Bashir's village. There was concern Bashir may not come back alive. When he entered the village two of Bashir's Hindu friends were waiting for him and shouted out to the neighbours that he was safe. They all embraced. Everyone was congratulating his parents, including his Hindu friends, on his return. 'I forgot everything that had happened, that had been in my mind. I said well, how can I kill them?'

When partition did arrive in August 1947, Bashir was in his village. He called everyone to come out. The men came out of their homes and there was a procession through the streets celebrating the independence of Pakistan. It was triumphant, he reminisces. Everyone was excited. However, he adds, around only 10 per cent of people in the village were educated and knew what was happening. Most people had never even seen a British person. Bashir explained to the others the significance of the moment. But there were still people, Bashir recalls, who didn't understand what was happening.

Gujranwala and the surrounding villages including Maan became part of Pakistan. Bashir assumed life would carry on as before. He had no inkling of what was to come next. 'But then it started to happen.'

One day a group of Hindus and Sikhs were migrating to a transit camp where they thought they would be safe. They were waiting for the Indian Army to take them across the border. (Both countries, in the weeks after partition, agreed to organise the transfer of populations to ensure their safety.) On the way there, they were attacked by a mob of Muslims. Caught up in the assault was a very good friend of Bashir's, a Sikh named Bhagwan Singh who lived around seven miles away. 'I had told him [Bhagwan] that if ever he felt unsafe, to come up to my place with your [his] parents,' recalls Bashir. When the family fled, they passed by the village of Maan, and enquired if Bashir's father was at home. He was visiting a neighbouring town, and Bhagwan's father refused to allow his family to stay in Maan without Bashir's father there. He was no doubt afraid to be a Sikh in a Muslim-majority village. Bhagwan was then killed en route to the camp a mile and a half away from Bashir's village. He thinks it must have been by a mob who came in from the city. 'That was a tragedy. That really affected me very much. So that really made me very sad. It was a horrible moment. In my own village!'

Eventually, the movement of Bashir's Hindu and Sikh neighbours started. He watched them move out peacefully. 'We were sad, they were sad that they were leaving. I remember when the [Indian] army trucks came and they ordered them in there with the little belongings that they could take and we were embracing each other, crying.'

As the Hindus and Sikhs fled with whatever few bundles they could take with them, most of the houses were left as they were lived in. At night the looters would come and raid the homes of their former neighbours. Bashir says he and some of his friends tried to stop them; mostly they weren't very successful, as between the friends they couldn't cover the entire village at all times. But he, as a landlord's son, and his friends, also from influential families, were able to offer some resistance to the looters. They managed to save some contents: utensils, beds, sheets, bed covers. Evidence of a life lived, but too burdensome to take in the rush. A nearby Sikh temple was made into a store room, and the fragments of the life of the Sikh and Hindu families were put there. Bashir realised that when families migrating from India arrived they would at least have something to start up a new home. As the exhausted, traumatised Muslim refugees from India eventually trickled in, Bashir handed these all out. People who could not share the same land would be sharing something even more intimate: the bed and bedsheets of the other.

Bashir's first job was in Lahore, where he was in charge of a coal dump. He then took a job as a government clerk. But he was beginning to feel disillusioned with his new country, and its politicians. He also wanted an adventure. His younger brother was serving with the Pakistan Navy and had been chosen for training in Rosyth in Scotland – with the aim of returning home to Pakistan to educate the new recruits with his new-found knowledge. On a trip to Glasgow his brother had been surprised to meet a Pakistani in the street. They kept in touch, and on his return to Pakistan, he told Bashir about the man he had bumped into – a Mr Mohamed. Bashir then decided he wanted to go to Britain and carried on the correspondence with Mr Mohamed. Bashir was warned that life in Scotland was hard, but Bashir was undeterred. 'I am a Jat,[7] I know what hard work is,' he says.

Unlike so many who came in those early days after independence, Bashir's connection with Britain was not through a family member, or someone from the village who had come over, but through a random association. In 1953 Bashir arrived in Glasgow, only intending to stay a few years. He was shocked by what he saw in the country of his former rulers. 'It was ingrained in my mind that it was the land of milk and honey. Then I came here and saw the dirt in the street and little boys playing in their bare feet. I thought "Oh my God!"' On Hospital Street he saw a briquette-seller covered black with soot – and the people buying the coal looked so sad. 'I was very surprised these were the kind of people who were ruling over us. Over there they were dressed up and clean, and then over here this was the situation.'

He lived in a house with other pedlars who sold knick-knacks door to door, sharing a bedroom with another man.

Bashir thinks there were only around 300–400 Pakistanis in the city when he arrived.[8] Nearly all were pedlars, a job vacated by Jewish immigrants. There were no other opportunities available then for South Asians. When he started hawking, his English was rusty, but it soon improved as he was speaking to Scottish people all day. The work was relatively lucrative, so he carried on for ten years selling clothes door to door. He sent home money every month, and saved the rest. Even when he was a pedlar he continued his studies at night, and gradually became vocal in the press in talking about community issues. In 1969 he was persuaded to stand as a city councillor for the Scottish Labour Party. To his astonishment he beat four native Scottish candidates and became the first Muslim in the country in that position. It was, he laughs, almost like a 'miracle' that he won. 'In those days we were so looked down upon, racism was rife, and coloured people were hated. But they voted for me.'

Bashir brought his wife over from Pakistan in 1961. His four children, grandchildren and great-grandchildren all live in the UK. Though he only intended to stay a few years, he has now spent the majority of his life in Scotland, though you could not tell from his accent. There is not even a slight Glaswegian twinge. He says Scotland has given him more opportunities than Pakistan could. He describes himself as Scottish Pakistani. Home is Glasgow. Even though he returns to the village of Maan in Pakistan every year, after a few weeks away he yearns to come back. He misses his friends, interests, even the Glaswegian weather.

At the age of ninety-one he is still planning to return to Maan. He enjoys the simple life there. 'I go to the places that I liked to play in my childhood,' he says. 'My school where I used to go. And the other places – a pool, a water tank, built by a Hindu financier, that is a very good place to sit and bathe. I like to go back. Old memories, those childhood memories. When there were no concerns, and you were just playing, that's all.'

The man who campaigned with the Muslim League for an independent Pakistan, now says that with the benefit of hindsight it would have been better if India had stayed together, and given guarantees to its Muslim citizens. The houses of Hindus and Sikhs, left seventy years ago, still stand in Maan – solitary reminders of a time when this land was lived on not only by Muslims. 'We were all disappointed by what happened, because none expected it would come to this.'

Bashir Ahmed Maan CBE was born in 1926 in the village of Maan, British India. He moved to Glasgow in 1953 where he started life as a pedlar travelling door to door, selling clothes from a suitcase. In 1969 he became the first Muslim to be elected as a city councillor. He went on to become prominent in Scottish politics and in the Scottish Labour Party. He was awarded a CBE in 2000 and is the author of a number of books on Muslims in Scotland. He died in December, 2019. The First Minister Nicola Sturgeon described him as "a trailblazer and role model in the Scottish Muslim community."

5

Fishing with Dead Bodies

Ken's first memory is the smell of mustard oil on his ayah. Old Bhutair, as she was known, would rub it into her skin as protection from the sun. 'I grew up with that smell. I liked it. It was familiar to me. It eased me.'[1]

Old Bhutair was from Bhutan, an elderly woman with dark skin who always wore a white sari. She was at Ken's disposal day and night. If he woke in the early hours, it would be Old Bhutair who comforted him. The first words Ken spoke were Hindi, taught by her. To communicate with his mother, the ayah would translate Ken's words into English. She would sing nursery rhymes in Hindi, which he still remembers to this day, and recites with a strong Dundee brogue.

Nini baba nini
Makkhan roti cheene,
Mackhan Makkhan roti hoa gia,
Soja Baba Soja,
Mera baba soja,
Ninnie Nina baba so gaya, gaya.

Sleep baby sleep,
Butter, bread and sugar,
Butter and bread are finished
Sleep baby sleep,
My baby sleep,
Little baby has gone to sleep.

She bathed, washed and cleaned Ken. She treated him like a prince. Ken remembers watching her take the skin off an orange for him 'in only the way an Indian ayah could peel an orange, not only the skin but the membrane of the orange, so I was just given the beads. Delightful.' He was told later that she used to put opium under the very fingernails that would peel his orange.

Ken is talking to me in the living room of his bungalow in Dundee. The winter sun is streaming in so forcefully, we move around the room so it does not blind us. I can see how much he enjoys remembering his childhood days. He is talking while holding black-and-white photographs from his youth on his lap. He is dressed smartly in a cream shirt and trousers with a paisley cravat. His voice is easy to listen to; it has a lyrical cadence and great warmth to it. His wife Patricia comes in to give us tea and cakes, and he says she too shares his affection for India, the place of his childhood.

Born in 1937, Ken grew up in Meghna, twenty miles north of Calcutta on the east bank of the Hooghly river. His parents, John and Elizabeth Miln, were from Scotland and were known as 'jute wallahs'. They had been in India since 1923. By the early twentieth century Calcutta was the main centre for the processing of jute. Many of the overseers, managers and mechanics working in the Bengal jute mills were, like the Milns, from Dundee. John spoke fluent Bengali and Hindi. He ran the Mackinnon Mackenzie jute mill in Meghna, where stems from jute plants were processed ready to be turned into rope, canvas, twine or woven into sacking. The mill was in a compound, where they and other European families also lived. It was surrounded by three high walls. The remaining side led directly onto the Hooghly river.

Just outside the compound was the Jagatdal bazaar, with its fresh fish and food stalls, fakirs – religious people – and loud Bengali music playing. Elephants and water buffalo would wander around, drinking from the nearby Hooghly. There was an ornate mosque and two Hindu temples nearby.

As a young boy Ken took part in daily baat (conversation) sessions with the family's Muslim and Hindu servants after tiffin, a light lunch, had been eaten. Sitting on the back veranda among them all, including his beloved ayah, the khansama (male cook), bearer (a household servant), and dhobi, who looked after the laundry, he listened as the servants gossiped and reminisced about life back home in the state of Bihar, or the cities of Dhaka and Khulna. Relaxed, the servants sat back smoking their bidis, made from a traditional mixture of betel nut, spices and herbs wrapped in a leaf. Ken would join them on these smokes from the age of eight. Sitting amongst the servants he noticed ostensible differences. The Muslims wore lungis, the traditional sarong, and Hindus dhotis, material from the waist covering their legs. Neither religious group ate together, 'but I cannot remember any animosity between them', he says.

The only people living in the compound were Brits and some other Europeans. 'I wouldn't call it exactly apartheid, but there were no Indians in the compound' – other than the servants, of course, and they slept elsewhere. He remembers Indians never came to the house for dinner. It was not a company rule; it was just not done.

His early schooling was at a convent school in the French colony of Chandernagore (now Chandannagar) across the Hooghly river, which he attended with some of the other British children from the compound. From the age of seven he was sent to board at St Paul's School in Darjeeling. Situated nearly 7,000 feet above sea level, on a hill named Jalapahar, it was famed for being the public school at one of the highest altitudes in the world.

In his first weeks there, free-spirited, with a strong tan, and fluent Hindi, Ken overheard some of the boys describing him as a chi chi – a derogatory term for an Anglo-Indian. 'I was horrified, I thought, "My goodness I'm part Indian, that's a horrible thing."' To be an Anglo-Indian meant to be an outsider. All Ken knew was that these people, who were often redheads with freckles, sometimes blond, and nearly always striking-looking, were forbidden entry to any of the smart expatriate clubs like the Calcutta Swimming Club, the Bengal or the Tollygunge Club. Their crime: to have a mixture of British and Indian blood.

Holidays back on the compound were a carefree time. 'We were used to open doors, lots of space, lots of air, lots of colour, bright sunlight, butterflies, cannas, poinsettias, bougainvillea, dragonflies, fish. I used to love fishing.'

Ken was told not to go down to the Hooghly, but from an early age spent most of his time there. 'I went down and fished with the fishermen, I went on the dinghies with the manjhis, or boat-men, and swam in the river.' He'd also 'palled up' with some local Bengali boys and would go to the Jagatdal bazaar, where they would look at the colourful stalls together. 'I did all these things and I had total freedom, I did what I wanted to, I was utterly spoilt in that respect.'

The Second World War passed Ken by. Some of the British in the compound joined up and served with the Bengal Horse Artillery, including his mother. She drove a lorry in Barrackpore, which worried Ken as he didn't think she even had a driving licence.

Things began to change in 1946, however, when Ken was nine. There were rumours that Hindus had slaughtered a pig and thrown it into the Jagatdal mosque, and the Muslims had slaughtered a cow and thrown it into one of the temples. The baat sessions ended abruptly. There was no more chat, no lazy afternoon meetings, just division between Hindu and Muslim servants who'd once been friends.

The trouble escalated fairly rapidly. At night Ken would hear screams and could see fires burning beyond the compound: 'Terrible rumpus let's say, even gunfire at times out in the bazaar.' Gurkhas protected the compound, however, so Ken felt safe there. The British were not the target and, despite the rioting, work at the jute mill was rarely affected. There were days when the rioting prevented a shift or two from operating, but there was little more disruption than that.

In the summer of 1946, Jinnah, the leader of the Muslim League, called a day of action which descended into the Great Calcutta Killings, leaving thousands of Muslims and Hindus dead. The riots affected Ken's village, not far from the city. He still has nightmares about a particular incident he witnessed. Some of the workers from the jute mill had got into a fight. They then burst into the compound area in front of his house. Ken doesn't recall whether they were Hindu or Muslim. 'There were two men with lathis – bamboo poles – and they beat the other two over the head. They killed them. And I can recall that just yards in front of me.'

The situation deteriorated in Meghna in the lead-up to the division of British India. Meghna was within tidal influence of Calcutta, even though it was around twenty miles north of the city, and around sixty miles from the Bay of Bengal. Bengal was so flat that tidal influence extended up to 160 miles inland. When the tide went out, dead bodies were exposed. Nine-year-old Ken watched the pariah dogs as they tore at the human flesh.

At the end of the jetty in the compound were large cranes that would lift the bales of jute up into the barges. From there they would go on to a railhead to be processed. Underneath the jetty were two huge pipes which would suck the water for the boilers and the reservoir tank. They had filter cages around them with steps leading down to the dinghies where the manjhi wallahs, fishermen, would sit. Ken recalls going down the steps and seeing a group of labourers fishing out body parts which had jammed the filter cages.

None of this, however, stopped Ken from enjoying his favourite activity – fishing with the manjhis. Ken even fished as bodies passed him, floating down the river. 'On one occasion I actually pushed the body off with the butt of my fishing rod. I didn't think too much of it at the time. I was obsessed with fishing and I was concentrating on catching a big fish. That may sound awful,' he says, 'but we got that used to seeing bodies, not only in the river but on the streets. In Calcutta and the bazaar, the place at times was littered with dead bodies, and children's bodies too. So a dead body, although an awful thing, didn't really terrify me and sad to say I became used to it I suppose to a degree.'

Ken watched as a number of the Muslim workers and servants left Meghna, and possibly even India, with their tin trunks and bullock carts. His family stayed on after Meghna (and Calcutta) became part of India following partition, and he recalls no animosity towards them as Britishers. Ken continued at St Paul's School in the Himalayas. The Muslim khansama stayed on, as did some of the Muslim workers at the mill. But Ken noticed more guards around the compound after independence, and things were not the same among the workforce: the Muslim and Hindus acknowledged each other but that was their only interaction.

Towards the end of 1949, Ken's father made the decision to leave India. Not because of partition, Ken points out, but for the education of his children. 'I do remember my cook saying to me I'd be "going to Blighty" and I didn't have a bloody clue really what he was on about.'

Ken and his family first went to live in Beckenham, Kent. It was cold, damp and crowded. Houses had little rooms where people sat around drinking tea in front of the fire. He'd been used to open doors, outdoor space, colour. 'That was dreadful, being in a confined, closed-circuit little environment, I didn't like it at all.'

He always missed India – 'I still miss India very much.' He has travelled back often in his lifetime, and lived there twice with his own family. His first job was back in Meghna in 1959 at the same jute mill his father oversaw. He went back to install and commission machinery. While there, he found an old footprint of his on the back veranda which he'd made as a boy while they were laying down cement years back. Another time he worked near Lahore as a project engineer at a new jute mill. 'I felt I was going home right away. I was stepping back home and have always felt that when I go.'

He still has dreams he is in India, living as an Indian. He has nightmares too, where he is being chased down a street, where someone is pulling at his legs to bring him down. He thinks it could stem from the days of the rioting. 'But it doesn't terrify me now; it used to, but it doesn't now. It just comes up now and then. I deal with it.'

Ken moved to live permanently in Dundee almost three decades ago, the place of his forefathers, the city of the jute wallahs. He speaks with the broadest of Scottish accents, as if he'd lived there all his days. You could never imagine his first words were in Hindi, that he spent his early years fishing with the manjhis on the Hooghly and milled amongst the stalls of fresh fish and vegetables at the Jagatdal bazaar. In fact, he says nowadays no one really remembers the many centuries of connection with India and Calcutta. Commercial jute production in Dundee came to an end in the 1970s. Of the city's 130 jute mills, many were demolished and around sixty former mills are now flats or commercial premises. But the legacy from the time of the jute wallahs is still there – in the chimneys that dominate the skyline, the parks paid for by jute wealth, and the university, founded in 1881, with money from the family of one of the most powerful jute barons, William Baxter.

We walk down Monifieth Street together, near his home, which is enveloped by the Sidlaw Hills. Hills Ken still climbs. He pops in to buy a newspaper at his local shop, greeting some of the shopkeepers in Urdu which he learned while working in Lahore. He doesn't want it to go rusty. 'Spiritually, if you like, I'm an Indian. By pure bad luck or administratively I'm British.' He rolls back his head and laughs.

Kenneth Miln was born in 1937 and grew up in Meghna, near Calcutta. His family returned to England in 1949. He worked as an engineer at jute mills in India, Pakistan and Kenya. He now lives in Dundee with his wife.

6

It Was Magic

In the summer of 1944, nineteen-year-old Denys Wild boarded a scruffy steam train heading around 150 miles north of Delhi towards Dehradun, in the foothills of the Himalayas. It was home to India's Military Academy (IMA), where officers were trained for the British Indian Army. At around four in the morning word came round that everyone had to get off. The engine was struggling, and the passengers, including Denys, were made to push the train up to the top of the hill. Then they all jumped back on and went on their way. This is Denys's first memory of India.[1]

Denys arrived at Dehradun in June. Since the early 1930s the IMA had trained a handful of Indians to be officers. Denys was among the first group of British officer cadets to be trained alongside them. At the entrance to the building is an engraved plaque, reminding cadets of their duty:

The safety, welfare and honour of your country comes first – always and every time.

The safety and welfare of the men you command comes next – always and every time.

Your own welfare and safety comes last – always and every time.

Training lasted six months. Denys learned to swim, drive, use a weapon, plan for battle, and how to speak Urdu, the lingua franca of the Indian Army. He trained, ate and lived alongside the Indian cadets: 'We got along very well.' Every Saturday morning there was a parade: 'It was all very pukka, with a band.' Denys was a colour bearer, carrying the regimental standard, alongside another cadet who held the Viceroy's colour. 'We thought it was very grand because as we stood in the middle of the parade there is a certain stage when whoever the inspecting officer was had to stop and salute us. Well, he wasn't saluting us, of course, he was saluting the flag, but it was quite nice to think he was saluting us. And when Field Marshal Sir Claude Auchinleck, who was the Commander-in-Chief in India came along, he then stood there and saluted us. I think we were quite proud of ourselves.'

Following his training, Denys had a choice: to be with the British Army, the British service attached to the Indian Army, or with the Indian Army. Denys chose the latter. His Urdu, thanks to his munshi's (teacher's) tutelage, was fluent. The Indian Army paid more, was prestigious and frankly quite 'exotic'. But there was something deeper too. Denys had grown up near Addiscombe, in Croydon, Surrey, which was once home to the British military academy that trained the private army of the East India Company. The streets near his childhood home had names such as Outram, Havelock, Elgin, Clyde and Canning – after soldiers and politicians prominent on the British side during the 1857 Indian uprising. Growing up, hearing this history, Denys believes something rubbed off on him, and influenced his decision to join the Indian Army, a decision which resulted in a lifelong relationship with India.

On 10 December 1944, Denys joined the 13th Frontier Force Rifles, which was part of the Punjab Frontier Force. He proudly has his regimental tie on when we meet. He was first sent to the command centre in Abbottabad, seventy-five miles north of Islamabad, where he was responsible for training new recruits. There were four main separate companies of Indians: the Pathans; Muslims from Punjab known as 'PMs' – Punjabi Musalmans; the Sikhs; and the high-caste Dogras who were nearly all Hindu. Denys recalls that during inspections you could not allow your shadow to fall on the Dogras' cooking pots otherwise they would have to throw the food away.

Denys stayed at the command centre for just a few months before being sent on jungle training, and was then finally sent on active duty, first to Burma, along with the PMs and the Sikhs of his regiment, then on to Singapore, Sumatra and back to Burma again. When the war ended Denys held the rank of captain, with three pips on his shoulder.

In July 1945, in Britain's first general election for ten years, Clement Attlee's Labour Party came to power with a mandate to withdraw from the subcontinent at the earliest opportunity. End of colonial rule in India also spelled the end of the existing British Indian Army and its administration. Field Marshal Auchinleck oversaw the division of this force. Around 260,000 soldiers, mainly Hindus and Sikhs, went to India. And around 140,000 soldiers, nearly all Muslims, went to the Pakistan Army. The Brigade of Gurkhas, recruited in Nepal, was split between India and Britain.[2] Denys's regiment was disbanded. He and his good friend Major George Bowyer offered to take the troops in their regiment back to their families in Punjab and make sure they were all properly paid and pensioned. For their part, the sepoys invited Denys and George – the sahibs – to visit their villages in Punjab. Over a period of twenty-eight days on the eve of independence, Denys and his friend travelled across Punjab to bid their men farewell.

The homes of the sepoys, Denys remembers, were mostly mud houses built of wattle and cane. They had thick walls and were cool inside. Family members would splash water on the outside walls to keep them fresh. He remembers these mixed communities where the village well was a meeting place, just as post offices were in English villages. He vividly recalls a modern canal system – gesturing as he describes to me how each village well had a sophisticated system of buckets in a circle and how a camel or bullock would walk around as the buckets entered the well and came up with water. It was a simple life. And that life was good. It appeared that everyone got on. He and George visited the mixed village of his Sikh naik (corporal), who was getting married. It was a boisterous affair, as many of the Sikh males 'had been on the booze' and got on horses and rampaged through the village past the Muslims while they were observing Ramadan. Denys felt their Muslim neighbours may have been offended, but no offence was expressed. He reflects that it is hard to believe that in just a few weeks' time these lands of Punjab were to become execution grounds.

It is the visit to his batman, or orderly, Mohammed Sarwar, however that Denys particularly cherishes. Sometime in late July or early August 1947, Denys travelled by rail from Lahore a hundred miles north to the village of Pindi Hashim to visit him. As the train passed through the stations he noticed huge crowds. After making some enquiries he discovered that Mahatma Gandhi was on his train. Denys says he thought he may have been travelling through Punjab appealing for calm in the weeks ahead of partition. When the train stopped Denys got out to see what all the fuss was about, and there he saw the Mahatma standing on the steps of his carriage. Denys was in his jungle-green uniform – the only Britisher around. 'I swear he [Gandhi] looked up and saw me and winked. But I may be quite wrong. I have always had that feeling that he winked at me.'[3]

Mohammed Sarwar had spent two years as Denys's batman, travelling everywhere with him. 'He made sure my uniform was in order, that I had a cup of tea in the morning; he was the chap who kept me on the straight and narrow.' Every officer had a batman. Denys communicated with Mohammed in fluent Urdu. He describes Mohammed as 'quiet, unprepossessing, gentle. Just very respectful.' Denys stills keeps a photograph of himself, Mohammed, George and Nihal Singh, his Sikh batman. The black-and-white image of the four men in their uniforms – Mohammed in a crisp white shirt, his head covered in a white headdress – hangs proudly in his study today.

Denys insists on getting all his old photographs out from the loft to show me. He climbs up a rickety old ladder, and I am worried this ninety-two-year-old will hurt himself. I needn't have been concerned. He returns with a cardboard box full of pictures: the officers playing cricket, a class photo of the Sandhurst cadets and the 1st Battalion, the Burma Regiment. Sitting in the centre is Captain Wild. Mohammed Sarwar is in the back row, standing on the far right in his regimental uniform.

Denys says he spent some of the most memorable days of his time in British India in Mohammed's village. Pindi Hashim was surrounded by the lush Punjabi plains: 'It was magic, actually.' Each evening Denys would carry up a charpoy, a light bedstead, onto the flat roof where he would sleep under the stars. 'It was lovely. It was nice and warm.' Mohammed showed him around. Denys had never ridden a horse before, but went, carefully, alongside the more experienced rider, Mohammed, with people waving to him on his way. In the evening the two men sat side by side on the earth, a British officer and his batman, eating a simple meal with their fingers of local vegetables and fresh chapattis, made by Mohammed's wife.

When Denys and Mohammed parted, they both knew it was for the last time. 'I don't remember discussing it at all, but I'm sure we all knew in our heart of hearts that we wouldn't see each other again,' says Denys. 'I couldn't put my hand on my heart saying I remember being in tears or near to it saying goodbye, but I'm sure I was. Everything seemed to be happening so quickly at that stage. India was part of the British Empire. Then it suddenly became independent and everything sort of happened bang bang bang on top of the other. And I think there was probably very little time for emotion.'

After they said their goodbyes, Denys started his long journey back to England. On Independence Day he and George found themselves stuck in Lahore. Two days later it was announced that Lahore was to become part of Pakistan. The two men stayed at the prestigious Faletti's Hotel on Egerton Road, just off the city's historical boulevard, 'The Mall'. The hotel boasted electric lights and fans in every room.[4] Out on the streets, Denys saw how the locals they came across 'were full of joy at being independent'. He recalls people coming to shake his hand, saying to him: 'Thank you for making us independent.' They were not able to leave the city as the train station 'was knee deep in bodies. Nobody could move.' He was told: 'Sit tight until it clears.'

One day a man charged into the hotel. It was Sir John Bennet, 'Inspector General Police in Punjab, big wheel'. He had with him his Hindu driver; 'probably hid him under the bed or something like that' to keep him away from the mobs, Denys presumes. During this time, he and the other army officers, who were mostly the occupants of the hotel, kept out of sight as much as possible: 'One just laid very low. Not for fear of any sort of reprisals or antipathy towards us, but the opposite, really. I don't think we felt any fear of what had become Pakistani people attacking us or being nasty to us or anything like that. I think we just laid low because there was so much of a problem going on elsewhere.'

After the officers received the all-clear to leave for the train station, Denys and George began their journey back to Britain. They travelled through Lahore, Delhi and Calcutta. But Denys has little recollection of witnessing any horrors. 'I think people of our age in those days were not exactly overburdened with thoughts about what was happening elsewhere in the country of India or what had become Pakistan. I think we were, it sounds self-centred to say so, almost ignorant of what was really happening on the nasty side.'

There was no question of Denys (or any British officer) going out to help subdue the disorder. He and George were on their own, using up the last days of their leave, his regiment about to be disbanded. 'We were fairly thin on the ground by that time. Certainly British troops would have left India. British officers would have been in the process of being taken over by their counterparts of India (and Pakistan). Maybe they could have done more.'[5]

With Indian independence, some British Army regiments were already on their way back to Britain. The alternative British initiative to quell the growing unrest was a limited military force operational from 1 August 1947. The Punjab Boundary Force was at its peak a 50,000-strong contingent, led by British officers. The majority of the troops on the ground were from the polarised Punjabi Muslim and Sikh communities. It was a 'toothless and dreadfully inadequate response to Partition's violence'.[6] They policed a 37,500-square-mile area with a population of 14.5 million across the twelve districts of central Punjab. However, by 25 August the Boundary Force was fatigued and their mood explosive.[7] The force was disbanded just two weeks after partition, and had been active a mere thirty-two days. The two new dominions took responsibility for the security of refugees on their respective sides of the border. The remaining British Army units had strict instructions to intervene only to save British lives.[8] By February 1948 all the British military units had left.[9]

'I think we all, sort of people like myself and other British officers, felt that partition was a huge mistake, but I think we also felt that the whole thing was too quick,' says Denys. 'It was speeded through. They should have taken a bit more time. The whole thing was not thought through. I think the British government of the day were anxious to get it done quickly and Mountbatten was a pretty ruthless man. And he backed that and made sure it did go through quickly. And it was a great mistake. If everybody had taken another six months or so, a lot more could have been sorted out. That's my – that was the view we all held.'

Denys returned to the 'dreary' port of Liverpool, demobbed, with a longing for India, and no idea what to do with the rest of his life. He spent most of his £50 war gratuity on going to the 1948 Summer Olympics in Wembley every day. It was four guineas a day to enter: 'It was the best money I ever spent.' Yet all he wanted to do was return to India. His dear friend George from his regiment suggested a job at a tea plantation, and so in 1949 Denys returned to India, and spent the next twenty-five years in Assam.

Denys is ninety-two when we meet, a very sprightly ninety-two. He lives in Dorset, in a picture-perfect English cottage. It is touching to hear of his deep affection for India, the place he spent his formative years, where he saw active service, made his career, met his wife Elizabeth and raised their four children. The only time he gets to try out his Urdu and Hindi now is when he is speaking to an operator at an Indian call centre, to complain that his broadband is not working. Denys is one of a vanishing generation, an old-school British gentleman. If you passed him on the street you would not know part of him belongs to a foreign land, a land he still holds dear. 'India means a lot. I would love to go back, actually, I'm getting too old to do it now. I have a great sort of feeling for India.'

Denys Wild OBE was born in 1925 in Addiscombe, Surrey. He served as a captain with the British Indian Army during the Second World War. From 1949 he worked in tea plantations in Assam, becoming a general manager. On his return to the UK in the 1970s he worked in the Foreign Office, specialising in Indian affairs. He was awarded an OBE for his work as chair of the Assam Branch of the UK Citizens Association and for helping evacuate UK citizens during the secession of East Pakistan from Pakistan in 1971. He died in July 2018, aged ninety-three.

My father, Ravi Datt Puri, as a young man. Born into a Hindu family in Lahore, he and his siblings were sent to live in safety with their grandparents shortly before partition.

My father waited until he was eighty-two to fully describe what he witnessed as a boy in India in the days after partition.

Pamela Dowley-Wise with her Raleigh bicycle. She was pushed off it in Calcutta in 1946, being told to 'Quit India' by the man who attacked her.

Pamela was in Calcutta during the Bengal famine, the Japanese air raids of the Second World War, and the Great Calcutta Killings. She left India in 1946 for England, but returned often in her life, and says she always retained her love for the country.

As a Hindu, Ramen Bannerjee had to leave his home in Dhaka when it became part of East Pakistan. 'Partition shattered my life,' he said.

Bashir Maan watched as all the Sikhs and Hindus left his village in West Punjab. Six years later, he started a new life in Scotland, selling clothes door to door. He would eventually become the first Muslim and British Pakistani to be elected to political office.

As a boy in Meghna, Ken Miln was obsessed with fishing in the Hooghly River. Even bodies washing in from the 1946 riots in Calcutta failed to deter him.

Ken's family moved to the UK in 1949, when he was twelve. He still misses India and feels that 'spiritually' he is Indian.

Denys Wild became a captain in the British Indian Army in 1944.

Captioned 'Officers and their Orderlies', this image shows Denys front left. His batman – or personal servant – Mohammed Sarwar stands back right.

Although he returned to England after partition, Denys moved back to live and work in Assam in 1949, where he married and raised a family. He stayed for twenty-five years.

As a young boy in East Punjab, Gurbakhsh Garcha witnessed appalling scenes of sadness and cruelty as his Muslim neighbours were forced out.

Gurbakhsh says that after what he witnessed during partition he realised 'human beings are very fragile – it doesn't take long to turn them into beasts'.

Karam Singh Hamdard (second from left in the front row) standing next to his father. His mother sits at the centre. An event in his village days after partition would change his family for ever.

What happened to Karam Singh's family during partition was so traumatic that he still finds it hard to recount some incidents.

Swaran Rayit, aged five, sits in the front row between his father and grandfather, dressed like an English boy.

Today Swaran, who saw terrible scenes of murder during a revenge attack on Muslims, still thinks, 'Why this partition?' Seventy years later, it makes no sense to him.

Harchet Singh Bains was one of hundreds of thousands of Sikhs once living on the Pakistani side of the partition border. His family walked for days in a long line of people to reach safety in India.

Khurshid Begum was a Muslim living in a village that became part of India. Her grandmother stood up to the male relatives, insisting they should all leave for Pakistan rather than stay and fight.

Mohindra Dhall's family had to leave Lyallpur when it became part of Pakistan. He still dreams that the Punjab will become 'one Punjab', not divided by religion.

PART II

PARTITION

7

Partition

On the stroke of midnight on 15 August 1947, India and Pakistan officially gained their independence and became dominions within the British Commonwealth. Britain had surrendered the keystone of its empire and its rule over almost 400 million people. In Pakistan celebrations took place a day earlier in the new capital, Karachi, presided over by Mohammed Ali Jinnah and the Viceroy Lord Louis Mountbatten. In Delhi, official events occurred on 15 August. Some princely states, including Hyderabad and Kashmir, were of uncertain status having refused to accede to either country.

Astonishingly, millions of people had no idea at the moment of freedom whether they were in India or Pakistan, as the boundary lines in the provinces of Bengal and Punjab had not yet been made public. This uncertainty aggravated the chaos and panic. Sir Cyril Radcliffe, the British lawyer tasked with demarcating the boundary line, had never previously been to India and was given a mere forty days to decide on the border. He spent much of his time in the confines of the Viceroy's House in Delhi, surrounded by maps, submissions and reports. He did not once visit the actual communities he was dividing.

The border was not announced until two days after independence on 17 August. 'Nobody in India will love me for my award about the Punjab and Bengal,' Radcliffe wrote to his stepson a few days earlier, 'and there will be roughly 80 million people with a grievance who will begin looking for me. I do not want them to find me.'[1] Following the announcement, Radcliffe promptly got on a plane back to England, apparently burned all his papers, and never returned to India.

The new border crossed agricultural land, cut off communities from their sacred pilgrimage sites, paid no heed to railway lines, and separated industrial plants from the agricultural lands where raw materials such as jute were grown.[2]

The two states were divided broadly along religious lines. Punjab in the west and Bengal in the east were split into two according to their Muslim and non-Muslim majority areas. West Punjab, along with Sindh, Balochistan and North-West Frontier Province together with East Bengal formed the new Islamic state of Pakistan. East and West Pakistan were separated by nearly a thousand miles of Indian territory. Travelling by sea between Pakistan's two major ports of Karachi and Chittagong took around five days. Jinnah described his country as 'a truncated, moth-eaten' territory.[3]

A month before division, the future governments of India and Pakistan issued a joint declaration saying that violence would not be tolerated. They imagined the local police and the Punjab Boundary Force would be able to take care of any difficulties that arose. There was no plan in place for the widespread murderous rampage that took place, particularly in Punjab, or for any potential mass population exchanges.[4]

The calculation of partition, which depended on head counts and the percentages of people living in districts, now came into full effect. Intricately entwined communities were to become for ever ripped apart. The intensity of this unpicking had been catastrophically underestimated by the new governments and the colonial authorities.[5]

The numbers killed in partition violence will never be known. Monsoon floods, mass disposal of bodies and administrative collapse meant corpses could not be fully recovered or enumerated.[6] Figures range from the low estimate of 200,000 by the British civil servant Penderel Moon, to up to 2 million by some South Asian scholars.[7] Many historians have settled for a figure of between half a million and a million.[8] Tens of thousands of women and girls are believed to have been raped and abducted, mostly by men from the 'other' religion.

In *The Partition of India*, Ian Talbot and Gurharpal Singh differentiate the 'end of Empire violence from traditional communal violence' that preceded it, in a number of ways. There was a desire to squeeze out, or ethnically cleanse, minority populations; violence occurred within the context of the end of Empire, and the contest for power and territory; partition violence was more intense and sadistic than anything that had preceded it; the violence spread to the private sphere: women and children were caught up; and finally the violence evinced a high degree of planning and organisation by paramilitary groups, assisted by the quiescence if not active involvement of state agents.[9]

Violence differed across northern India in its intensity but also its timing. It peaked in Bihar, Bengal and Uttar Pradesh in late 1946. It only began in Punjab in March

1947 and continued until independence. In Sindh in Pakistan and in Delhi, the capital of independent India, it only started with the arrival of partition refugees following independence.[10]

The resulting migration in response to violence or the impending threat of violence (though of course some chose to leave) is the largest single movement of people outside war and famine in human history. It is estimated that between 10 and 12 million migrated at the time of partition, though the precise numbers will never be known.[11] The majority of those fleeing in August 1947 and the immediate months after were from Punjab. Millions had no choice but to move as they found themselves on the wrong side of the border. The two-way flow in Punjab peaked between August and November 1947. Once the violence started, governments on both sides of the border, shocked at the scale of the killings and huge influx of refugees, set up Military Evacuation Organisations (MEOs) in India and Pakistan. They organised the movements of people, taking them across the border.[12]

Between 1946 and 1950 rioters wreaked havoc in many cities. Riot zones were declared in Delhi, Bombay (now Mumbai), Karachi and Quetta, in towns in Uttar Pradesh, the hill stations of Simla and Dehradun, Ahmedabad, Khala Ghoda and Vadodara in Gujarat, Ajmer and Udaipur in Rajasthan. Each riot had its own causes, but the social dislocation of partition in areas beyond Punjab and Bengal generated individual economic crises, refugee upheavals and visible destruction in every area affected.[13]

This movement of people transformed the new states, as well as the individuals. Cosmopolitan cities such as Delhi, Bombay, Karachi, Amritsar and Lahore lost their citizens, and were shaped by an influx of refugees. But these newcomers did not always have the skills to fill the gaps left by those fleeing. The economy and the functioning of the state in both countries suffered.

The governments of India and Pakistan assisted, as far as they were able, with the rehabilitation of the refugees from the Punjab and other areas they deemed exceptionally disturbed. But all other refugees had to rebuild their lives using their own networks and often modest personal resources. Some did so with remarkable success. However, the poorest among them fared less well, some living for years in very basic camps. Some of these camps still exist in India, particularly in divided Bengal.[14]

Many people ask why Bengal receives less attention than Punjab in partition discussions. Much of this has to do with how convulsive the violence was in Punjab at the moment of partition. In Bengal there was less bloodshed around 15 August 1947 and the migration flows were lower at that time. However, mass migration continued for decades to come, peaking during communal disturbances.[15] East and West Pakistan were united by religion, but profound differences in language and culture proved stronger. In 1971 the Bangladesh liberation war resulted in an estimated 10 million people fleeing for their lives from East Pakistan to India, as West Pakistan brutally suppressed the secessionists. Hundreds of thousands of people were killed.

Partition changed the demographic make-up of the Indian subcontinent. Today only 2 per cent of the population of Pakistan is Hindu (Sikhs were not considered in the most recent census). The latest Indian census shows there are, however, up to 180 million Muslims living in the country, just under 15 per cent of the total population. There is a Hindu contingent in Bangladesh (former East Pakistan) of nearly 9 per cent, though it is rapidly declining. But in Punjab, partition saw the virtual depopulation of Muslims in East Punjab, and Hindus and Sikhs in West Punjab by a state-assisted transfer of the population.[16] Punjab today is almost completely segregated. The existence of communities that had lived together for centuries, with a shared language and culture, can only now be learned of in history books.

8

My Faith in Humanity is Shaken

It is the spring of 2017, a few months shy of the seventieth anniversary of partition, and I am sitting in the morning sunshine eating freshly made ginger cake in a garden in Lewisham, south London. The birds are singing. It is a picture of peace only occasionally disturbed by the sound of low-flying aeroplanes. Gurbakhsh Garcha, smartly dressed in a Nehru waistcoat, exudes gentleness and calm. A calm that must have been tested many times during his tenure as Mayor of Lewisham, navigating the local politics. He has a look of nobility; in his comportment, the way he speaks and moves. The story he tells me will never leave me. It is one of the most shattering I have ever heard. He speaks quietly, pausing often, he paints vivid pictures as he talks. I can see the scenes so clearly, though there are times I wish I could not.

Indian sweets were handed out to all the schoolchildren. It was 15 August 1947. India had won its independence and there was a break from lessons to celebrate. Twelve-year-old Gurbakhsh did not really know what all the fuss was about. He, like the rest of the villagers, had only ever known a time when they had been ruled by a monarch. He had overheard some elders in the village say independence now meant India's new leader, Jawaharlal Nehru, must be the new King of India.[1]

Dhandari Khurd in Punjab was a small village of around 150 people: mostly Sikh – like Gurbakhsh – a quarter Muslim, and one Hindu family. They shared with each other their own distinctive Punjabi culture, and spoke Punjabi with one another. The village was just five miles from the main city of Ludhiana. Politics had not really bothered many in the village. The British Raj was accepted as a fact, and they did not know much about the independence movement. Most of them had never even seen a Britisher.

Two days after independence, Gurbakhsh and the rest of the village crowded around the one wireless in Dhandari Khurd to listen to All India Radio. Citizens of this small Punjabi community were no longer ruled by the British but the new borders of Punjab and Bengal had still not been made public. Gurbakhsh, like millions of others, had no idea which side of the line his village was on.

The atmosphere was tense. It was clear to the people of Dhandari Khurd that Ludhiana would be in India. Then the announcer declared which country the city of Lahore had been awarded to. There were gasps of disbelief all around. Some men started crying.

Lahore was one of Punjab's most cosmopolitan cities, with a large Hindu and Sikh population. Since March 1947 it had seen some of the worst communal fighting on the Indian subcontinent. Sir Cyril Radcliffe had decreed that Lahore was to be part of Pakistan. The villagers did not want Lahore to go, it was a big prize. They felt the British had betrayed them.

Gurbakhsh's home was in a picturesque village amid the fertile plains of Punjab. The region was laced with five rivers, stretching from the Himalayas in the north to the Thar Desert in the west. The villagers farmed wheat, corn, cotton and groundnuts. A scene unchanged in centuries. Years later, Gurbakhsh Garcha would write of the idyll of his childhood days:

> Magic was the air of Punjab
> And as sacred nectar Dhandari's water
> Where my playmates used to dwell.

He would run around the open streets. There was a not a tree he had not climbed. He played kudukundi, a local game, with a home-made ball of rags and a branch from an acacia tree for a hockey stick. He would take his yellow kite out to fly. He felt free:

> Wire fashioned into hoop and hook;
> Running free in the fields all day,
> Playing hide-and-seek at night
> Sleep pursued us in vain.
> Food merely an afterthought
> Magic was in the air.

It was a harmonious and tight-knit community. Religious difference was barely thought about. No one could have believed that one day they would separate from each other.

Just before partition, Gurbakhsh noticed posters going up around the village inciting bloodshed against the Muslims his family had lived alongside for decades. They said that anyone demanding India should be split to create Pakistan would get 'kabristan' (a Muslim burial ground).

Gurbakhsh never thought his peaceful village would be touched by any kind of violence. But then the Sikh gangs arrived, carrying swords and spears. They were on the lookout for Muslims. One day a group approached Gurbakhsh's grandfather. They called out to him, asking if there were any Muslims working on his land. His grandfather responded that it had nothing to do with them. 'We want to kill Muslims,' they shouted back. 'They are my children,' Gurbakhsh's grandfather told them. 'They have been working with me since they were little boys. You will have to kill me before you touch them. If you touch me, the whole village will be here and you won't escape.' Gurbakhsh's grandfather was an imposing figure. He was six foot tall and well built. The men hurled abuse at him but then left. The Muslim farm workers were terrified. Not long afterwards they left their village, and India, for good.

By the time of partition, many of the Muslim neighbours began to move out too. But there is one goodbye Gurbakhsh can never forget. His uncle's mother had died many years before and one of her best friends, a Muslim neighbour whom they all called Mai, had raised Gurbakhsh's uncle as her own. So close were relations that Mai had even been his wet nurse. Gurbakhsh would often see her while he played with his cousins. She bathed him as a little boy. Mai's sons would carry him across the fields to their farm. Gurbakhsh felt part of her family; she part of theirs.

It soon became too unsafe for Mai's family to stay in the village. They told Gurbakhsh's uncle they needed to leave. He borrowed an Indian Army truck and with sadness loaded up their belongings. The Sikh villagers gathered around the Muslim family on the day they parted. They were all crying. Mai took Gurbakhsh into her arms, reassuring him they would soon be back. He felt her warmth for the last time.

The villagers watched as the uncle drove Mai and her family to a safe transit camp for Pakistan.

Mai meant what she said – she believed she would return. She even handed the keys to her house to the uncle so he could look after it in their absence. He kept them for years afterwards, not allowing anyone near their home. But Mai never came back. No one heard from them again.

There were different posters now, plastered all over the walls of houses and pinned to trees. 'You are all Indians, whatever your religion,' they said. 'Do not fight each other. Allow the country to prosper without foreign leaders.' They were signed by Mohammed Ali Jinnah, Pakistan's leader, and Mahatma Gandhi, the spiritual leader of India's ruling Congress Party. It had been unthinkable to the Pakistani and Indian political leadership and colonial authorities that so many, in their millions, would move. The partition plan had assumed that groups of religious minorities would remain on both sides. This plea for unity was too late.

Dhandari Khurd was on the main railway line from Delhi to Lahore. The track meandered through the plains of Punjab. One of Gurbakhsh's family fields, where he would play, was just twenty yards from the railway line. Trains were now full of refugees from both sides of the border. One day, while milling about with friends, a train passed by, slowly. The doors were open, revealing men, women and children, some dead, some dying, covered in blood. Twelve-year-old Gurbakhsh watched the scene in horror. There had been rumours of trains loaded with the dead, butchered by fanatics from both sides as they tried to escape across the border.

From that same field, weeks later, Gurbakhsh saw another of these ghost trains arrive, but there was something unusual.

Life amidst death. A dishevelled and distressed woman with two small children fell off the train and made her way erratically across the fields towards his village. Gurbakhsh ran towards her, where a crowd had begun to gather. It became clear she was a Muslim. The Sikh women of Gurbakhsh's village took the woman and her children to a farm building for their protection. They brought food and clothes. They reassured the woman that even though she, a Muslim, was in a Sikh village in India, she was now safe. They hid her and the children in a barn used for storing animal fodder, hoping the Sikh gangs would not find them there.

Gurbakhsh saw how the Sikh women of his village were touched by the plight of this stranger – a Muslim, the so-called enemy. 'People hadn't lost their humanity, especially women who saw a woman with children – small children. Your motherhood comes first.'

Safely in the barn now, among the fodder, the Muslim lady was distraught. She was crying continuously, clinging on to her two children, repeating: 'Allah will help, Allah will save us. It's Allah's will.' She refused the offers of clothes and food, only accepting milk for the children. Gurbakhsh had been watching all of this. She looked so afraid, he thought, her future so bleak. A few days later the villagers arranged with the police to take the woman and her children to a safe camp near the border. No one knew what became of them.

Across Punjab, in both directions, millions of refugees fled not only by train, but also on foot. This mass of humanity – caravans of people – could be many miles long. Gurbakhsh was a witness to one of the largest mass migrations the world had ever seen. He saw these lines of exhausted people, travelling together for safety, with their bullock carts and whatever possessions they were able to grab before they left their homes. He saw how they would sleep on the road, some camping in his family's groundnut fields, the same place he would play and help on his grandfather's farm.

A year later he and his grandfather were weeding together in fields near the railway line. The grandfather noticed that the groundnut crop grew surprisingly lushly in certain, seemingly random, patches of the field. They discovered that the crops had been fertilised by human bodies, refugees who had died on their journey – the sick, the elderly, the young – buried in shallow graves. His grandfather told Gurbakhsh not to disturb them. 'It is their place of rest,' he said.

To Gurbakhsh, the childhood of running carefree through the fields and playing hide-and-seek with his friends suddenly felt like a dream. The magic in the air lost for ever. He now felt his whole being had changed with all he had witnessed. He got used to seeing bodies exposed, used to seeing death all around him. He was now numb to it.

What was unthinkable before became permissible. Gurbakhsh recalls that during the massacres, Muslim women were taken by elderly Sikhs who wanted a wife. He noticed how they would take the young pretty Muslim girls. He heard the same was happening in Pakistan, with Hindu and Sikh women being taken by older Muslim men. He observed how some of these relationships became permanent and accepted by the women and some did not.

Another uncle of Gurbakhsh's, a young and handsome Sikh man, saved a young Muslim woman after her family had been massacred. Gurbakhsh saw how over time the two grew dependent upon each other. She then converted by choice and married him – he had become her protector. She had nowhere else to go, no family left, and no wish to go to

Pakistan as she had no relatives there. Gurbakhsh would see them together, many years later: this Muslim woman who was now a Sikh and had become a fully accepted member of his family. He always thought how happy they looked together.

Yet there was another, more sinister side. Gurbakhsh also remembers the house of one of his cousins. He was from a much wealthier family and he had the one thing Gurbakhsh craved – a library. One day Gurbakhsh was visiting and there was an elderly Sikh man there too. He recognised him as one of the men who had been involved in carrying out massacres against the Muslims. He always carried a sword and spear. That day he'd brought with him a young, attractive woman, who appeared to be in great anguish. Gurbakhsh could see she was terrified and how the elderly Sikh wanted her to obey him. In front of everyone he taunted her, held out a spoon covered in pork fat and demanding she lick it. Gurbakhsh knew that pork was forbidden. There were no pigs in the village out of respect for their Muslim neighbours. But the young Muslim woman had no choice. She licked the spoon in front of the spectators. Gurbakhsh burst into tears and went straight home. He could taste her humiliation. He felt hatred towards the old man. Weeping, he told his grandmother what he had seen. She knew this man. 'Oh, they are barbarians,' was her response.

Gurbakhsh now assumes the woman must have been raped by the elderly man and believes the rest of the village knew that. They accepted it, he says, as they knew the Muslims were doing it to Sikh women.

After partition, Gurbakhsh heard of abducted women who had been rescued by the authorities. He learned that the young Muslim woman taken by the elderly Sikh had been one of those saved. She had returned safely to Pakistan. He was relieved.

There were now just a handful of Muslims left in Dhandari Khurd. Gurbakhsh's teacher was a Muslim called Umarbaksh. He lived in a neighbouring village and had taught at his school for many years. He was being protected by the village headman, Zalidar Shamsher Singh, who was well known in the area and had influence with officials and the police. One day, Umarbaksh was threatened by a Sikh gang in his village. He told them: 'If you want to kill me, ask Zalidar first.' The gang took him and two of his sons from their village towards Dhandari Khurd, ostensibly to meet Zalidar. Then they stopped at an area lined with trees, between the two villages, near the road and the railway line. They took out their knives and killed the three of them in cold blood. Gurbakhsh's great uncle heard about this and rushed to the scene to try to resuscitate them, but it was too late. Their throats had been cut. Some of the adult villagers came out and gave the slain men a burial where they had fallen.

The place they were laid to rest was just a hundred yards from Gurbakhsh's school. Everyone there knew where their schoolteacher now lay. One of the sons who had been murdered was a classmate of Gurbakhsh's – they were the same age. Gurbakhsh says he was very disturbed by these deaths. The next day at school, the schoolteacher's only surviving son came in crying uncontrollably. A new teacher at the school, a refugee from Pakistan, said to the boy: 'I feel very sad looking at you. The cruelty you are suffering we have suffered on the other side the same way. It's a very nasty world. I wish I could give you more comfort.' The lone son stayed some days, then left for Pakistan.

And that is what happened in Dhandari Khurd. After Umarbaksh was murdered all the Muslims left. They could no longer be protected by the villagers. Families who had lived on the land for generations fled and never came back. Their homes were soon taken by refugee Hindu and Sikh families coming from Pakistan. The villagers of Dhandari Khurd still thought one day their old Muslim neighbours could return. But the new occupants put that thought to rest. 'Be under no misconception,' they told them, 'they are never coming back. We can't go back to Pakistan, they won't come back.' Most of the new arrivals had no experience of farming. The Muslim land was divided amongst the long-time Sikh and Hindu families.

Gurbakhsh didn't see any of his Muslim friends again; the ones he'd climbed trees with since he was a boy, and with whom he'd played hide-and-seek on the undivided Punjabi plains. He did receive a letter from Pakistan from one of his closest friends. Gurbakhsh answered, but they never wrote again.

His grandmother felt the loss of her best friend, Ehsa. 'Ehsa would have said this or done that,' she would say to Gurbakhsh. At Eid she would sigh: 'We have no Indian sweets this year from them.' Ehsa is still vivid to Gurbakhsh. When he was a toddler she would take him in her arms if he had hurt himself in her house, comforting him. Gurbakhsh remembers her smell. There is no trace now that she had ever lived in his village.

Years later there were floods and Gurbakhsh and his friends saw the skeletons of his teacher and sons exposed in shallow graves. A ghoulish reminder that Muslims once lived in Dhandari Khurd. But this story is not one Gurbakhsh has ever talked of. It is too painful to recount. His children didn't ask. And, anyway, he did not want to expose them to things he had witnessed.

He is still angry at the way and manner of the British withdrawal. Gurbakhsh calls himself an agnostic Sikh. He feels his faith in humanity has been shaken, that human beings are fragile. How little it takes to turn them into beasts.

Gurbakhsh Garcha was born in 1935 in Dhandari Khurd, British Colonial India. There are no Muslim families in his birthplace today. He came to Britain in 1958. He was a technician in a brain research laboratory, and Mayor of Lewisham from 1994–95 He died in September 2018.

9

Desh

'Collect as much as you can and go to the square.'[1] It was a summer's evening in September 1947, and eleven-year-old Harchet Singh Bains was confused at this instruction from his father. He walked towards the village square, the most notable feature of which was the communal well. The area was full of people, people Harchet had never seen before. Mostly there were Sikhs, but also Hindus, children, women, entire families. He waited with them, unsure as to what was going on, and after some hours, fell asleep on the ground where he stood. He was woken early the next morning and told to prepare to leave.

The family took their cart, pulled by two oxen, laden with whatever food and clothing it could hold, and some fodder for the animals. Harchet managed to take some books, and a little wooden spinning wheel, stuffing them into his trouser pockets. He watched as his father locked the house up. The key was given to their Muslim neighbour, Inyattollah, for safe keeping. Harchet overheard his father giving instructions about feeding the animals, and the time of day to milk the buffalo. Inyattollah reassured Harchet's father not to worry about his home, it would be well looked after until he was back. 'Nobody was aware that we were leaving for good.'

Harchet had not a clue what was going on. He was told they were going to desh (homeland); the place, the village you are from. He was bewildered: 'I am from the village I have just left. That is my home.'

It had been such a happy childhood in western Punjab, in his village near Okara in Montgomery district. Harchet's father was a successful farmer; they had a large house known as a haveli, with land. They kept buffalo and oxen, and had carts and farming equipment. Politics never touched his life. Harchet hadn't even set eyes on an Englishman.

There were no radios in the village. Occasionally an Urdu newspaper would be brought from town, when the farmers sold their produce at market, and read to the mainly illiterate villagers. Harchet had overheard the adults speak of Jinnah and Gandhi but didn't know who they were. At the gurdwara there was talk of independence, but to Harchet it meant little, there was never a sense that it would mean being uprooted.

Evenings were spent crowded around the one gramophone in the village, where Harchet, his neighbourhood friends, and their families would sit together and listen to old folk songs. There weren't many records, so they would play the same few over and over again. 'Pagdi Sambhal Jatta' is the one he remembers. A song about a farmer's life, a difficult life, during the time of British India. A man who has debts to a moneylender.

Harchet is a youthful-looking eighty-two. A statuesque, dignified man, his only ailment is the arthritis which niggles him when he gets up off the floor of the gurdwara he established near his home in Hertfordshire. He still sits cross-legged for prayer at his place of worship, and wears a turban, as his father and forefathers did. He works now to improve interfaith relations among the British South Asian community around Hitchin. As a child he remembers that those of different faiths mixed freely in his village. He went to the mosque to celebrate festivals, and the Muslims came to their home to mark Diwali. The communities didn't intermarry – other than that they were 'very, very friendly'. His best friend was Mohammed Azeez, a Muslim boy. They played kabaddi, a team game involving tagging each other, picked fruit from the trees, sharing the spoils, and spent their time 'just making mischief as all children do'. In the rush to leave there had been no time to say goodbye to his dear friend Mohammed.

Around half a million Sikhs lived in parts of Punjab that were now on Pakistan's side of the partition line, including Okara and Harchet's village. Pakistan became home to some of the holiest Sikh pilgrimage sites including the birthplace of Guru Nanak, the founder of Sikhism. Sikhs were leaving not just their homes but also their most sacred places.

Harchet and the throngs of people – minorities in this new country – started walking in a long line, a kafila. Harchet learned that they had to flee, as Hindus and Sikhs in nearby villages had been attacked and killed, and they were no longer safe. They had to move quickly and were told to stay close together. In the chaos of leaving two of Harchet's cousins, aged four and three, went missing.

On the second day of their journey by foot, Harchet saw parts of the human line come under attack from Muslims. It was only then that he and his family realised they would not be returning to their village again. Two retired Sikh army officers on horseback, with rifles on their shoulders, were all there was to protect the group. The two rode back and forth along the line of people. 'I remember the army men telling us, "Be close together, it's very dangerous. It is firing going on, people are killing other people, so be very, very vigilant." ' When a Muslim mob approached to target the kafila, on seeing the armed men, they would back off. They focused their attack on parts of the line where there was no one patrolling. Often grown men in the caravan would carry lathis – bamboo poles – as they walked, to defend themselves and their families.

People tried to help one another as best they could. 'The younger and fitter people used to help the very frail,' says Harchet. 'My grandmother, who was quite frail, she did survive all the journey but very slowly, so we were trying to help. I couldn't help her because I was too young but I used to lay my hand on her and say, Dadi, Grandmother, we will soon reach.'

Harchet crouches down as he shows me now how he and his siblings were told to walk underneath the horse cart, while the adults of the family walked around the wagon to protect them. 'It was difficult to walk like that while you're crouching but it was so terrible situation that we were made to do that for our safety.' As they walked they were told to say prayers so God could save them during the journey. They recited the 'Mul Mantar' in Punjabi, the first composition of the Sikh holy text 'Japji Sahib', a prayer every Sikh child knew:

> There is only one God,
> Eternal truth is His name,
> He is the creator,
> He is without fear
> He is without hate,
> Immortal, without form,
> Beyond birth and death,

He is the enlightener,
He can be reached through the mercy and grace of the
true Guru.

The rains soon came and it quickly became muddy and difficult for the bullocks dragging the carts. They threw out some of the heavier belongings to help the animals, but eventually as the rain came down harder it became impossible to move, and the carts and their contents were abandoned. Harchet's books in his pockets and the wooden spinning wheel had long been jettisoned. It was now a matter of survival. All Harchet and his family had with them were the clothes on their backs.

The food they carried had run out. It is the persistent hunger that is the abiding memory for Harchet of that journey, and his crying to be fed. Harchet's parents would pick tender leaves to eat from plants or trees – wherever it was safe to get them. These leaves had now replaced Harchet's belongings in his pockets. The children hated eating them, they tasted of nothing – so his elder sister found some spicy chilli leaves which they would rub on the other leaves to make them more palatable. 'It looked at that time very, very tasty because the tasteless leaves were so horrible to eat, but to fill your stomach up you had to eat something. We were crying and we were not happy and saying how come we eat leaves but that was the only thing available so we had to make do with that … so we had to survive like that.'

One day the elders went to find water, and found corpses in the well. After that, the children were told to drink from the puddles, even if they were muddy. Muddy water was preferable to water which had lain with decomposing bodies.

As the caravan went on it picked up more and more people from the villages along the way, until Harchet believes it was miles long; as a child he said it felt never-ending.[2] As they walked they would hear cries of people who were hurt badly, lying along the roadside. Harchet assumes many had been attacked by the mobs as they walked, and most likely eventually died where they fell. But they could not be carried or cared for, so the caravan moved on past them. 'I saw somebody; his throat was cut and he was lying backwards and I could see the blood coming out and he was trying to speak but obviously he couldn't. All I remember was he was making some kind of sound and I don't think he survived very long.' They felt sorry for these discarded people, but soon they began to see them so frequently that they barely noticed them.

Harchet finally knew he was safe when he was handed roasted chickpeas and nuts by villagers in Fazilka, which he discovered was in India. He laughs as he recounts stuffing the morsels into his mouth. The first decent food in days. Harchet is still unsure how long the journey was by foot – he thinks maybe four or five days. They were relieved finally to be safe. But his two little cousins were still missing. He remembers loudspeakers overhead advising the incoming refugees to take a bus or train to their intended destination in India – and that travel was free. From Fazilka they boarded a train 'which was so full we were made to sit on the top of the train, on the roof, and lucky [if] nobody fell off. We held each other as we sat on the roof.' They were bound for the district of Hoshiarpur – where the family had originally come from generations back. Desh.

They entered the village of Khera barefoot. The men had lost their turbans; their shirts and kurtas (tunics) were torn. This is how they walked towards their desh.

They were given a house which had once belonged to a Muslim family, but it had no doors. The rioters had burned them. There were literally just bricks and walls. Inside, there were no cooking utensils, bedding or clothing. This was no place for children, so Harchet and his four siblings were billeted temporarily with other family members who had been housed nearby. Eventually they were allotted a small plot of land in Garhshankar, where Harchet resumed his schooling. But there was no respite. The schoolchildren from the area, Hindus and Sikhs, laughed at Harchet and his brothers with their bare feet, and old clothes, calling them refugees and displaced, as if they did not belong there.

Sometime later, Harchet is not sure whether it was weeks or months, news came that his little cousins were safe. Members of his family, along with the Indian authorities, had gone back to their village in Pakistan to look for them. They learned that the children, terrified by the noise made by the villagers on the day they all left, had run back to their home, only to discover it locked. Inyattollah, the Muslim neighbour who had kept the keys to Harchet's house, had looked after something far more precious than the building. The children had been safely cared for by him, and he now handed them over to their parents. It was to be the last time any family member ever returned to the village.

Eleven-year-old Harchet only wrote Urdu when he arrived in India, so he had to learn to write in Hindi as well as Punjabi. He was a good student and won scholarships to study further, qualifying as a teacher. One day he saw an advert by the

British High Commission saying teachers were required in Britain, so he applied and got a voucher to travel. Maybe he wouldn't have come to Britain if he had stayed in his home village in western Punjab, he muses.

Harchet arrived in Southall, west London, in 1964, but there were so many Indians, and so few jobs. He heard there were factories and foundries around Hitchin in Hertfordshire, so he tried his luck there. His first job was as a foreman in a flour mill, where he worked for seven years. After his shift he taught English to new immigrants on the 'Make Yourself at Home' scheme at a college of further education in Hitchin. And then he went to night school for five years, at the end of each working day in the factory, to learn electronic engineering. He lived in difficult conditions, three to a small room with one bed, and there were some in the town who would shout out racially abusive names to him in the street. He fought against discrimination in pay, and against the National Front, taking part in demonstrations. When he qualified from night school he worked till retirement as an electronic engineer for Granada Television.

In the years after he arrived in Hitchin, he wrote a letter to his schoolmate Mohammed Azeez, but never heard back. He applied to go to Pakistan to see if his friend was still alive, but was refused a visa. It's unlikely now that Harchet will ever return to the place he grew up, to see the fruit fields where he played kabaddi, at a time when a Sikh and Muslim could be best friends, a place where for generations his family had farmed the land.

'They say we are independent now, but what good it was when you have lost everything?' says Harchet. Even today he refuses to celebrate Independence Day on 15 August. It is a painful reminder of all his family had lost. 'It was a great tragedy, and we didn't like being friends one day and enemies the next … we will always curse the authorities, the British or Indians, the politicians who made this mess. I will never forget these tragic events. Always remember. I will take these things to my grave, so to speak, they were bad things. But they happened.'

Harchet Singh Bains was born in 1935 in Keba, Montgomery district, British India. He moved to Garhshankar in India following partition. He came to Britain in 1964 and worked in a flour mill factory, and then for Granada Television as an electronic engineer. He is a prominent member of Hertfordshire's Sikh community and established its first gurdwara, in Hitchin in 1976. He has been active in interfaith work for many decades.

10

My Mind is Still Confused

Karam Singh Hamdard is the interviewee I think about the most and who left me, and still leaves me, feeling unsettled. We were contacted by his grandson, Jasmeet, who said his grandfather had a story to share. Karam Singh, now a widower, lives in south-east London, and two of his four children live nearby. He moved into his Victorian terrace in 1971, when to be the only Asian family in the street was an open invitation for trouble. There are pictures all around his living room of his family, including his beloved wife, whose death four years before he has clearly not recovered from. Grief, though, is a condition Karam Singh has been acquainted with from a young age.

Karam Singh grew up in the small village of Mulewal Khaira in Jalandhar district, in East Punjab. There were around 200 people in the community in 1947. It was known to be a mixed village, of Sikhs, Muslims and Hindus. 'We were like one family,' says Karam Singh wistfully.[1] 'They were joining us, we were joining them, everybody joining each other in their sorrows and happiness and weddings and all those things.' When partition became a reality, his father, Labh Singh, joined a peace-making committee which met at the local police station every fortnight, where people would discuss how to keep order in the villages in the area. However, it was soon disbanded after disagreements. One particular member, Aslam, was fervently in favour of Pakistan and for all of Punjab to be part of it. It was an ominous foreboding of what was to come.

In the days immediately after partition little seemed to change in village life. Independence Day was barely acknowledged. News of where the dividing line was drawn eventually reached the village, but knowing they were in India caused not one of their Muslim neighbours to leave for Pakistan. 'Up to the last day of the last minute of the attack, there was no such thing as animosity.' But after the day of slaughter – just nineteen days after partition – no Muslim would ever live in Mulewal Khaira again.

On the morning of 3 September 1947, Karam Singh's mother injured her hip and was in terrible pain. His sisters administered a local remedy of hot milk, tamarind and ghee. But there was no time to recuperate. Just hours later – in the late afternoon – huge numbers of men streamed into the village from all directions. They were Muslims, Karam Singh says; he believes some were from nearby villages, others from the city. But they were also joined by people from his own village.

Mulewal Khaira was in newly independent India, but Karam Singh believes the mob were still hoping that Jalandhar district could be part of Pakistan. Karam Singh's family were Sikh, and now in danger. His mother, unable to move because of her injury earlier that day, was carried by her daughters upstairs and locked in a room for her own safety. The girls then fled for their lives.

Karam Singh's mother, still writhing in pain, must have been bewildered and scared. Alone in her house, she heard a familiar voice outside. It was that of a Muslim neighbour. 'There's an old woman in there,' she heard him say. 'I came to see her this morning. She is hurt and is in a bad condition.' But his message was not one of concern. 'Put the fire here then she will burn in this house.'

When Karam Singh tells me the story of his mother trapped in the house, hearing the voice of their neighbour-turned-murderer, he shudders. This is our exchange:

Karam Singh:	He was a Muslim from our village.
Me:	So, it was one of the people that you knew?
Karam Singh:	Yes. He was very close to us.
Me:	But he wanted your mother to die?
Karam Singh:	I don't know. This is the thing which, in my mind is still confused, why people changed so quickly from [the] positive to [the] negative side straight away.

'My mind is still confused.' Seventy years on it is incomprehensible to Karam Singh how this could have happened. How people who lived side by side with each other, who shared in each other's sorrows and happiness, could want a middle-aged woman to be burned alive in her own home. Karam Singh later tells me that same neighbour had come over earlier that day, before the attack, to enquire after his mother's injury and wish her well.

The question I am asked most about partition is the one that still perplexes Karam Singh today: how was it possible for people who once coexisted peacefully together to murder each other, and so viciously?

It is a question historians cannot answer definitively and still debate. Yasmin Khan says: 'Much evidence points not to the crazy and inexplicable actions of mad, uneducated peasants with sticks and stones, but to well-organised and well-motivated groups of young men, who went out – particularly in Punjab – to carry out ethnic cleansing.'[2] Historian Andrew Whitehead agrees: 'This was not a civil war with battle lines and rival armies – but nor was it simply spontaneous violence. On all sides, local militias and armed gangs planned how to inflict the greatest harm on those they had come to see as their enemies.'[3] That certainly explains the mentality of the mob who entered Mulewal Khaira on 3 September 1947. But for Karam Singh's neighbour, the turning of the individual, who has intimate knowledge of the victim, Professor Khan acknowledges: 'In other places, it was a case of neighbour turning against neighbour, often in a deluded form of "self-defence" or revenge, sometimes as a cover for resolving old family feuds, for getting back at a mercenary landlord or as a chance to loot. In the main, people were whipped up by demonisation of the other, encouraged by the rhetoric of politicians and a feverish media.'[4]

When the mob entered the village, Karam Singh was with his father. He watched as his father, one of the community elders, approached some of the Muslim men, imploring them not to attack, to go away. They didn't listen. Father and son then spoke a while, before Karam Singh's father said to his boy: 'God bless you.' He then walked away, by himself, towards their outer house, where the animals lived. Karam Singh watched as his father freed their cattle – so they would not be burned, he believes.

Karam Singh was now alone, and amid the panic and confusion, started to run. He heard a gunshot, then a split second later saw his school friend, who had been in front of him, lying on the ground. There was a black hole in his forehead – the mark of the bullet which had killed him. The mob were well armed. Karam Singh needed to hide. He ran to a nearby house. There were a group of people already sheltering there. But they were soon discovered. The mob shouted, threatening, banging on the windows. They were coming in, smashing the glass as they entered. Karam Singh felt a spear in his arm. He has no recollection of what happened next. 'They left me as dead ... I don't know how long I was unconscious. When I came around, there was a lot of weight on me and I was lying underneath it, under the dead bodies.'

Slowly, he freed himself. He tried not to look at the fresh corpses. Only one other boy had survived, though he had a terrible head injury. Karam Singh was so scared that he moved from the place of bodies to an empty house, and hid until daybreak. He recalls an eerie atmosphere in the village. It was completely deserted. Injured, Karam Singh left his hiding place to where a few people had started milling around. He was comforted by them and was put onto a bullock cart along with the boy with the head injury, and taken out of the village for safety. They were given food and beds and a doctor called to attend to them. Karam Singh was to be the only survivor of the attack in the house. The young boy died from his injuries. He didn't even live to see the next daybreak.

Karam Singh's family were by now all scattered. The mob had, on the neighbour's instigation, set fire to his house, intending to kill the 'old woman'. His mother, who had been trapped on the first floor, had seen through the cracks in the door the smoke rising. Realising she would be burned alive, she jumped out of the window, and survived. 'I don't know from where my mother got that strength, it must have been a miracle from God.' Karam Singh was later reunited with his mother and other family members. One of his sisters was saved by a Muslim family from the village who protected about thirty to forty women in their home. Another sister had a lucky escape, and was safe.

Local scores were settled that day too. Karam Singh heard that someone from a neighbouring village with a grudge against his uncle killed his cousin. The day of slaughter was about petty grievances, as well as who would control the land, and hatred of the 'other'. The mob were organised and well armed: the attack had been planned. Karam Singh heard rumours later that a Muslim inspector at the police station had been supplying weapons to some of the mob, including Aslam, the man who had been on the short-lived peace committee with his father.

It is only towards the end of the interview that I learn what happened to Karam Singh's father after they parted, once he had asked God to bless his son and freed the family's cattle. Karam Singh's daughter, Charan, is talking to me about her father's recollections, when she says: 'He didn't see his dad again.'

Karam Singh's father was the first to die at the hands of the mob that day. He was shot with a rifle. Seven decades on it is still too painful for Karam Singh to tell me this. His father's blessing were the last words he would ever speak to his child. I wonder if he gave that blessing knowing what was to befall him.

I think of Karam Singh the most because of how raw his emotions still are. 'When I remember, my body shakes,' he goes on to tell me. His children advise him to live in the present, but he mostly remembers at night. 'If I had a bad dream of that time I really wake up shaking.' He then rolls up his shirt sleeve to show me the scar of the spear that entered his left arm when he was attacked in the hiding place. The spear had been tipped with poison, 'very serious poison', Karam Singh adds. The scar is a faint but clear white line, just longer than an inch. It is seventy years old. A permanent, physical reminder of that day. If I touched it, I could almost touch that day of death. Karam Singh says the physician who treated him said: 'You are lucky, a day or two more and you would have gone with the blood poisoning.' He pauses and I think he's coughing. He tells me this story twice. It is only later, when I watch the video recording of our interview, that I realise he's not coughing, but making a sound I've never heard before. It is visceral and deep – both an intake of breath and a convulsive sob. It was too much, even now, for Karam Singh to recount the details of what happened and how he himself nearly died that day. A day that saw his father murdered at the hands of a Muslim mob after he freed his cattle so they would not be burned. The same day his sister was given sanctuary by a Muslim neighbour.

After speaking to Karam Singh I did wonder if it was the right thing to be asking people to remember such traumatic events. I kept in touch with his daughter to check up on him. But Karam Singh wanted his story heard and preserved. Yet it was revealed with such profound sorrow.

The mob fled after the attack, and were never seen again. All the Muslims of the village left. How could they ever feel safe, fearing reprisals? There were no goodbyes. As with so many villages on both sides of the now divided Punjab, refugees soon took up the recently vacated houses.

'We were better off during the British time because everybody was in peace,' Karam Singh tells me in his soft voice. 'Nobody had any fear or anything and [the] general public thought after independence we can speak freely and do what we want freely and everything. But that did not happen.'

Karam Singh Hamdard was born in 1931 in Mulewal Khaira, Punjab, British India. In 1949 he went to Tanzania. He moved to the UK in 1970, going on to live in south-east London. He worked in hospital maintenance until his retirement. He died on 3 May 2022.

11

I Have Seen This

How do you begin to talk about partition when you or people in your family committed atrocities? I spoke to many people who witnessed violence, but very few admitted to wanting to take part or actually participating in it. Bashir Maan spoke of feeling so incensed with the butchering of Muslims on a train which arrived in Lahore that he wanted to kill all the Hindus in his Punjabi village, though he never did. Ramen Bannerjee admitted to throwing nail and petrol bombs at a Muslim mob in East Bengal, an act he says now fills him with remorse, but at the time he says he had no choice.

In a suburban street near Slough live three generations of the Rayit family. The elder was born in Punjab, his son in Uganda, the grandchildren in Britain. Swaran Singh Rayit, a proud Sikh, is gently spoken, with a kindly look. He tells me that in the summer of 1947, aged fifteen, he was part of a murderous raid against Muslim villagers.[1]

Desi Radio, the Punjabi-language station based in Southall, in the London borough of Ealing, is Swaran's channel of choice. It is playing from the large flat-screen television in the living room. A petite, well-dressed man, he has a long, white, immaculate beard. I can see his hair must be very long. It is in a knot or joora just covered by his white turban. Like many religious Sikhs, Swaran observes the commandment not to cut your hair: kesh. It is the practice of growing your hair naturally as a symbol of respect for the perfection of God's creation. It is one of the external symbols ordered by Guru Gobind Singh to profess the Sikh faith.

The presence of the tenth guru and spiritual leader, Gobind Singh, is very much felt in the house. There is a sweeping, vibrant canvas filling one whole wall in the living room, the guru at the centre. It is a scene from 1699 when the guru requested Sikhs to congregate at Anandpur Sahib on Vaisakhi (the annual spring harvest festival). It is on that day that he founded the Khalsa five commandments of what Sikhs should wear, which includes kesh as well as carrying the kirpan or sword. The picture shows the guru wearing a stark orange kurta, tunic, and matching turban in a sword-giving ceremony to Sikh warriors. Khalsa Sikhs are expected to embody the qualities of the 'saint-soldier', with the courage to defend the rights of all who are wrongfully oppressed regardless of creed. They, like Swaran, are meant always to carry a sword.

*

In the days after partition, elderly Sikh members from the village of Jasso Mazara in Indian Punjab took the decision that one member of each household would join a revenge attack for the recent slaughter of their people.

Fifteen-year-old Swaran, as the elder son of his family, was chosen. Carrying his sword, he walked with the men from the village for over an hour. Sikh men from four or five other villages joined them along the way, all with their swords. It felt like there were hundreds of them marching towards the village he knew as Kangroad. Swaran knew this village was Muslim. He says they took the swords for killing but also for protection.

When they arrived there was panic. The Muslim villagers tried to escape. One of the adults Swaran was with, a heavily built man, tried to behead a Muslim. But his sword was damaged in the act. He shouted to Swaran, who was just ten yards away from him, to hand over his sword. Swaran said the man was much older than him, and he had no choice but to give it to him. The young man watched as his sword was used to murder a Muslim, not far from where he was standing.

The day of killing will never leave Swaran. He can still visualise how the older Sikh villager took a cloth to wipe the fresh blood off the murderous blade and then handed the sword back to him.

The scene was one of chaos. There was frenzied killing, blood in the street, bodies on the ground. 'Maybe fifty to a hundred people they killed in that village.' Swaran insists he did not harm anyone, that he had no choice but to go along with the other men.

The group returned to their villages that day jubilant, some with property looted from the homes – silver trinkets and jewellery belonging to the women. How did ordinary people become murderers? Swaran thinks it was the refugees from the western Punjab who came with their stories of horror that turned minds. But he is not really sure what happened. There was no way he could have stopped them. He said nothing, just followed.

He shows me a black-and-white picture of three generations of his family taken when he was five. In the front sits Swaran, formally dressed as a proper English boy would be. He has Fred Astaire two-toned brogues, embroidered knee-high socks, a white shirt, tailor-made shorts and an oversized blazer. His father, who he says liked to dress 'posh', is wearing a white suit and has a black turban. His grandfather's angular face, not dissimilar to Swaran's now, has a flowing white beard. He wears a tailored suit over smart traditional pyjama trousers. His father was in Karachi hundreds of miles away, working as a carpenter, the day Swaran was chosen as the eldest male in the family to go on the raid; otherwise the young man would have been spared.

'We never thought this would happen,' Swaran says. Jasso Mazara was mixed, pretty much equally, between Sikhs and Muslims. Sikhs lived on one side of the village, Muslims the other. There hadn't been any trouble there before. His best friend was a Muslim, Gulam Rasool. They played together, went to each other's homes, knew each other's parents. Though they never ate together. Guru Gobind Singh forbade the eating of halal meat.

From the age of eleven the two had gone to high school together, six miles away in the city of Phagwara. Swaran, along with the other Sikh boys, stayed in a hostel during the week, as the journey was too far to make every day from the village. Gulam didn't have a bicycle to make the trip back home, but the owner of the boarding house was reluctant to take him in, as it was only Sikhs who stayed there.

Swaran argued successfully with him that Gulam should stay there too. The boarding-house owner was worried Gulam would be preparing food in the kitchen. Sikh religious rules prevented a Muslim cooking food for them. Swaran reassured the owner that they would prepare food for Gulam, that he would not be making it, though they would all be eating together.

Since the announcement of partition things had grown tense in the village. There was concern about which country the village would be in. Swaran's family had even packed belongings in case they needed to move. Swaran remembers choosing which clothes to take. At school he had no interest in politics. He had never been involved in the freedom movement, though he was aware partition was coming. He says the Sikhs and Hindus wanted the Ravi river, so that Lahore would be part of India.

On Independence Day there were no celebrations, everyone felt fearful. They waited for the announcement about which country the village would be part of from the local newspaper. No one had a radio. The family were relieved that Jasso Mazara was awarded to India, but concerned for their father, who was still in Karachi, now Pakistan's new capital.

Attacks against Muslims nearby had already started, so the Sikh villagers told their Muslim neighbours it would be difficult for them to protect them, and it was better they head to the camp a mile and a half down the road for their safety. It was guarded by Indian soldiers and was a transit point to Pakistan.

Swaran remembers saying goodbye to his Muslim 'brothers' in the middle of the night. He can still recall the sadness he felt at their leaving. 'We were very disturbed, we had all been living together for hundreds of years.' He carried some of their belongings to the camp.

Gulam and Swaran hugged as they parted. It was an emotional departure. It was too hard to say anything to his best friend, Swaran says. He knew even then that Gulam and the others weren't coming back. 'Why this partition?' Swaran says seventy years on as he remembers this scene. It still makes no sense to him.

Schools were suspended after partition as there were so many disturbances. Swaran thinks he was off for around four months. A male from each house now patrolled individual homes each night in case there was trouble from the Muslims. It was around this time the murderous raid happened.

As Muslims left the surrounding villages, looting took place of their houses. Swaran was part of these raids, but insists he didn't take anything. Jasso Mazara was on the road where many refugees passed by, heading for the camp. Swaran says he saw two or three Muslim women who were on their way there with their families, forcibly taken by elderly Sikh men. He remembers the girls crying, but they could not put up a fight. He says the men who abducted them were not from his village, he did not recognise them. The Indian Army seeing these incidents just fired into the air, they did nothing. No one saved these women. Swaran has no idea what happened to them.

Both sides did these things he tells me. Muslims wanted to brand 'Pakistan Zindabad' – Long Live Pakistan – on women's bodies and their chests. His future wife was a girl of ten at the time of partition, travelling from Montgomery district in western Punjab with her family in a truck towards India. She told Swaran years later that Muslims were going through the vehicles looking for girls. She was hidden by her family in the gap between the trunks in the boot. 'They are doing things with these ladies,' Swaran says. Then he stops. I am sure he remembers I am much younger than him. Maybe he does not think it appropriate for me to hear, or for him to be telling me the details. 'I can't say these things at present, these things are so bad.'

Gulam's home and all the others were quickly taken over by refugees from western Punjab. They came with their carts, exhausted and angry, full of stories of what was being done to them in the name of religion and nationhood.

While school was suspended, Swaran still went to Phagwara where a centre had now been set up to distribute clothing and food to the many refugees arriving there. He shows me a picture, which I recognise as one of the iconic ones taken by the American photographer Margaret Bourke-White for *Life* magazine. It shows a train bursting with passengers, people hanging out of the doors and windows. And sitting on the roof of the train were hundreds of refugees. Swaran's mother prepared chapattis and he would take them and throw them up to the refugees who were on the train's roof – like those in the picture – as they pulled into Phagwara station. Sometimes they caught them, sometimes they did not. Chapattis were the only food that was light and easy to throw.

Swaran has still kept a tattered 'social service' certificate from 1948 which notes his work over a ten-week period in helping the new arrivals, handing out clothes and food to people who had lost everything. He went on to graduate from high school the same year, and matriculated from East Punjab University. Swaran explains even Punjab University was split into two at partition – east and west.

Ironically, his own life would later be uprooted. Swaran emigrated to Uganda in 1951 with his parents, in search of a better life. He worked his way up to being a grade VI clerk with the East African Railways and Harbours Corporation in Kampala. However, his job was abruptly ended in 1965. He still has a letter from the chief operating superintendent, which he shows me. It states: 'Due to the policy to replace non-African officers with Africans ... you shall be called upon to retire ... to make way for a suitable African officer.'

In 1972 Swaran, his wife and three children, fled Uganda after they and other Asians were expelled by President Idi Amin. The family arrived in the UK, first spending a few nights at a camp in Newbury, before heading off to Wolverhampton to be with his brother. Like those refugees to whom he threw chapattis, Swaran Singh Rayit had now lost everything. He was lucky, though, to have been able to bring £50 with him from Africa. But he had to start life from scratch.

He blames the last Viceroy of India, Lord Mountbatten, for hastening the departure of the British and precipitating the disaster that followed. However, he no longer holds grudges, as it was the British who gave his family refuge after they were kicked out of Uganda – a decision he is still grateful for. He admits that if it had not been for partition and the upheaval that followed, the family may never have left for Africa in the first place and then ended up in Britain, where they have all thrived.

Swaran settled in Hayes, Middlesex, shortly after arriving in the UK, as there were more opportunities there. After quickly completing a maths and English test he found a job working night shifts at a packing company, and was soon promoted to quality control inspector – a job he did for twenty years. All his three children graduated from university. His son, Tejpal, who he now lives with, qualified as a chartered engineer.

He says he only told pieces of his story to his family. Having had to restart his life twice, there was not much time to think of the past. Swaran is not a man of many words, nor one to mull over what has happened. He has a particularly close relationship with his grandson, Manveer, who is now in his thirties and runs his own company. Swaran taught him Punjabi, the only grandchild who can speak it fluently. They would often chat over a cup of warm milk in the evenings about his early days in British India. He had never mentioned the murderous raid to his grandson before, however. Swaran says this incident, the murder and the sight of the dead bodies did not really trouble him. After some delicate questioning, he admits that yes, perhaps he was a little affected by it all. I say to Manveer that his grandfather is such a kindly man, it is hard to imagine him being part of it, and seeing the things he did, on that day of killing. Swaran's grandson says maybe that is why he is so gentle.

Swaran did tell his grandson of other aspects of his life in his Punjabi village, and about his friends. Manveer knew his grandfather had tried many times to find his best friend, Gulam Rasool, but with no luck. It is still painful for Swaran to remember the day they parted. Swaran wonders out loud, half under his breath, if he is still alive.

Every morning eighty-six-year-old Swaran rises at four and recites his prayers for half an hour. He makes himself some porridge, listens to Desi Radio until nine, then goes back for a quick sleep. There is not a day he does not go to the gurdwara. He drives himself or takes the bus. Every Thursday he goes to meet his friends at the East African Asian Senior Citizens Association at the Southall Dominion Centre. The day we meet is 'Pizza Thursday'. He's the vice-chair there. It's a mixed group of South Asians: Hindus, Sikhs, Muslims and Christians. They organise events like watching films and poetry readings. Manveer says the Asians that came from Africa were not discriminatory. They all had to get on together over there; they didn't bring the same prejudices as those who came to Britain directly from Pakistan and India had.

This quiet man lives in an ordinary suburban street in Britain. Swaran, a witness to a massacre in the fledgling country of India, a lifetime ago. 'I was a student ... I did not want to kill people.' Then he adds slowly and deliberately: 'But I have seen this.'

Swaran Singh Rayit was born in Jasso Mazara in 1931. He left for Uganda in 1951 where he worked as a clerk, and came to England in 1972 after Asians were expelled from the country by the dictator Idi Amin. Swaran settled in Hayes with his wife and three children. He worked for twenty years as a quality-control inspector. He is now the vice-chair of the East African Asian Senior Citizens Association.

12

She Took a Stand

One of the hardest stories to tell is also one of the most shameful aspects of what happened during partition: how men of all religions targeted women and girls of the 'other' religion to rape and abduct them. Women of all ages, class, caste and ethnic groups were victims. Some women were forced into marriage and made to convert. Bodies were branded with nationalist slogans. This happened on a huge scale. It is estimated that around 75,000, mainly women and children, were kidnapped and raped.

Urvashi Butalia in the seminal book, *The Other Side of Silence*, was one of the first to document so extensively the experience of women during partition.[1] When we met in London she told me how women became property to be fought over and exchanged. It became a show of masculinity and manhood to pick up the 'other's' woman, the other's property, to violate her. 'Their bodies became the battleground on which these men of these two newly formed nations fought their battle. So it wasn't only that they were raped and abducted ... They had marks of the other religion tattooed and stamped on their bodies. Their breasts were cut off, all kinds of humiliations were heaped upon them. And it was just part of this whole thing of treating women as property and as chattel.'[2]

As early as September 1947 the prime ministers of India and Pakistan, in a rare show of unity, met at Lahore and issued a joint declaration. 'Both the Central Governments and the Governments of East and West Punjab wish to make it clear that forced conversions and marriages will not be recognised. Further, that women and girls who have been abducted must be restored to their families, and every effort must be made by the Governments and the officers concerned to trace and recover such women and girls.'[3] Later that year both governments agreed through the Inter-Dominion Treaty 'Central Recovery Operation', comprising women social workers and police, to set up machinery to rescue abducted women and girls from each other's territories, ensuring they would be brought back, if necessary by force, to their 'own' homes. As Butalia emphasises, this meant the place of their religion.[4]

In 1949 the Abducted Persons (Recovery and Restoration) Act, passed by India and Pakistan, stated that any conversions and marriages after 1 March 1947 would not be recognised, and also that these individuals were considered 'abducted persons'.

Gurbakhsh Garcha had strong memories of being a child growing up in a small mixed village in Punjab, of the young Muslim woman who was abducted by an elderly Sikh and forced to eat pig fat. He was enormously relieved to hear later that she had been rescued by Pakistani police; she had seemed so unhappy. However, difficult as it is to imagine, not all women wanted to be repatriated. Some, like Gurbakhsh's aunt (who he says willingly converted), would no doubt have refused to go with the Pakistani authorities, as she grew to love the Sikh man whom she saw as her saviour, who had protected her after all her family had been slaughtered.

Other women had been left behind and their husbands and children had fled for a new country. Some of these women had children of their own with their new 'husband'. Would they have to abandon these children too, only to be taken to a new country, and for their first husband to reject them? If a woman was found by her relatives to be pregnant by the 'other', they most likely had to give up their child for adoption or have an abortion. In India, abortion was illegal at the time, but the government financed mass abortions specifically for this purpose.[5]

Gandhi and Nehru made appeals to families to reassure them that the women who had been raped and kidnapped remained 'pure'. 'I hear,' Gandhi said, 'Hindus are not willing to accept back the recovered women because they say that they have become impure. I feel this is a matter of great shame. These women are as pure as the girls sitting by my side. And if any of those recovered women should come to me, then I will give them as much respect and honour as I accord to these young maidens.'[6] Butalia says the accounts suggest the issue of 'purity' held more importance within India, to Hindus and Sikhs, 'perhaps because the Hindu religion places such great emphasis on purity and pollution'.[7]

The recovery operation continued for nine years after partition. In all 30,000 women were removed on both sides (22,000 Muslim women and 8,000 Hindu and Sikh women were recovered). As time went on, Butalia observes, the process became more difficult: 'The greatest hurdle in the way of forcible recovery was the women's reluctance to leave their children.'[8]

Ashrams were set up across northern India to house women whose families could not accept them, were destitute or orphans. Astonishingly, some women were still living in ashrams as late as 1997. In an extraordinary interview for the

BBC World Service series *India: A People Partitioned*, Andrew Whitehead spoke to a woman who lived in the Gandhi Vanita Ashram in Jalandhar, Indian Punjab.[9] She was a Hindu brought up in Pakistan. She arrived at their door as a twenty-year-old woman, pregnant and alone. Her son and husband had been butchered while they were hiding in a paper mill in Sheikhpura. At the time of the interview, in 1997, she had been living there for fifty years.

Understandably, the experience of women is a difficult story to tell through direct first-person testimony. When we were looking for interviewees, overwhelmingly those who would volunteer were men. Looking back at the transcripts, the stories of women are always there, albeit in the background. Many were reticent to go into details of sexual violence, about what they saw, or what they knew may have been going on. I think they were also mindful of the invisible mores that govern the British South Asian community. I am a British Asian woman who could be their daughter or granddaughter; such things would not usually be discussed openly.

Swaran Singh Rayit saw two or three women near the transit camp near his Punjabi village being taken away, and remarked how no one, not even the authorities, did anything to protect them. He stopped, not wanting to say any more. Another interviewee, Iftkahr Ahmed, remembers walking across Delhi in a group when young Muslim girls were picked up and taken off. He still remembers their cries and those of their parents. These are told almost as incidental stories from that time. In the recounting, it was one of the many horrific things that happened. Khurshid Sultana, a schoolgirl in Delhi whose story we shall come to, spoke of hearing that her friend had been abducted and kept by her schoolteacher – but it wasn't mentioned before the interview, and barely came out during it; I needed to go back gently over the incident once it had been disclosed as an aside, to understand what had happened.

These stories, the rapes and abductions, have not emerged in the individuals' own words in Britain. They may never now be told. This is hardly surprising. There was and is a huge amount of shame attached to sexual violence within the British South Asian community, especially among that generation. Of those who migrated to the UK after independence we may not ever know the extent of the sexual violence they experienced during partition. Silence has pervaded so many partition memories, but these will always be the hardest silences to break, if they will ever break. I feel we have to respect this silence.

There was naturally fear amongst families of all religions that their women who upheld the honour within the communities would be disrespected – by being kidnapped, impregnated or physically disfigured by men of the 'other' religion. To protect them against such 'dishonour', violence would be committed within some families. Female family members would be killed by brothers, fathers and uncles to save them from being violated.

There are well-documented cases such as those in March 1947 around the villages of the district of Rawalpindi, in Punjab. When partition became a reality, Sikh villagers came under attack by Muslims. This was said to be in retaliation for Hindu attacks on Muslims in Bihar. In the village of Thoa Khalsa, it was reported that around ninety women jumped into a well and drowned themselves. They martyred themselves so as not to stain their honour, that of the family, and their religion. Three survived as there was not enough water in the well to drown them all.

Bir Bahadur Singh's mother was one of the women who survived jumping into the well in Thoa Khalsa. Other females aged between ten and forty years old had gathered to hide from the attackers. Sixteen-year-old Bir saw his father call out to his older sister, Maan Kaur, who was one of them. He recalls clinging on to his father's kurta and watching as his father swung his sword to behead his sister.[10] However her dupatta (headscarf) got in the way. He watched as Maan Kaur moved her plait so that her father could have a clearer strike. Next he remembers his father angrily moving her scarf clear of her neck. He then saw his father bring down the sword, and the head of his sister roll and fall. Bir crept away weeping and sobbing; all the while he could hear the swinging and striking of the sword, as other male family members joined in. He says he believes twenty-five young women were killed that way.

Decades later Bir still remembers that day: how no one made a sound, how none of the women protested: 'All you could hear was the cut, cut, cut sounds.'[11] They just chanted God's name. This, he says, was martyrdom: 'All honour to those people who killed their own children, who jumped into wells. And they saved us.'[12]

*

Khurshid Begum is in her early eighties, and is quite frankly lucky to be alive. She was saved by a remarkable woman. Today she lives on the outskirts of Cardiff in a quiet street. She speaks no English, conducting the interview in Punjabi, with her son translating.[13] She wears an elegant, thin, purple chiffon dupatta, which falls over her right cheek and is wrapped around her shoulders. As she converses, her daughter-in-law keeps a supportive hand on her shoulder.

She was born in the Muslim-majority village of Langeri, around five miles from where Swaran Singh Rayit grew up in Jasso Mazara. Theirs was a large family, eleven uncles in all, and they owned a lot of land. She remembers the Sikh and Muslim parcels of land being quite separate. Each knew which belonged to whom. She lived in a large house as part of a joint family.

She has no memories of Independence Day, and her village officially becoming part of India. But she does remember overhearing conversations amongst the men, whether to stay or go. She recalls her grandfather and some uncles saying, 'Why should we leave, this is our home, where would we go to?' 'Come what may, we will live here and die here,' they would say. Other uncles wanted to leave straight away. In the end, in the days immediately after partition, the men of the family agreed they would stay in India, despite being Muslims. They would fight it out.

Khurshid was no longer allowed out into the fields by herself. She was told it was not safe. There were rumours of what was happening to women in other villages, though Khurshid says she never saw anything. The males of the family discussed what they should do with the females, to protect them. Twelve-year-old Khurshid heard some uncles arguing that they should all be put together in a room and killed, but other male family members disagreed. She was scared, she admits, though she was more worried about what would happen to the men without the women. There was no question of Khurshid having a say in whether she lived or died. 'No one used to speak in front of my uncles because they were the decision-makers in the family ... we left everything to fate.'

Khurshid's grandmother, Fatima, however, took a stand. 'I was quite young but my grandmother stood by us. She said, "It's their life and they also have the right to take a decision." ' She spoke to the two male elders of the family, sat them down, and talked sense to them. She explained that their family was too small to stand up to the mob. Spare the women, and migrate together, she told them. If you don't want to go, the women will go to the transit camp on their own. 'Grandmother literally ordered the men to leave, and they had to listen to her. She was a brave woman. No one used to disobey her.' The men did not concede to Fatima straight away; however, they eventually came round. She was, Khurshid says, 'like a man. Strong.' She admits that if it were not for her own grandmother she would not be alive today.

She thinks it was around two to three weeks after partition they all left for the camp at Behram, just a mile or so from Swaran Singh Rayit's village of Jasso Mazara, and the same camp where his best friend Gulam Rasool also ended up with his family. Khurshid's family were fortunate. A Hindu teacher who was a friend of the family came to their rescue, offering to take her family to his house, and helped them move their belongings to the camp. They stayed for around two-and-a-half months. Conditions were tolerable, though there was little food. They had only taken some lentils with them when they left. They felt safe in the camp, as all the Muslims from the surrounding villages were together. But it was dangerous to leave alone or in small groups. They heard stories of some who had ventured beyond the camp and were killed. One of Khurshid's uncles was friendly with the Indian police and would go with them to collect their food rations.

The family went to Pakistan in two groups; they ended up in Lyallpur (later Faisalabad). An influential uncle with an important government job already lived there and had ensured that land was allotted to the family. Adjusting to life was not so bad, though food was scarce.

'My real home was in India,' says Khurshid. 'I remember every corner of my house in India. Now home is here, Wales, where we are settled.' Her soul is still there, her son interjects: 'It's very sentimental you know, when she talks she gets emotional. But she thinks partition was a good thing.'

Khurshid Begum was born in 1935 in Langeri, British India. She came to Cardiff in 1979 to join her husband, who was a bus driver. She is a mother and housewife.

13

The Good Old Days

'Heart to heart I wanted to see the place where I was born, and whence I left. I had memories of the game that I used to play with other kids there.'[1] This deep urge to see his childhood home led Mohindra Dhall – three years ago – to become the only one of his family in almost seven decades to return to the home they had originally fled. He joined a group from his university days in India who were all retracing their origins in Pakistan. He took with him a map of Lyallpur in western Punjab, which had been hand-drawn by his father. This was the city where his father grew up, and where Mohindra was born and lived as a small boy.

When we meet at his home in Edinburgh, Mohindra is dressed in a traditional white linen kurta pyjama with a Nehru waistcoat. He is greying but still has some black hair left; the wrinkles of this seventy-six-year-old are deeply etched into his face, yet he still has the air of a much younger man. He smiles easily and has a deep, lyrical way of talking.

He carefully unfurls the map of Lyallpur, and many years after it has been drawn, it bears hardly any creases. It is detailed, and intricate. This map is a love letter. 'My dad did this because he loved the place ... he wanted to keep in his memory how the city looked.' It was drawn in the 1960s, and was the Lyallpur of nostalgia. Mohindra only learned about the map's existence two decades later, when his father gave it to him, along with a book that he wrote about his life in Pakistan and how the family escaped.

Lyallpur was named after the Lieutenant-Governor of Punjab, Sir James Broadwood Lyall, for his services to the colonisation of the Lower Chenab Valley. His surname Lyall was joined with pur, meaning 'city' in Sanskrit. It became one of the first planned cities in British India. Completed in 1895, the layout of the city centre was designed to replicate the design of the Union Jack. Eight roads extended from a large clock tower at its epicentre. They developed into eight separate bazaars, leading to different regions of Punjab. Mohindra points to the map, showing me his father's drawing of the famous eight roads, which decades later inspired Connaught Place in India's new capital, Delhi.

He shows me where his grandfather had a shop, right in the middle of the city, at Anarkali Bazaar. He took this map when he returned to Pakistan because it marked the place he was born. Surprisingly the house still stood, though Mohindra had only a few memories of it, but he knew it was the right place as his elder brother had described it in some detail, even the room Mohindra had been born in. As he approached the house of his birth, 'People were staring, looking and they were a bit scared and all that, who are these people...? And then later on we were told because some people who were using our property as a business were thinking that they were in illegal possession of their property and they were scared that someone may not come and whip them.' Even today, uncertainty over property claims linger.

Returning to the place he was born was a moving experience for Mohindra. 'It is difficult to express those moments,' he says. 'It is a very touching thing. But particularly when I went to the top floor, the toilets in that house is the same as it was seventy years back. They haven't even changed the flush system. In those old days the sweepers would come and clean your rubbish. The same thing is happening even until today in that house. In that particular house the owner actually has converted it into a printing press. It's no more residential.' The front of the house, where their buffalo used to be, is now an office.

But it is at the home Mohindra moved to as a young boy, in the nearby village of Pakka Dalla, where the memories come flooding back. His father worked in the Public Works Department as a subdivisional clerk, overseeing the canal in the village. The family lived in a compound there with other employees. Mohindra found the bungalow they had once lived in, but it was now dilapidated. The house of his father's boss was still there. He stood in the room he used to play in with the boss's children. It was the same room to which Mohindra and the group were taken as elderly men for tea and biscuits by the current subdivisional officer. He showed the visitors great hospitality, Mohindra recalls, giving them a tour of the site, including a visit to the school where he had learned to read and write. The layout of the compound was almost exactly the same.

*

Mohindra Dhall and his family had left their house in Pakka Dalla on Mohindra's sixth birthday, 13 September 1947. It was around seven at night when his father, Devi Dayal, rushed into their home telling the family to pack and leave. There had been incidents around the village against Sikhs and

Hindus since mid-August. But the latest attack was too big to ignore. 'My father never wanted to leave Pakistan,' Mohindra remembers. 'He loved the place so much.' So much so, that when government employees were asked whether they wanted to remain in Pakistan after partition, he had even written 'in black and white' that he wanted to stay and serve in Pakistan, even though he was a Hindu.

The decision to leave, when it came, was abrupt. 'That particular night there was a very major attack on the biggest village close to us and then everybody in the village in our compound felt that there is no point continuing any more, we had to go. And that's how it was [a] very spontaneous decision ... to leave Pakistan.'

All of the forty Hindus who were in the compound grabbed what they could. Mohindra's family took a bicycle and one suitcase containing his mother's sewing machine, jewellery, a few clothes for the family and chole, cooked chickpeas. A whole family's life in a suitcase.

They walked past the place where Mohindra would play gulli-danda. His face lights up as he explains the rules of his childhood game to me. And then there was the tree his friends would chase him up. He loved this game. No one plays these old Punjabi games any more, he says ruefully. Decades later, when he returned, he saw that his tree was still there. A tree once played on by a Hindu boy, at a time when Hindus still lived in West Punjab.

He tells me how he, his four brothers and their parents, as well as the other Hindus in the compound, managed to escape. They began their twenty-five-mile journey towards Choorkana (now Farooqbad) train station. Mohindra's one-year-old brother was pushed on his father's bicycle. They trekked through the night along the single-track railway line that went from Lyallpur to Choorkana. Nearly seventy years later Mohindra was surprised to find this was still a single-track line and had not been upgraded.

At around six in the morning the next day, there was a commotion and a train sped by. The group dispersed in panic, fearing they may be shot at from the train. Mohindra hid in a bush until it passed. They then continued on their way until around eleven in the morning. They reached a village where they planned to eat something before heading towards a Hindu temple. But as they started to enter something was not quite right and the adults left quickly. Mohindra was told there were three dead bodies at the entrance. They made off to the next village.

Shattered, the family sat by a small pond and ate their lunch. Mohindra started throwing stones into the water. One of the stones had a scorpion on its underside which stung Mohindra's finger. He was in agony, and his mother rubbed her steel house keys against his skin to take the poison out. It worked. She had no idea this would be the last use of her keys. They would never again open the front door of the family home in Pakka Dalla.

Mohindra thinks they may have walked for another three to four days, sleeping where they stopped, under the trees and stars. Eventually the group made it to Sachar Sauda, a few miles from Choorkana, where the local Hindu subdivisional officer of the Public Works Department lived. The group bedded down where they could around his large house, and managed to get some sleep. They then carried on their way to Choorkana railway station. Relieved, they saw the train already there, but the station was full of people desperate to leave Pakistan. Everyone got on the train, except Mohindra's eldest brother – nineteen-year-old Bishamber Lal Verma.

In the tussle to board, there was no space left for him. As the train was about to go, Mohindra's father decided they all needed to get off to be with him. Unknowingly he had saved his family's lives. 'This last-minute decision just before the train left to just come out ... Only to find out the next day the train was totally butchered. Not a single person was saved, and many of our compatriots from the compound were there.'

It would be another three or four days before the family was able to get on the next train together. But Mohindra says this next part of their journey, from Choorkana to Lahore, was the worst experience of their flight.

The train was so packed. There was no danger of a stampede, but they were all stuffed into the carriage for hours. They stopped over in Lahore station, arriving at around six or seven in the morning. They were all told to get out. The Pakistan Army took the women and children, separating them from the men. Mohindra was with his father and three brothers. Only his one-year-old brother remained with his mother. The whole day passed like that. There was no food or water, or explanation of what was happening. The army removed all the ammunition, knives and swords which people had been carrying to protect themselves. Mohindra's eldest brother, a member of the Hindu nationalist party Rashtriya Swayamsevak Sangh (RSS), was carrying a large knife which he was forced to hand over. The army then let them back on the train and they went on their way.

Just a few hours later, the train stopped at Shahdara in Pakistan. It was where the railway engines would come from India to take people across the border. A Pakistani engine could not go beyond Shahdara and enter India. So for a day or two Mohindra and his family were waiting on the ground by the station (there were no platforms). He estimates around two thousand people were on the train – there were up to fifteen carriages and hundreds on the roof. This mass of humanity sat on the recently named Pakistani earth, waiting. The women cooked with what little they had. Mohindra's mother had just a few chole remaining. So the family went a day or two without anything much. All around there were the cries of children. Some were clearly dying of diarrhoea. Eventually the Indian engine arrived, to carry the Dhall family to Amritsar. India soil. Their ordeal was over.

The family first went to Ferozepur and moved into a large house that had been vacated by Muslims. Mohindra's family took over the larger section of the house. His maternal grandparents and uncle joined them later. He doesn't remember anyone apportioning the house to them. It was empty and so they moved in.

Mohindra went to school and learned to read and write in Hindi. His elder brother Bishamber had almost completed his degree at Punjab University but had not been able to finish his practical exams in Lahore. He was allowed to do 'social service' in Ferozepur, helping refugees in lieu of the missed exams. The family stayed for over a year before moving to Delhi.

Mohindra is still angry with the last Viceroy of India, Lord Mountbatten, for moving the date of partition from June 1948 to 15 August 1947. Raising his voice, he asks: 'Why should we have been forced out of Pakistan? At the end of the day we were living a very peaceful, happy life ... my father's love of the place, there is no reason for us to just be thrown out. It was of course religious-based killing that started it, but a lot of it had to do with the land grab.' He suspects people on both sides of the border cynically used partition as a way to expropriate land.

When Mohindra returned to Pakistan three years ago, he took a brick from the bungalow in Pakka Dalla, the house he fled. A friend took a photograph of him removing it from the arch of the doorway. He was helped by some of the Pakistani workers there. This rose-coloured brick is now the centrepiece of his Edinburgh living room. It sits on a coffee table, carefully displayed in a glass case. He takes it out to show me, insisting I carry it. It is heavy. He proudly tells me that's because bricks from the 1920s and '30s were of superior quality. He took this brick as a keepsake he says, 'because there is a personal attachment to the place where I was just six years old playing in a little compound. I did feel that this will keep me reminding from the good old days and there is that personal attachment to that particular village.'

Over seventy years after he left that home in Pakka Dalla, he keeps a small piece of it in his living room in Edinburgh. He likes the conversations the brick starts; to be able to tell the story of his past, whether to his grandchildren, or his Scottish friends. And they all ask about it. How could they not? It is very touching to see this physical reminder of a bygone time. The only tangible evidence that he once lived in a Pakistani village – which had a tree he would play in, where he laughed as he was chased up it, before he was forced to flee on his birthday, having just turned six.

Mohindra says it was easier for him to recover from the trauma of leaving because he was a child. But his father was unable to. In fact, all his life, Mohindra's father regretted leaving Pakistan. He always wanted to go back and see the land he left behind, but never did. His sadness at leaving Pakistan

THE GOOD OLD DAYS

for India meant he didn't once visit his son in Edinburgh for fear of dying in *another* foreign land. 'He [Mohindra's father] said, "I still regret leaving Pakistan, I do not want to leave Delhi and die at some other place. I have been here [India] out of compulsion but that's [Pakistan] Motherland to me, so I'm sorry I will not come on holidays."'

Mohindra turns towards a corner of his living room to reveal an ornate gramophone. It is from Budapest, he tells me proudly. He picks out some old vinyls that he used to listen to in the 1950s and early '60s in India. Urdu songs. The language of Pakistan and the first language he learned. He puts on one of his favourites: 'Yeh Ishq Ishq hai Ishq Ishq'. He sings and in his chair dances – moving his upper body in tune, arms in the air, clicking his fingers. He loves Urdu music, Punjabi food, and he has an affinity for the place of his birth in Pakistan: it's almost – I say – as if partition hadn't happened. 'Absolutely,' he replies. 'You see, the culture, the language, the food, the habits, even the rituals, for example weddings, are all common. If you see a Muslim wedding or a Hindu wedding, there are loads of rituals which I can tell you are all common. It has nothing to do with religion ... because they belong to that particular land, the particular place that you come from ...'

Land. The way he says the word is long and meaningful and almost reverberates. He says land, not India or Pakistan. 'It has to do with the land from where you were born ... I still dream sometimes that one day perhaps Punjab will become one Punjab.'

Mohindra Dhall MBE was born in 1941 in Lyallpur (now Faisalabad), British India. He moved with his family to Ferozepur in Indian Punjab in September 1947 and then to

Delhi. He worked in banking in India and then Africa, and came to Scotland in 1992 where he founded the Ethnic Enterprise Centre in Edinburgh and in 1994 the Scottish Indian Arts Forum; he is also the founder of Edinburgh Diwali. He was awarded an MBE in 2006 for services to the arts in Scotland.

14

You Had to Choose

Haroon Ahmed was playing cricket with friends in his garden in Windsor Place, Delhi, in July 1947 when his uncle burst into the house, wearing a revolver in a holster. 'Jump into my car,' he heard him shout. 'Take the children. Jump into my car. Come, come, come.'[1] There was panic and confusion. Haroon's mother went to find her handbag and gather some belongings, but was told to hurry. Haroon, his three siblings and mother climbed into the uncle's Morris Traveller and sped off.

Eleven-year-old Haroon was wearing shorts even though he had just graduated to wearing trousers. On the car journey his overriding memory was wanting to change into his trousers. As they drove, the streets of Delhi were disarmingly still. 'The city was quiet. Would you believe it? It was quiet everywhere. I remember that. Normally it was very crowded as Indian cities are. But on this occasion it seemed to be deserted.' His mother tried to cover the eyes of the children as they drove. But they still managed to see, through the cracks in her fingers, dead bodies and injured people lying, casually discarded, on the streets.

They arrived at Keeling Road (now Tolstoy Marg), at the grand home of Haroon's wealthy grandfather, who had once worked with the renowned architect Edwin Lutyens. The manicured gardens were now covered in tents housing Muslim refugees, and armed men were patrolling the grounds using hunting rifles from Haroon's grandfather's collection. These were the same lawns where until recently peacocks had strutted and Haroon and his friends had played hide-and-seek. The ten acres or so of the estate included a mango grove which led to spacious outbuildings, which were rented out to tenants, including a Hindu family.

Haroon was bundled into a crowded room where there were 'a lot of children and women. The men were all outside. I remember the smell of excrement. It was just impossible,' Haroon remembers. 'Everyone in there was wetting themselves ... and there were not enough facilities. The first impression, I am sorry, it's a very strange impression to give, but it could have been the smell of fear. You start sweating, you are upset, and your tummy goes. So there is this smell that is the child's predominant memory. Then the crying ... some of the women were crying because they [had] lost things or relatives.' Haroon's mother was crying too. This was the home of her childhood, and was now a makeshift refugee camp. But she was also crying for her husband, Haroon's father, who was still not with them.

Earlier that same day Haroon's father, a liaison officer and one of the people responsible for dividing up assets between the soon-to-be independent countries of Pakistan and India, had been leaving work with his chaprasi (attendant), who was carrying his files. He left the Secretariat building on Raisina Hill, close to the Viceroy's House, climbed into his Austin car and drove off. However, he was being followed by a group of Sikhs and the vehicle was intercepted. Haroon's father responded by accelerating into them. He and his chaprasi then escaped on foot to the local police station, which was fortuitously very close by. He telephoned Haroon's uncle, telling him to take his family to a place of safety, fearing they could be targeted too – which is how they ended up living in one room, with other Muslims, fearing for their lives. Haroon tells me now that he believes his father was being pursued by an extremist group who wanted to prevent him from doing his job, in order to damage the process of partition.

At his grandfather's house, Haroon remained trapped in the room he had been originally bundled into. It was crowded and he was desperate to get out. 'It was a house where I had lorded it and there had been servants who would bring you a glass of water when you felt thirsty and there was grand luxury in that house,' he says. 'I am now very aware of how wealthy it was because he [his grandfather] had all these luxuries. But suddenly those luxuries had disappeared. There was even a shortage of food. We were eating dhal and lentils from plates on the floor instead of formal meals in a sumptuous dining room. So it was a very big transition. But not being allowed out was the worst for a little boy – to be confined in that area and virtually nothing to do.'

However, there was one time he was able to leave. Outside the room, on the veranda, was an armed man keeping watch for trouble. The guard, seeing this tall youth, presumed Haroon to be older than his eleven years. 'I will teach you how to fire this gun,' the man said to him, 'because you are to take it if I am killed. I have to teach you so you can protect the others.' Haroon was told not to tell anyone about the conversation. He never did tell his parents about this encounter.

Haroon had had no idea that trouble was brewing in the city. His father took *The Statesman* of Calcutta and the *Hindustan Times*, and he would read them too. He had seen the reports of vicious rioting in the eastern part of the country, the murder and looting, as well as in the province of Punjab, but had seen no evidence of that in Delhi – until the day his uncle burst into the house with a revolver and came for his family.

At his grandfather's house he would ask his parents repeatedly: 'Why aren't I with the boys I played with before?' Previously, he'd enjoyed games of cricket, teaming up with the Hindu, Sikh and Christian boys in his neighbourhood. 'Now they were enemies. It wasn't that gradually we became less friendly or moved away from people, nothing like that. It was so sudden. In my experience you were there at St Columba's School studying and playing together and then it was all over.'

By July 1947 Muslim families like Haroon's were starting to be targeted, but Haroon only understood fully what was happening once he moved into his grandfather's house. 'I was very aware that there was this rioting going on and people were being killed,' he says. 'I know that my sisters were saying that awful things were being done to women. It was a very early awareness that awful things could be done to women. It was very much something we feared … All I can say is that I was very aware that this was being done in the name of religious belief and extreme religious belief, rather than normal religious belief which is perfectly without any violence in it.'

By mid-September 1947 nearly all the Muslims in India's capital had left their homes and clustered together into refugee camps in the city, particularly the Lal Qila (Red Fort). Hundreds of thousands would end up leaving – a third of Delhi's population,[2] including the six members of Haroon's family.

Haroon's not sure how long he stayed at his grandfather's house, but he is certain that partition had taken place when he was once again bundled into a car. He was told to lie flat on the back seat with his siblings, their mother on top of them. His father was driving them to Willingdon (later Safdarjung) airfield.

Single men driving a car were relatively safe. The gangs of Sikhs and Hindus roaming around independent India's capital were looking for Muslim families who were trying to flee. 'This is communal rioting. You kill the other religion. And the other religion was fleeing,' says Haroon.

As they left, Haroon's parents tried to hush their crying children, telling them to keep quiet. Once the car reached the outskirts of the city, the children and their mother were finally able to sit up. As they were affluent, they were put into one of the guest houses of the airport. But late that night they heard shouts of: 'Out, out, out!' The guesthouses were being attacked by Hindu and Sikh rioters and they had to flee to the hangar in the middle of the airport where a guard of troops and some British officers were set up. The family slept on the floor of the hangar overnight – a fitting end to their last day in a country that had been home to generations of their ancestors; they said their long goodbye laying their cheeks to India's earth.

The next day they managed to get onto a Pakistani 'mercy flight', a Dakota DC4, meant for women and children only. But Haroon's mother fought hard for her husband to travel with them, and won. He was put in charge of organising the passengers on the flight. Haroon sat squashed into the middle aisle with people stepping on him. On landing in Karachi he threw up because of the motion of the plane, and was promptly accused by Pakistani officials of bringing cholera from Indian refugee camps into the country.

The family arrived in Pakistan with little more than the dirty clothes they had been wearing since they fled in the Morris Traveller months earlier. Life in a new country was difficult in the beginning. Most of the houses of the Hindus and Sikhs had already been taken by refugees who had moved to the new capital before them. But, in time, Haroon's father's job was restored to him; they no longer had to share accommodation with other families and were allotted a government bungalow. In the early days, Haroon's father cycled to work, but eventually he bought a car, and life started to become more comfortable, though nothing like their Delhi existence. Haroon found he didn't really miss his former home that much, but he did miss his cricket bat and teammates he had left behind. He felt safe in Pakistan, and had proud nationalist feelings for his new country: 'There was all this tub-thumping and a lot of newspaper reports about how important it was to be Pakistani.' But for Haroon's mother it was hard to accept their new life; she had never wanted to leave India in the first place. 'Why would she? She was having a great lifestyle, great luxury. It was her home ... she was certainly not into going, she didn't want to at all. And she returned afterwards to India on a couple of occasions. My father didn't, he had opted for Pakistan. You had to choose.'

This sense of loss pervaded his mother's whole life. 'We were well aware of my mother bemoaning the fact that she had to leave India. All her life she regretted it. She was full of sadness at what had happened and didn't ever completely accept that she had lost everything until many years had passed.' Haroon's wife Anne recalls how her mother-in-law always carried her large handbag everywhere, keeping it with her at all times. It contained her jewellery and large amounts of cash. She assumes it was in case she ever had to leave again in a hurry.

In 1954, aged seventeen, Haroon moved to England with his family. He describes it both as an awakening for him, but also as more dislocating than having gone through partition. The prejudices he encountered – prospective landladies refusing him board because of the colour of his skin, fighting Teddy boys, the institutional racism within academia in his early days at Cambridge University – were stronger than anything he had personally experienced before. However, England also proved to be an intellectual homecoming. He discovered the local public library in Acton, west London, near his first home. The kind librarians soon became his mentors. Haroon would also cycle to a nearby bookshop, where he became friendly with the owner, who told him about Foyles, the largest bookshop in the world. Soon he was frequently taking the bus to Charing Cross Road to stand by the bookshelves at Foyles and reading, as he didn't have enough money to buy all the books he wanted. He recalls his grandfather's wonderful library in Keeling Road where he first developed his love of reading, and stills feels a deep regret at the loss of the collection.

Following his A-level exams, Haroon went on to study electrical engineering at Imperial College, London, and won a postgraduate scholarship to study at King's College, Cambridge. He has lived in Cambridge ever since. Haroon was the first person from an ethnic minority to become a lecturer and teaching fellow in engineering. He went on to become a professor and master of a Cambridge college. He proudly shows me his portrait, which hangs amongst those of the other masters in the dining hall of Corpus Christi College. It is noticeable that he is the only non-white face among the men who have run the college since 1352.

Haroon is in his eighties and exudes good health. He plays golf, cycles around Cambridge and checks daily that he has reached his 10,000 steps target on his Fitbit. Recently I received an email from him. Seventy years on, the process of remembering what happened had 'awakened many buried and very devastating moments in my life and even more so the lives of my parents'.

He is writing a memoir now, for his family, about his life, to be read after his death. One of his daughters, a Cambridge academic, tells me that her father had rarely spoken of this time before, but something stirred within him during the marking of the seventieth anniversary. Haroon is now planning to take his two daughters and wife back – for the first time – to the land of his birth, and the home of his dear grandfather in Keeling Road. The grand house, which still has so many of the original features, is now a guest house with a four-and-a-half-star rating on TripAdvisor. He has been looking at it online, remembering. A home that once entertained the great and the good of Delhi society. The house was abandoned in 1951 by his grandfather. He had gone to live in Dhaka with his son, who had emigrated before partition after he had caused a scandal by eloping with the Hindu daughter of one of their tenants. 'She had come-to-bed eyes,' Haroon chuckles. She chose to convert and they lived a long, happy life together.

In 1951 the keys for the grand house on Keeling Road were left with the Hindu tenants. Nothing from the grandfather's home or the one on Windsor Place was ever recovered by Haroon's family. Discarded homes and lives. But, for

Haroon, partition had unexpected consequences. It was the making of him. If he had stayed in Delhi, he says, with all his grandfather's wealth, he may have been 'like the idle rich. I would have been a feudal landlord running round the estates.' He acknowledges that if partition had not taken place his family would not have emigrated to England. 'I would not have been here in this capacity that I have loved so much. I have loved my life in Cambridge. The legacy of partition for me has been quite wonderful because it brought me here. But this is only chance. The same thing did not happen to everybody. Of course, to my parents and grandparents' generation, the consequences of partition were lifelong disasters.'

Haroon Ahmed was born in 1936 in Delhi and left for Karachi, Pakistan, in 1947. He came to Britain in 1954. He obtained his Ph.D. from Cambridge University in 1963 and was appointed a faculty member of the Engineering Department where he worked for twenty years before being promoted to Professor of Microelectronics; he was the head of the Microelectronics Research Centre until his retirement in 2003. He is a former fellow, Director of Studies in Engineering, and Master of Corpus Christi College, Cambridge. Since retirement, he has published a number of acclaimed books on the local history of Cambridge.

15

Horrible Days

The telephone rang at the residence of Ratendone Road, Delhi, at eleven at night. Maneck Dalal picked up the receiver to hear a voice say: 'We're coming to kill you.' Maneck thought it was a friend playing a prank. 'Look, I'm very tired, please don't fool around,' he said. But the man repeated the threat: 'We're coming to kill you.'[1]

Maneck's English wife Kay was pregnant with their first child, and he was concerned enough to call friends, who invited them over to their house to spend the night. The next morning, back at the residence, their chowkidars, nightwatchmen, said a gang of men had come to the house asking for him. Later that day a large black square with a black cross was found on the front door. It was 'the practice at that time, particularly for Sikhs, to mark their victim', Maneck says.

In September 1947, twenty-eight-year-old Maneck Dalal, from the small minority of Parsees – so, technically, above the fray of communal fighting – was a wanted man. As manager of Air India in the capital, Delhi, he was responsible for ensuring that Muslims left the city safely. 'It infuriated some of the extremist elements [Hindus and Sikhs] who did not realise we were acting on government orders.' After the threatening phone call, Maneck and his wife moved temporarily to the Imperial hotel, and then to a second-floor flat in Connaught Circus in the centre of town.

The weeks after partition were 'a time of chaos and mayhem,' remembers Maneck, 'it was intense ... and extremely frightening. Murder was commonplace. Houses were looted.' Just weeks earlier, he and Kay had been on the streets of Delhi with thousands of others shouting 'Pandit Nehru ke jai!' (Long live Pandit Nehru!). It was a day 'full of joy'; everyone, regardless of their backgrounds, was jubilant at independence. But soon the bodies of dead Muslims began to appear outside the gates of their compound. In the centre of the city, Maneck saw more and more corpses: 'They just lay there, because no one dared to pick them up, in case they themselves were fiercely attacked.'

Maneck worked long days at Willingdon airfield – the same airfield that Haroon Ahmed and his family went to when they fled Delhi for Karachi. Each morning Maneck would be given a list, provided by the government, of people who had been prioritised to be transported on the Air India Dakotas from Delhi to Lahore or Karachi. Muslims would come to his office, begging him to take their families, offering huge sums of money. They were desperate to leave quickly, and Maneck remembers they were not all rich people. 'But it was a question of life and death.' He was never tempted to take the bags of money. Instead, he would patiently explain the government rules of prioritisation. 'Often they would get furious and abuse me and swear at me. They would say things like, "Have you ever seen your mother killed? Have you ever seen your sister raped?" This was a very tough period.'

Maneck would insist that Muslim women and girls wore a tika (the small dot on the forehead used by Hindu women), and gave them Hindu names to protect them from the Hindu and Sikh mobs watching the airport.

Muslims who were leaving Delhi went from 'Hangar A'. Hindu refugees arriving from Pakistan came into 'Hangar B'. One evening, to Maneck's horror, he discovered one of his uniformed staff mistakenly leading the Hindu passengers who had just come from Lahore into Hangar A. Maneck was able to stop them in time, avoiding what he believes would have been certain carnage.

While the Dalals were still living at the exclusive Ratendone Road (now Amrita Shergil Marg), Maneck arrived home for lunch one day to find four Sikhs bearing swords outside the gate. He drove in calmly, only to be confronted by a friend of his Muslim cook screaming in Hindi that 'these bad villainous, wicked men' were being threatening. 'Get inside, you fool,' Maneck shouted at him, and the young man, looking hurt, went back in. 'The truth was, I was worried for his life,' he adds.

Maneck went inside the house and pretended to phone someone, all the while keeping a lookout through the French windows. 'There was no point in actually telephoning the police, who were notoriously partisan.' He watched for the reaction of the four armed men. 'At first they didn't move, but after a few minutes they decided to leave.'

Maneck was born in Bombay in 1918, a month after the end of the First World War, to a Parsee family. The origins of the Parsees in India date back to the beginning of the eighth century when a group of Zoroastrians fled religious persecution in Iran and arrived on India's west coast. They settled in Gujarat. In the seventeenth century they began to migrate to Bombay, where they built their fire temples, and formed alliances with the British. This small minority of nearly 115,000 by the early 1940s were a privileged group.[2]

Maneck's father was in charge of the largest gin distillery in India, and was the first Indian to be captain of the Western India Golf Club. Maneck grew up in a large house, amid acres of land with mango groves, custard apple and mulberry trees, and a rose garden. There was a tennis court, and a rough-and-ready hockey pitch. There were buffalo too, and he would watch as they were milked and the produce churned. He and his siblings would then drink the fresh buffalo's milk.

He read law at Trinity College, Cambridge during the Second World War. It was in 1943, while in England, that he met his future wife. He was at a university dance when he first saw 'a blonde blue-eyed young girl'. Nearly seventy-five years on from that meeting, he says, looking over with pride at his wife: 'I thought she was very pretty ... she was a stunner to be honest.' Sometime later he invited Kathleen Richardson, whom he quickly began to call Kay, to the Cambridge Arts Theatre for a show and dinner. 'Despite the fact she had never met an Indian before we got on really well.' Kay was reading social sciences. She was technically at London University, but had been evacuated to Cambridge because of the bombing. They would go punting on the River Cam, and play matches of mixed-doubles tennis. They danced together at 'The Dorothy', or 'The Dot' as it was affectionately known, a posh tearoom that was also a dance hall.[3] One evening, as they walked across Jesus Green, Kay suddenly turned around and they kissed. They were soon engaged, but her father, unimpressed with the impending union, told Maneck to get a job first, and if they still felt the same after a year, he would support their marriage plans.

So Maneck returned to India and secured his first employment in Bombay as a station superintendent with Tata Airlines in February 1946. Tata was owned by a prominent Bombay Parsee family. A few months later the company became Air India. 'This was the propeller age and our fleet of planes were modern for the time … It was a new and exciting field. Of course only the wealthy or staff of the business could afford to fly.' By September 1946, aged just twenty-seven, Maneck was the manager of the Air India office in Delhi. He was in charge of the town office and airport, and had a staff of around eighty people.

One day the chairman of the company asked him to visit Mahatma Gandhi. He wanted Maneck to collect Gandhi's articles from his weekly publication *The Harijan*. Gandhi's writings focused on India's social and economic problems. Maneck arrived at Birla House in the capital wearing a silk shirt, bow tie and very tight-fitting trousers, the fashion of the day. 'When I called on Gandhiji [Gandhi], he looked this young Indian up and down, taking in the tight trousers and the fact he clearly fancied himself in Western clothes. He invited me to sit next to him. He, by contrast, was bare from the waist upwards and wearing a snow-white dhoti. He was also sitting on a very low seat. It is impossible to sit on the floor in extremely tight trousers. I tried. Gandhiji cackled with laughter. He told me in Gujarati how silly it was to wear such impractical clothes.' He laughs out loud as he remembers the scene.

Maneck went to see Gandhi every week to collect his article for his journal, but after the first meeting chose to wear loose trousers and a bush shirt. 'He [Gandhi] had a delightful sense of humour and he gave you the feeling that he was always on your side.'

By the end of the year Maneck had received a letter from Kay's father saying that 'though he was not at all enamoured of the idea, if we still wanted to get married, he would arrange it all. I was impressed by how very honourably he had kept his word, particularly given his lack of enthusiasm.'

They married at Barnet Methodist Church on 8 March 1947, just a few weeks before Mountbatten announced the partition plan. Sitting in his home in leafy Hampton, London, Maneck shows me their wedding photo album with pride, and it's no exaggeration to say the two look like film stars of their era. Handsome, and in love. A love that was sustained almost seventy years. It is very touching to see how Maneck, throughout our meeting, asks for advice or approval from Kay, who has now lost her short-term memory. His respect and tenderness for her is clear.

When Maneck returned to India with his new bride in the spring of 1947, they were part of a Delhi set that saw the British and Indian elite mixing together.

By the time of partition, Maneck was helping Muslims escape not only by plane, but train too. And Kay was helping him. A colleague of Maneck's, a man called Bradshaw who was the English managing director of Air India, had eight Muslim servants. The Dalals helped them to safely leave the country to get to Pakistan. 'The last person we took, that's what I remember very clearly, was a very smart young chap ... in his early twenties.' The couple dressed him in Maneck's best clothes, and tie, and took him by car to Delhi station sitting in between Kay and Maneck. They walked from the car to the station – the servant in the middle of the couple. They watched him board the train as it pulled away from the platform. Maneck remembers to this day how the young servant stood out of the train to look at them. 'I was quite touched by that because this was his farewell.' When Bradshaw visited his servant in Pakistan he sent a message of thanks to the Dalals. When I ask what would have happened if the Muslim servant had stayed or been discovered, Maneck replies unequivocally. 'They [Hindu and Sikh extremists] will kill him without hesitation. They were mad at that time. They were absolutely mad.'

Maneck was still a wanted man – even after he had moved out of his house on Ratendone Road where he had received the threatening phone call. One day Maneck returned from work to the new flat in Connaught Circus. At the bottom of the stairs outside the front door was another large black square with a cross. From that day Maneck decided to employ a Sikh chowkidar at the property; they also gave sanctuary to a Hindu refugee family who had fled from Lahore to show they were not partisan. 'The large black square with the cross mysteriously disappeared,' Maneck reflects. 'They were horrible days. There were days which were horrible for the reputation of both India and Pakistan, if I may be blunt. Horrible days.'

I leave Maneck and Kay as they are about to have lunch. I glance at them sitting side by side at the kitchen table. He is eating an Indian meal, she an English one, as she does not like the spices. This union, which came together in the month before partition was announced, between a gentlemanly Indian and his elegant English wife, has lasted for almost as long as the continent has been divided. Witnesses to the bloody division of a country as Empire ended, yet also a happy marriage between a former subject of the Raj and a woman from the colonial ruling class.

Maneck died two months after our meeting. A man possessed of exquisite manners, natural charm and wit. I felt privileged to have met him.

Maneck Dalal OBE was born in Bombay on 24 December 1918 and died 6 March 2017. In 1946 he was the manager of the Air India office in Delhi. After partition, Maneck came to London to open Air India's offices overseas. He worked with the company until 1977. He was chairman of a number of Indian cultural committees, including the Bharatiya Vidya Bhavan in London, of which Lord Louis Mountbatten was a patron. He wrote a memoir with his daughter Sue Dalal, entitled An Indian in Britain, *published in 2019.*

16

India Was Mine as Well

The majestic Red Fort palace in Old Delhi, with its imposing red sandstone walls, is where India's first prime minister, Jawaharlal Nehru, and every prime minister since has raised the Indian flag each year on Independence Day, before delivering an address to the nation. Built by the emperor Shah Jahan, it shows the Mughal Empire at its political and cultural apex. It is fitting that this Muslim fortress should be the place that officially heralded independence, a nod to the broader origins of the fledgling country.

It was within sight of the Red Fort, amidst the bustle of the Chandni Chowk marketplace, that seventeen-year-old Iftkahr Ahmed went to watch the fireworks and independence celebrations in 1947. He was a Muslim in now independent India, but the creation of Pakistan meant nothing to him. 'India was my home.'[1]

The city was all lit up. 'It was just like Christmas time.' He was delighted the British were gone. He laughs as he remembers how they all sang good riddance to the British. He sings that same song to me, first in Hindi, and then in English: 'You don't have to be afraid any more, the English boy is gone!'

They were happy days, Iftkahr recalls. However, he admits there was a fear in the heart of Delhi's Muslims that something was going to happen in the city, as even by mid-August there was already trouble on the outskirts. But he never believed anything would happen to him.

I meet Iftkahr in his living room in his home in Hove, Sussex. He is wearing jeans and a navy turtle-neck jumper and smart, leather slip-on shoes. He is the kind of person you'd want to have a drink in a pub with. Scattered around the house are his medical pills; his life is now peppered with hospital appointments for his many ailments. His son, Nick, is with us. He is in his early fifties and is an attentive, dutiful son. He is about to take his dad to a hospital appointment: we don't have much time and Iftkahr is keen to tell me his story, the story of his escape from India.

Iftkahr had moved to Delhi from his village in Gangoh, Uttar Pradesh, at the beginning of 1947 to live with his elder sister and brother-in-law. He quickly found a job as a machinist at a weaving factory, near to his home, in the area of Roshanara Bagh in Old Delhi. He was one of a handful of Muslim boys working there. One day, Iftkahr told the Hindu boy who wound the cotton for his sewing machine to 'hurry up'. The Hindu boy didn't like being told what to do by a Muslim, and a fight broke out between them. The boss, a Hindu, was 'a good guy'. He told Iftkahr not to get embroiled with the Hindu boy. 'Trouble is going on everywhere with the Hindus and Muslims and you are fighting a Hindu boy? You want to get killed?' Iftkahr listened to the owner, but from that moment, 'I knew something was going to happen.'

By early September 1947 the factory closed due to the growing disturbances in India's capital. Iftkahr had no work to go to, and was now alone in the city, and scared. His sister and her husband had left the capital some time back for a family visit, and were now too afraid to return. It was becoming too dangerous for Iftkahr, a young man, a Muslim, to be living by himself in Delhi.

He found sanctuary with other fellow Muslims. Opposite his house was a big yard of buildings with two large entrances where many had congregated – including women and children. Iftkahr knew a lot of the people there. At night they used horse carriages and barrels to barricade themselves inside this makeshift safe house and block off the gangways. However, the barricades were frequently set alight by the Hindu and Sikh mobs trying to flush them out. When the curfew was lifted during the day, Iftkahr could move around his area. He was in desperate need of a haircut so one day he visited the barber's, but just as he sat down, a group of Hindus came in; scared, he ran back to his hiding place in the yard. At night time the group could hear screaming and shouting. Iftkahr lived like this for three days and nights, until around fifty of them decided to move towards the great mosque, Jama Masjid, for safety.

They walked during the day. Mostly the mobs came out at night. As they travelled they saw bodies littered on the street, 'like leaves from the trees. Everywhere on the roads …' He starts pointing as if he were on that very street: 'Children there, women, I can see the man. Because you are so afraid, you don't want to see them [their bodies] – but you can see them.' They reached an area which was a Muslim stronghold. On a corner house, the door was open. Iftkahr went in and fell asleep. The next thing he remembers was being woken up by an elderly man telling him: 'What's the matter with you? This place is on fire.'

They were walking again, this time through an area which used to have a wholesale vegetable market, but which was now closed. They stopped there a while, but needed to keep moving as darkness was approaching. They came across a large Muslim home with three big gates. Inside it was bustling with Muslim families, all eating and cooking. What has stayed with Iftkahr is the gnawing hunger, and how no one offered him any food. Eventually, someone did give him a scrap of bread, but it was inedible. 'It was so dry, I could not swallow it ... It was like a stone. I couldn't chew it or anything like that. So I chucked it away.'

They carried on walking through Old Delhi, from Subzi Mandi towards Pul Bangash then on to Sadar Bazaar. In normal times these were mixed areas, though he notes that Muslims and Hindus lived on different sides of the streets. It rained continuously. 'We Indians believe that when God is pleased with you he gives you rain. We were in a horrifying place – no place to live, no place to sleep, no place to cover ourselves. And it was raining, raining, raining.' The roads were disarmingly quiet. Deserted. 'There was not a soul around the streets. Not a fly.' He then made what he describes as 'the biggest journey' of his life.

The group walked through a Hindu area, from Char-khiwalan Gali to Ballimaran Road, which was just a short distance. In every doorway there were men with 'tied white cloths on their heads', a symbol of being Hindu, holding knives and swords. 'They were dying to get us,' he recalls. 'We dared not even look up at these men, as eye contact would have meant certain death.' As they walked, being watched from the doorways, Iftkahr thought with every step he took that he could be killed at any moment. Then the Hindu men moved in. 'They picked up the young girls,' says Iftkahr. It is the sound of their screaming, and that of their parents, which he cannot forget. Iftkahr just carried on walking, looking straight ahead. He thought it was a matter of time before he and the other Muslims he was travelling with were attacked, and most likely killed. Yet all the men and older women managed to get past unharmed. 'It was the most frightening moment of my life,' he says. There was no option but to walk on by. To protest at the taking of the girls was certain death. 'You were for your own life ... we were just walking.' He tells me he has two younger sisters, and he was thankful the girls being taken were not them. 'I couldn't do anything about it. That's all I can tell you. It was so horrible. I cannot describe to you how bad it was.' He has no idea what became of those abducted girls.

What was left of the group eventually made it to the vast Jama Masjid. Built by Shah Jahan in the seventeenth century, it was jammed full of Muslim refugees, sleeping on the floor of the religious building. This was the fifth day since Iftkahr had left his home and he was desperate for food. The only advantage to being hungry was he did not need to go to the toilet, and there was nowhere to go anyway. He and the others only stayed a night in the mosque as the conditions were so bad.

The group journeyed on foot to another refuge they had been told of. Conditions at the sixteenth-century Purana Qila (Old Fort) were even worse. 'Oh boy, the people up there, it was almost like the whole of Delhi was there ... It was so horrible that time there.' Iftkahr was shocked to see women so desperate they were selling themselves for half a piece of bread to give to their children. It is estimated that up to 200,000 Muslim refugees fled there and to the nearby Mughal monument, Humayun's Tomb, in September 1947.[2]

Convoys of lorries, organised by the Indian Army, were coming to take people to Pakistan. He helped some passengers load up their luggage and was given a rupee. Iftkahr managed to buy a plain chapatti. The first proper food in days. The following day he heard a tannoy announce that a train was leaving the nearby station of Pragati Maidan and heading into Pakistan. He overheard people muttering: 'The trains will never reach Pakistan. Don't take them.' The next morning, he decided to get on the train. He sat in the packed compartment, aged seventeen, too exhausted to care if he even made it over the border. Whether he lived or died no longer mattered.

On the way, the train stopped in Saharanpur, the district of his village Gangoh. He tried to get off but was told by a soldier to stay on the train, he would be killed out on the streets. He listened, and stayed. After what seemed like three days he arrived in Atari, just a few miles from the Pakistani border. Everyone got out. People started cooking. Iftkahr had nothing, so he just milled about trackside. Another train pulled in. It was full of Pakistani soldiers on their way to the border. There was an English commanding officer who was marching up and down the train, walking with a very straight back. Iftkahr asked one of the Pakistani soldiers if he could travel with them, saying he was on his own and had no luggage. When the commander went out of view, the soldier said, 'Jump in.' Iftkahr did so and the soldiers pulled him inside, hiding him under their seats. He was given dried biscuits and a cup of tea – 'a hell of a lot'. One of the soldiers gave him some advice. 'When you come to Pakistan you will find nothing there. It is like India – everything is shattered. But don't stop in one place. Look for where you can find something for you.' Words Iftkahr has never forgotten.

It was night when the train pulled into Lahore station. The soldiers said to Iftkahr: 'Son, this is Pakistan. This is your world – do whatever you want to do.' He got off the train, and the soldiers continued their journey. He finally felt he was no longer in danger. 'As soon as I came into Pakistan I was safe in my mind. I was in the place where I am a Muslim and no enemy here like there was enemy in India. No enemy in Pakistan to kill me because I am a Muslim.'

All he wanted to do was sleep. So he put his head down on the platform and closed his eyes. At around five the next morning he awoke feeling something wet. The platform appeared full of people and there was a torch-light flashing – Iftkahr demonstrates with a hand movement how an Englishman was shining a torch on the platform. He then got up and saw that he had been lying amongst dead bodies. 'Children, women all cut up their faces, women cut up, all the details. That was the last time I was there. I took off from there and never looked back again.' The wet he had felt on waking was their blood.

'I used to think that I would never reach Pakistan … could be round the corner my death. Waiting for me. So when I got to Lahore that morning and found all those dead bodies I didn't worry about them, I worried about myself.' He is sure that the bodies on the platform were from the train he left at Atari station. He overheard people on the platform say that everyone on the train had been slaughtered. Everyone, that is, except the train driver. Someone had to take the corpses to Pakistan. The bodies must have been unloaded onto the platform while he was sleeping, he imagines.

When he walked into Lahore he was shocked by what he saw. 'Lahore was all burned. Wherever I looked it was all burned … in Anarkali [a predominantly Hindu area] [the] complete town is burned. That's what the Pakistanis did – they burned the houses and the people in it. That's what they did ... India did it to us, Pakistanis did it to them the same.'

Iftkahr's son Nick is listening, taking it all in. 'It's quite emotional and even now you well up because I might not be here ... it's like oh Christ ...' He breaks off apologising, and is in tears. It is difficult to hear these stories, especially when you are just learning the details of them. And Iftkahr's story is such a dramatic one. What upsets Nick is that his father was so young and alone. 'We as a family are very proud of him. We struggle to imagine what he saw with his own eyes and how life was and to look at him now, and what visions he has in his mind, that can never be erased, is very sad.'

As Iftkahr talks he remembers other memories. But sometimes we lose him altogether. I see him drift off, staring outside somewhere beyond the window. We are all quiet, respectful. We all feel it. It is as if he is picturing it all again. I hope the retelling is not too much for him. He had told his beloved late wife Sandra fragments of the story, but not the children. 'If things happen to me I want to forget it ... It was such a bad dream that I don't want to think about it.' Even now there are things he won't talk of. The first four months in Lahore and what happened to him, and why he left for Karachi to be with his sister.

These stories of his journey from Delhi, Nick tells me, were buried so deep. 'We never knew about the nightmares ... He had these flashbacks that he was being killed. He never told us. We never knew till literally a couple of years ago.' He compares his dad's generation to the men who lived through the First World War and how most of them couldn't speak of the enormity of what they saw. 'They just bottle everything up. I think it's hard to offload that.' Growing up, Nick knew nothing of partition. Only that his father was a Muslim, from India. He did not really understand the Pakistan connection, it was completely unknown, though he adds: 'Even if it was known – what did it mean to us? Didn't mean anything. We just wanted to go and play football in the park and eat pizza.'

Nick and his younger brother Marcus suffered racism when they were at school in the 1970s. He says he wishes he had known of the adversities his father had been through; it would have given him strength to deal with the bullies. He doesn't carry the same surname as his father. After the terrorist attacks of 11 September 2001 Nick changed his name from Ahmed to Yearwood, his wife's maiden name. 'I had foresight – anticipated everything would get worse for Muslims, not just in the UK but elsewhere. It was also about racism. I had learned from my diversity and equality training at work that people make an impression of you based on your surname. I didn't want them [his children] to be discriminated [against] or suffer bullying at school just by having that name, Ahmed.' Both his parents supported him, but it was a traumatic decision for Nick. What he feels he has lost by the absence of his surname, is his identity. 'Who am I if I'm not an Ahmed?

He is now helping his father write a book about his life, his early days in India, his flight to Pakistan, and coming to England. 'His story is one of struggle, survival and a journey to keep striving for success.' His father is writing his memories in Urdu, by hand. Nick is planning to get them translated, and hoping to learn more about his father's life story as there are still so many gaps for him. Nick wanted to find the family of the man he believes changed his father's life, a Pakistani known to his dad as 'Saddar'.

Iftkahr came to England in 1951 after he was told of a man who was travelling to Britain and was looking for staff. He queued in line for an interview at the Taj Mahal Hotel in Karachi and got the job. He was told his general duties would include gardening and being a butler. Mr Saddar, his new boss, a Pakistani, took him to the expansive home he shared with his English wife, Marie, in Caterham-on-the-Hill in Surrey. It was a positive experience for Iftkahr. He was treated well by the family, and remembers no discrimination towards him in the local area. After some years he wanted his life to progress, so he handed in his notice and was told to leave immediately. Walking into the town centre with a small suitcase, Mr Saddar's neighbour, Harold, an Anglo-Indian, shouted out: 'Johnnie [as all non-whites were called], where are you going?' He took Iftkahr in for a few weeks, fed him, and gave him money for cigarettes, until he moved again, this time to Brighton where he has spent the rest of his days. He met and married his English wife there and raised their two sons.

Iftkahr is very clear about his roots. The UK – where he has lived for over sixty-five years – is his home, but so too is India, even if it was a land he was forced to flee. The cherished memories of playing in the Gangoh alleyways, with his Hindu friends Jagdeesh and Jahon, are still with him. The three would play gulli-danda and delow with a tir jute stick. He never felt Pakistani, and has always described himself as Indian. In fact, he jokes, 'I'm English, I am born in the British Raj!'

His home is here now, but the pull to India is visceral. 'The village [in Gangoh] is like a memory you never forget. I am Indian. India was my home. Whenever I go to India I always smell my home that I was displaced [from] … India was mine as well. I was born there, my grandparents born in India, and their grandparents. India will always be where my mum was born. No one can take that away. That's what I feel about India.'

India was mine as well. I cannot fail to be moved by this. An elderly man's insistent claim that the land he was forced to flee, and the earth where his parents are buried, also belongs to him. Iftkahr's health is failing him now. Walking is a struggle. When he leaves the house he uses a mobility scooter. He has returned to India often, both Delhi and his village in Gangoh. He wants to go back one last time to bid it farewell. 'My village is my dream ... How long am I going to carry on living? So I say to my son, next year this time I want to go to India to say goodbye to India, to my village, my school, my alleyways, my mum, my dad ... They are all buried there. So I want to go to India again – one more time.'

We go to the beach at Hove just at the end of his road. He drives past the brightly coloured beach huts on his scooter. Looking out to sea, he says, 'I never stopped.' Just like the Pakistani soldiers told him at Lahore station: *Don't stop in one place.* 'From there I never stopped. And today I am in England. I have passed many years ... since 1951 I have lived here ... seventy years ago that journey started. So here I am ... one way or another I got the chance to go to England and that was the end of my journey. And here I am. I am so happy. I survived to come here. I have grown up, got married with English girl, I have two beautiful boys ... It's a beautiful journey where I end. I am so happy to be in England.'

Iftkahr Ahmed was born in 1930 in Gangoh, Uttar Pradesh, British India. He moved to Pakistan in September 1947 and came to the UK in 1951. He worked in the hospitality and catering industry for many decades, and ran a small convenience shop called 'Zippys' in Hove. He married Alexandra (Sandra) in 1961, and has two sons, Nick and Marcus, and five grandchildren.

17

They Become Like Animals

There is a creased black-and-white photograph showing a five-year-old girl holding a piece of fruit in her right hand. Khurshid Sultana is posing with her little brother Yusuf and their servant, a thin man with a slim moustache. It was taken to remember their employee, who was leaving the household. But this photograph would come to symbolise so much more.

Ten years after that photograph was taken, Khurshid Sultana's father turned up at her school in Delhi. Mohammed Hussain Sultan told his daughter to leave with him immediately. He had already warned his child that if he were ever to appear and ask her to come out of class, she must do as he says. No questions.

Mohammed was a Muslim civil servant working in the Imperial Secretariat Service. Days earlier he had been tipped off by some Dalits, untouchables, whom he had been giving charitable assistance to, that there were to be riots in the area he lived in. 'Leave quickly,' they told him. He arranged to send his family to Karachi; only Khurshid would stay with him, as she was about to sit her school exams.[1]

His wife and eldest daughter, dressed in saris to look like Hindu women, made their way to Delhi station, bound for a new country. Khurshid's mother was carrying a newborn, and in her purse she kept the photograph of five-year-old Khurshid holding a piece of fruit, and her son Yusuf. Yusuf had died years earlier and was buried in India. She took the photograph as a reminder of the son she was leaving behind in India's earth. It would be the only keepsake the family would take to their new life in Pakistan.

Now, a short time later, it was Khurshid and her father who were heading to the railway station with nothing but the clothes on their backs. She has no idea whether this was before or after partition, but she remembers hearing of the riots at the Jama Masjid in Old Delhi, which started in early September. The train she boarded at Delhi station was virtually empty. Khurshid, separated from her father, sat in the ladies' compartment. She thinks there were one or two other women around, but she was so frightened she cannot quite remember. In all that time, she never spoke a word, such was her terror. Occasionally there were warnings from the guards in the carriage, and Khurshid would hide under her seat. She understood that as a woman she was vulnerable to attackers. Convention meant she was unable to see her father and enter the male carriage during the many hours that passed.

When I meet Khurshid, who is now eighty-five, she is wearing a cream-coloured salwar kameez with delicate red and white flowers. Her head is loosely covered with a matching chiffon dupatta. She has gold hoop earrings, no make-up. She is serious, and carefully spoken. She is not expansive in the way she speaks. Her granddaughter, Sarah, sits close by her. Khurshid's fear – from the train journey she made – is still palpable. Until recently she had recurring nightmares of being fifteen, in Delhi, with no idea where to go.

Khurshid was born in her mother's village near Gurdaspur in eastern Punjab, but grew up in Delhi. Her best friends at school were Sarla and Santosh, Hindu girls. They regularly used to visit each other's homes. They did everything together, except the girls wouldn't eat in Khurshid's home. 'Hindu people don't eat Muslims' food. We don't mind. So they won't even touch the pots and pans. If we touch it they won't eat in the pans.'

She would encounter British people during her holidays in Simla, particularly while she was at Annandale, a flat area of land with deodar and oak trees where the British liked to play polo and cricket. Whenever she would see them she would automatically say: 'Good morning', or 'Good afternoon, memsahib, sahib'.

An India free from British rule was a concept she understood from a young age. At school in the early 1940s, she would go with her classmates and teachers out into the streets of Delhi in a procession demanding that the British leave. 'There was nothing like Pakistan or India in the beginning. We wanted independence ... India. There was nothing like partition or [being] separate. All Hindu, Sikh, Muslim, Christian, everybody – we used to be altogether, we used to all say we want independence – India is ours, India is ours.' They would sing 'Saare Jahaan se Accha', an Urdu-language patriotic song written for children by Muhammad Iqbal in the lyrical ghazal style of Urdu poetry. 'Religion does not teach us to bear animosity among ourselves,' they would chant. 'We are of Hind, our homeland is Hindustan' – both an anthem in opposition to the British Raj and an ode to Hindustan, the land comprising present-day Bangladesh, India and Pakistan.

Independence when it became a reality, Khurshid thought, would be peaceful. She never imagined that when she sang on Delhi's streets for freedom, that very freedom would mean leaving her friends and her home for a new country to live as a refugee.

When the train arrived in Karachi, Khurshid was finally united with her father and the rest of her family. Her mother and sister were in tears; they had thought they wouldn't see them again. Her baby brother was covered in blisters, as he had been wrapped so tightly in a blanket during the journey to Pakistan, their mother fearing his cries would draw attention to them all. The family were living in a tented refugee camp by the station, sleeping on the floor. There, Khurshid ate a chapatti and boiled green chilli, her first food in days. Despite this makeshift existence she felt relieved, safe even.

A month or so later the family were transferred to army barracks, firstly to the neighbourhoods of Jut Lines, then to Abyssinia Lines. They were given two rooms. Khurshid's father started a business supplying office machines to companies. It was a hard adjustment for the family given the huge change in their circumstances, but they felt grateful. Unlike so many other refugees, the whole family had survived, and had been reunited.

Slowly, they rebuilt their lives. They bought a gramophone. They had only possessed a radio in Delhi. Mother and daughter would play traditional songs while cooking. Mostly these were records by Surinder and Prakash Kaur, Sikh sisters who had fled Lahore for Ghaziabad, Delhi. The sisters sang mostly Punjabi folk songs in Punjabi, Urdu and Hindi – then recorded in India and heard by Khurshid and her mother in Karachi.

One day Khurshid received a letter from Sarla and Santosh, her Hindu former school friends. They told her about another classmate of theirs, a Muslim girl, who had stayed in India's capital. Khurshid tells me she does not want to mention the girl's name. This fellow student had been raped by a Hindu teacher at the school, became pregnant and had stayed with him. Her family had all moved to Pakistan, leaving her behind. Khurshid remembers being extremely upset at this news. 'I can't describe how bad I felt.' She replied to their letter, but didn't write again. 'I didn't want to know what happened to her and other things. Bas. Enough. I just stopped.'

When I express shock that it was a teacher who raped her, Khurshid says: 'That is nothing. I know the people living all your life like brothers and sisters, they attack each other.'

She then tells me her maternal home, the place she was born, in a village in Gurdaspur, was expected to have gone to Pakistan after partition. It was a Muslim-majority village. But it was awarded to India and lay just a few miles from the border. Her family had to leave immediately. Khurshid's maternal grandmother buried all her jewellery in the ground thinking she would come back. She and the rest of her mother's family headed to the River Ravi, which they had to cross to enter Pakistan. It was difficult to traverse, as it was heavily flooded, so, where they could, they crossed on their animals. Sometimes people came from the Pakistani side to offer assistance.

A year later, Khurshid met some of her mother's family who had managed to escape to Pakistan. Three elderly ladies told her how their sons had been killed in front of them by Sikhs or Hindus – she is not sure who. These mothers pleaded to be killed alongside their sons, but were told: 'You go to

Pakistan!' Khurshid's mother's cousin had been kidnapped in Gurdaspur along with her daughter. The family, once they were in Pakistan, asked the army to help find them. The authorities crossed the border and went to the village to make enquiries, but they were never found. To this day Khurshid has no idea what happened to them.

Khurshid is at pains to tell me, however, that there were good people in the village too. Her mother's sister-in-law was heavily pregnant. A Sikh friend of Khurshid's grandfather offered to look after her so the rest of the family could escape across the border without being held up. This young Muslim woman was left in the care of an elderly Sikh man. Word soon spread that a Muslim was being sheltered in a Sikh house. The elderly Sikh's son-in-law arrived at the place of sanctuary, demanding he make her leave or he would kill her. This old Sikh man replied that he had given his word, and that he must treat his guest as a daughter. He would not allow any harm to come to her. That night this elderly man took the pregnant woman to the border, where her relatives picked her up and she was saved.

Stories like these are, of course, impossible to verify, not least because Khurshid was not an eyewitness. However, what is significant is that seventy years on she has chosen to tell me this story, that it has survived the family's collective recollection of that time – and that in the retelling it is the so-called enemy who saved her mother's sister-in-law. It is important to Khurshid, like so many of the other interviewees, that stories of kindness and humanity are remembered amidst the terror. That 'some people were good on both sides too'. Proof also that deep ties and friendships did exist before partition. It is so easy for the horror and violence that then ensued to overshadow that.

Living in Pakistan, Khurshid was no longer afraid, but she never felt completely welcomed into Karachi society either. There was little mixing of the newly arrived refugees and Sindhis, the people already living in Karachi. Khurshid stayed within the army barracks and only met Sindhis when she started her medical studies at Dow Medical College. One day one of her Sindhi classmates told her they hadn't realised she was Punjabi, 'because Sindhi people say if there is a snake and a Punjabi, kill the Punjabi first, then the snake'.

Khurshid was seen as a Muhajir. They were Urdu-speaking refugees who migrated from India to Pakistan during partition, mostly from Uttar Pradesh. Many Muhajirs settled in the then capital Karachi and their presence transformed the city. By 1951 they comprised almost 60 per cent of Karachi's population.[2] The local Sindhis were largely rural, with fewer professionals; they championed the Sindhi language and had a well-developed sense of provincial politics. The refugees, in contrast, tended to be urban, well-educated, vociferous advocates of Urdu as a national language, and looked towards the national government as the guarantor of their interests.[3] At the heart of the difficulties that developed between the two groups were questions of who and what it meant to be truly 'Pakistani'.

Khurshid flinches and emphatically says she is not a Muhajir. 'Muhajir means you migrated. We migrated for good. With our own choice, now this is our country ... Why should we keep on saying we are Muhajir?' But it remains an unsettling issue, not only for Khurshid so many decades after she left Pakistan, but also in relation to the status of the Muhajirs and their families within Pakistan today.[4]

Khurshid left Pakistan over fifty years ago and now lives with her son and his family, including her granddaughter Sarah.

They live in a large house in a leafy part of Hertfordshire. It was her granddaughter Sarah who persuaded Khurshid to speak about her experiences. Sarah has just finished university and only recently found out about her grandmother's early life. While they were watching the Channel 4-aired drama series *Indian Summers* together, Khurshid had remarked that Simla didn't really look like that – and slowly her story emerged.

Sarah wants Khurshid's story to be remembered – 'a bit of emotional blackmail about recording it for my grandchildren ... It's important to have that sense of your family journey and your roots.' She, the third generation, feels disconnected, 'between two-worlds'. She doesn't speak Punjabi, Hindi or Urdu. She hadn't heard the term 'Muhajir' before the interview. She was interested by her grandmother's reaction, how her body language changed at the mention of the word, and is now curious to understand more. She wants to speak further about that after I have left.

I felt Khurshid's reticence to speak of what happened to her during the time of partition. Sarah noticed it too. It is hard to remember those times, sometimes it is easier to talk to a stranger, but not always. I did not want to push her for too many details. Like Karam Singh, there is a lot that is still raw. Khurshid's family were not touched in the same way Karam Singh's were; she did not witness the worst of what partition bore. But the memory of feeling fear in Delhi and the train journey to Pakistan, the sting of being regarded as a Muhajir is still there. By the end of our meeting Khurshid has relaxed. She proudly shows me an obituary of her father in December 1973, from a local Urdu newspaper in Lahore, which says he was the inventor of the Urdu keyboard for typewriters. The paper says he got in touch with a German firm and made an Urdu type-machine which became very popular in offices. It also says he was an adviser to Pakistan's founder, Mohammed Ali Jinnah, and that while a civil servant in Delhi, he campaigned for the rights of Dalits, demanding they have representation in parliament, and even organised a protest for them. The same group that warned him that trouble was brewing and made him swiftly take Khurshid out of school to go to Pakistan in 1947.

Khurshid hasn't been back to Delhi since the day she left as a fifteen-year-old. Nor has she been back to the village of her birth in Gurdaspur. She tells me that though she has Sikh and Hindu friends in Britain, there is a hesitation about returning to Delhi. 'I'm scared the people might kill me. Still.' She says it is what she remembers that holds her back. 'I think [the] same will be from their side.' Khurshid believes that Hindus and Sikhs must be afraid to return to the places they left in Pakistan too.

Even though Khurshid never felt completely accepted in Pakistan, partition for her was the best solution. 'In my village [Gurdaspur] we were like a big family, whether they are Hindu, Sikh ... very close. And then suddenly they become like animals. It is something very, very unusual. You can't think of these things. So then we think after that if we had lived with them there might have been trouble like that often. Because of the English people there was law and you know they were disciplined. There was no trouble like that. Ever.'

Khurshid Sultana was born in Gurdaspur, British India, in 1932. She trained as a doctor at Dow Medical College, Karachi. She came to Britain in 1961 and, over the next thirty years, worked as a gynaecologist, and then as a community health officer.

18

Mother, I Have Come Home

'That parting of each other was most unbearable. She was crying. I was crying.' Raj Daswani was fifteen years old and heartbroken at leaving his first love, Yasmin. 'We held hands again with each other. And slowly, slowly, slowly, slowly, slowly we left each other . . .'[1]

Raj was a Hindu and Yasmin a Muslim.

The two had known one another for five years, and lived in the same apartment block. They would meet in the evenings on the terrace, and hold each other's hands, and light a candle between them, in the shadow of the moon. Raj, eighty-five, cups his hands and raises his arms. 'I used to tell her, like putting my hands like this against the moon, that one day I'll give you the moon.'

They talked of their future, and how it would be. Whether they would be able to be together because of the difference in their religions. There was no precedence for a Hindu boy marrying a Muslim girl, and he feared that all the Muslim community would have opposed it. 'We used to talk about it and be very hopeful that since we are in real love we will definitely be able to come through and cross that bridge of religious difference.'

Raj lived in Sindh province, in newly independent Pakistan. He had lived there since he was adopted by his maternal grandparents at the age of two, after a devastating earthquake in Quetta, Balochistan, in 1935 had killed his parents and siblings. He lived with them for five years in Shikarpur, before moving to Karachi. On the day he left with his grandparents (whom he calls his parents) in September 1947, their Muslim friends and neighbours all came out. They were crying, imploring them not to go. 'They told us you are safe here, we'll safeguard you, don't leave.' But there was no option; they no longer felt safe. Since partition, 'The Muslim refugees from India, or the Muhajirs as they were known, had arrived [in Karachi] and were causing trouble for the Hindus left in Sindh province. Hatred was not there from Sindhi Muslims. Hatred was more from the Muhajirs. So, as they started to come, and many came to Karachi because of the port ... that hatred created fear.'

On the day he left, Yasmin came out too. Raj told her he had to leave because of the situation, and Yasmin implored him to return soon. 'I said I might come back, I might not. Because every Hindu was expecting this partition to be very, very temporary.' No one had sold their property, or belongings, they just left them in the care of their Muslim friends. Raj got into an open-top van, sitting in the back with his mother and their goods, his father in the front with the driver. 'I could see Yasmin looking at me till the end, till she could [no longer] see me.'

They drove to Karachi's port to board a ship for Bombay in India. At customs all their bags were confiscated. They had too many. All they took with them to their new life was one big tin of fried wheat flour, ghee and thirty-five rupees. Raj took with him a jar with the earth from his home.

'We were dumped in India, I would say.' Raj is still bitter at how many Sindhis were scattered around the new country. He was offered a certificate on arrival that showed he was a refugee and was eligible for free travel throughout India, but he refused it. 'I said that I am not a refugee. I refuse to be a refugee. Because before partition, Sindh was part of India. And we have come from one province to another province. So we are not foreigners. We have not come here to take the refuse [out]. We have come to live with you – our brothers.'

However, Raj felt they were not wanted in India. They were moved between camps until in early 1948 they finally settled in a big hall in a former military barracks at Kalyan military transit camp, later renamed Ulhasnagar ('City of Joy'),[2] nearly forty miles outside Bombay. It had been originally set up to accommodate thousands of soldiers from the British Indian Army during the Second World War.

Officially 80,000 people lived in the camp, though the true number was certainly far higher.[3] The mainly Sindhi-speaking Hindu refugees arrived after partition, many coming in the first months of 1948.[4] This deserted camp became their new home.

There were over 2,000 barrack blocks, many with large central halls. Raj's family was billeted in one of these halls. They used bedsheets to divide sleeping space between families, others used saris, tin, sackcloth and bamboo matting. The barracks were often windowless and without ventilation; some did not even have doors.[5] There were few toilets, if you could call them that, shared by around 500 people and located a long way outside, though the stench was ever present. Men and women both used them. Rats and snakes roamed around the latrines. Raj would get up early in the morning and stand in a queue to use the facilities before the crowds came.

The government provided free food rations to the barracks, which would arrive in the morning hours in a truck. It would bring onions, potatoes, lentils, rice and wheat. Raj says all the supplies were rotten: even the animals wouldn't eat such food. They lived like this until the early 1950s, when accommodation blocks were put up with sewage and drainage systems installed, and more toilets built. Raj says no national or regional political figure ever visited the camp: 'We were left just like orphans.'

As a boy in Karachi, Raj would sing the patriotic Urdu pro-independence song, 'Saare Jahaan se Accha', which begins:

Better than all the world, is our Hindustan,
We are its nightingales, and this is our garden
If we are away, the heart stays in our homeland,
Where our heart remains.
That mountain most high, neighbour to the skies,
It is our sentinel; it is our protector
A thousand rivers play in its lap,
Gardens they sustain, the envy of the heavens is ours,
O the flowing waters of the Ganges, do you remember
that day
When our caravan first disembarked on your waterfront?
Religion does not teach us to bear ill-will among ourselves
We are of Hind, our homeland is Hindustan.

As a teenager Raj would distribute bundles of independence leaflets – demanding the British leave – across Karachi. But he didn't think for a moment that independence would mean he would have to leave his beloved home for good, and live in squalor for many years in a refugee camp.

Life in India went on, however. Raj went to school, and had to learn Hindi, as his mother tongue was Sindhi. At the end of the school day he would leave the barracks and hawk knick-knacks – playing cards, buttons, cufflinks, combs, sewing needles. Whatever he earned he would give to his mother. His father was now bedridden following a fall, so Raj was the only earner.

One day, some years after they had first moved to the camp, they received a visitor from Karachi, a Muslim fisherman who had borrowed the significant sum of 1,500 rupees from his father before partition. He had managed to track down where the Daswanis were living. The fisherman had come all the way to hand-deliver the sum owed. 'I was at that time eighteen to nineteen years old. I could see [in] my father's eyes were tears that such people are also there in the world,' Raj remembers. They welcomed the visitor like a family member, and he stayed with them for a week.

The fisherman was shocked at their living conditions, asking them why they did not revolt against the Indian government at their treatment. 'He had seen our lifestyle in Karachi, and he was seeing the reverse, life in the barracks.' He told them their home was safe, that it was now occupied by Muhajirs. There were no riots in the town, but he lamented the loss of the Hindus. 'We lost our real brothers and foreigners have come,' he told the Daswanis. But the fisherman knew there was no possibility that the family could return. Karachi, a Hindu-majority city before partition, was virtually depleted of its Hindu population; it had become a city of partition refugees arriving from India.[6]

In 1951 Raj spotted a girl, Geeta, in one of the new blocks opposite. 'Within the first glimpse I could feel that she is the same as Yasmin. She was resembling her – features were the same, her colour was the same, her curly hair was the same – so I was attracted to her.' He was friends with Geeta's brother, so he already knew about her, but it took Raj a year to have the courage to approach her. She was a Hindi teacher, and he asked for help with his Hindi. She would one day become his wife.

She rolls her head back in their kitchen in north London and laughs now as she remembers: 'Hindi lessons! He used to chase me ... he played a lot of tricks.' Raj and Geeta had shared a passion for literature and plays, and with other young people would put on performances and recitals in Sindhi for the barracks.

Geeta was from Hyderabad in Sindh province, from a Hindu family. She arrived with her mother and two brothers in the barracks. They had left a few weeks after partition when it had become part of Pakistan, fearing trouble against them. Her mother was in sole charge of the children, as her father was abroad and she decided they should go. 'She thought ... "Okay, let me put my children in a safe place and then come back and sort things out." We had our property, our house, gold, silver, furniture, everything, bank balance, everything was there.'

Like the Daswanis, they imagined the move to India would just be temporary, so took only a few clothes with them. As they were waiting at Hyderabad station to board the train for India, men dressed in burkas entered the ladies' waiting room and robbed all the passengers. Luckily, they didn't have much to take. But her uncle (in the male compartment next door) had put his gold coins inside some home-cooked pakoras for safe keeping, and lost them all, as his tiffin box was taken.

In the scramble for the train, she and her brother were separated from her mother and other brother – and understandably Geeta was distraught, but no one helped them. 'Nobody has the compassion, nothing ... Nobody just had the little sympathy as to why these two children are there, no parents, nothing as such. Everybody was scared and thinking about themselves.'

On board the train they were crammed in 'like cattle, like you put goats and cows on there, we weren't treated like human beings. No food, no water, nothing was there.' She cannot remember how long she was on the train, possibly five or six hours or more, before it stopped at Luni station in Rajasthan, when she was reunited with her mother and brother on the platform, who in the rush to board the train had been forced into another compartment.

At first they lived in Madras with relatives, before moving a few years later to the Kalyan military barracks outside Bombay. Her mother was soon able to buy a bungalow in one of the new government-built blocks. Each had three rooms with a self-contained toilet. Geeta was then spared the treacherous journey to the filthy snake- and rat-infested latrine. Her brother used to accompany her and wait outside, to protect her modesty, as there was nothing so luxurious as a lock.

Raj and Geeta married in 1958. It was a modest affair. Only biscuits and tea were served after their ceremony in the small temple hall in the camp. Unusually, there was no dowry. Raj says he didn't ask for any, and her family were not compelled to give one. Their friends and family gathered; even though they were Hindus from different parts of Sindh province – she from Hyderabad and he from Shikarpur – there was no opposition to their union says Raj. It was only in 1959, eleven years after entering the camp, that Raj left, with his new bride, for Bombay, where he started working for the central government railways.

Restless, the Daswanis moved to Britain in 1974 after a brief stay in Sierra Leone. But their affinity for Sindh has never left them. Raj had a supermarket on the Finchley Road in north London and would note down the name of all his customers who were Sindhi so he could start a directory to put them in touch with one another. He amassed 1,200 names, both Muslims and Hindus. He and Geeta also founded the *Sindh Times* in September 1980, through which they campaigned for an independent Sindh, but following threats they were forced to close the publication some months later. They held Sindhi musical programmes at a church hall as well as at their home, and Geeta formed a teenagers' group called Anamika, so the next generation would understand their history.

In 1992, forty-five years after he left, Raj went back to Karachi. On the plane he says he had the feeling that he was going to meet his real mother, whom he had not seen for a very long time. The person sitting next to him on the plane asked why he was so gloomy. 'I told him that a few years back I left my mother in Sindh. I am going to see her.'

When Raj landed at Karachi airport, the first thing he did was take dust from the ground, kiss it, and put it on his forehead. 'I said, "My mum, I have come back."' He roamed the old streets where he had once played with friends, studied, and distributed Quit India leaflets. And he returned to the home he left in 1947. 'Oh, it was a dream come true. Of course the shops were changed, and the appearance of people were changed because the Muhajirs were different from Sindhis. But all was same. My place was same.' He looked up at the terrace where he would eat peanuts and sugarcane. The place where he and Yasmin would sit, talk of their future, and feel the moonshine. But he could not bring himself to enter the apartment, fearing he might burst into tears. He took a photograph of the outside for a keepsake and left.

On another visit to Karachi he discovered Yasmin hadn't married, and was living as a bibi, a recluse, having renounced the world. But she was alive and still living in the same apartment as when she was a young woman. Raj stood outside looking up at her window, knowing there were only twenty-eight stairs separating them, yet he dared not see her. 'I got married in India, and she didn't get married. It might be that if I see her because of those old memories and for whatever reason she did not marry and she renounced the world she might not be able to see me. And she might collapse.'

Raj returned to England with a heavy heart. He believes Yasmin somehow knew he had come back, just as she had asked him to, all those years back. He later learned that she died on 4 March 1998, the day his granddaughter Selina was born. 'I feel Yasmin had come back to me.'

Raj sings 'Nale Allakh Je Bairo Tar Muhenjo', a Sindhi folk song, one he and Yasmin used to listen to together. He translates for me. 'It means: "We used to pray to God to keep our life together, and sail together throughout our life." When I listen to [that] song, I remember that God didn't give us the blessings, he didn't make us together . . .'

Geeta and Raj have been happily married for sixty years now. A handsome couple, their home in north London is covered in pictures of their four children and many grandchildren. They speak Sindhi together. Raj writes essays and poetry, mostly about his beloved Sindh. Geeta is a formidable woman, with a cheeky sense of humour, keeping Raj, the dreamer, in check. It is wonderful to observe the warmth of their union.

Raj has returned to Karachi three times since partition, but Geeta has not been able to bring herself to return to Hyderabad. 'I thought the things won't be the same. And besides that I won't be able to find where my house was because things were changing, everything got changed,' she says. 'They changed the names, every single thing. And I don't know, maybe I got [a] terrible shock while leaving. So, I was thinking ... no, I won't see this land again which is not mine, it doesn't belong to me. When I go there, all those strange people will be there, nothing will be mine, so I just wanted to save myself from the pain. Again, the same wounds, I didn't want to open and suffer.'

But she still feels bitter that partition dispossessed the Hindu Sindhis almost entirely. 'Nobody looked after us. At least Punjabis, they got their own province, they are being looked after, but Sindhis [are] landless.' Strikingly she feels India is as much of a foreign land to her as England. 'From Sindh we went to India. From India, we are here, again to [a] foreign country which we just can't say it is our land. Still we are landless. If we go to India, we don't have any land, we can't go to our hometown because somebody else has taken it. So still we are just hanging.' Raj adds: 'Sindhis are scattered throughout the world, and our culture is becoming diluted day by day. The Sindhi community does not have any homeland.' Two souls, homeless.

After his final journey back, Raj wrote a poem addressed to Sindh. It began:

> In the end have realised this.
> In exile or forced to leave you
> Imagine the agony suffered by me
> Our flesh and blood, our kith and kin
> Suffering, in the name of religion.

The attachment to Sindh – its land, the culture and language – is so strong; according to Raj, it is stronger even than religion. If he had been an independent adult he says he would have converted to Islam so that he could have stayed in Karachi, where he grew up. 'Why did we leave our soil? Because our religion is more precious or the soil? Of course soil. If for soil you have to change your religion, I will go for it.'

He keeps and needs a physical reminder of his land. At first it was the earth from his homeland that he has taken with him. He kept it in a jar in the barracks and would touch it every day, 'as if I'm touching my own soil'. He had to relinquish it when he left for Africa in 1971. 'It was my own soil. This is not my soil, England or Bombay or India.' Today, in his study, he keeps stones which he took on his last trip to Karachi. He takes them out carefully, and puts them to his lips and kisses them. 'It is as if I am still connected to my soil.'

Raj Daswani was born in Quetta in 1932 and grew up in Karachi, Sindh province. He left for India in September 1947 and lived for twelve years in a camp on the outskirts of Bombay. Raj worked as a property developer and is a writer on Sindhi history. Geeta Daswani was born in Hyderabad, Sindh province in 1932. Raj and Geeta met in the refugee camp and married in 1958. They lived in Sierra Leone from 1971, before arriving in Britain in 1974. Geeta ran Sindhi language and cultural classes. They live in north London and have four children.

PART III

LEGACY

19

Legacy

The last UK census shows that there are over 3 million people in England and Wales with South Asian heritage (excluding 'other Asian' and 'mixed Asian' people). Modern Britain has been transformed by its South Asian population.[1]

South Asians have been living in Britain for over 400 years. A small population travelled as early as the formation of the East India Company in 1600. Some of the earliest known settlers were lascars (sailors) who travelled from Bombay or Calcutta, bringing tea, spices, silk and luxury goods to British homes. Some chose to jump ship because of harsh conditions, and settled in the ports of London, Glasgow, Liverpool and Cardiff.[2] It is estimated that around 8,000 Indians lived in Britain on the eve of partition.[3] As well as the sailors, there were ayahs, who travelled to be with their young charges, pedlars, students, doctors, as well as lawyers, and those from the British Indian Army.

However, the major flow began in the early 1950s in response to the call to help rebuild the UK economy after the Second World War. The 1948 British Nationality Act conferred the status of British citizenship on all Commonwealth subjects and those still part of the Empire. It recognised their right to work and settle in the UK. Over the next decade they came in their thousands from the Indian subcontinent to Britain.

The areas of India and Pakistan which were disturbed by partition and its aftermath were major contributors to this emigrant flow to Britain.[4] In the early post-war years many came from both Indian and Pakistani Punjab, which had experienced so much disruption. Sylhetis (who as sailors already had ties to Britain) from East Bengal, later Bangladesh, tended to settle in the East End of London. Following a local referendum in July 1947, Sylhet was detached from Assam and became part of East Bengal and Pakistan. Working in Assam or even Calcutta after partition had become too difficult.[5] Mirpuris were from a part of Kashmir that was actively fought over after partition, ending up on the Pakistani side of the ceasefire line. When the authorities decided to build the Mangla Dam, from the early 1960s, many thousands were made homeless, with some settling in Britain – particularly in the mill towns of the north and the major industrial centres of England.[6]

Clair Wills, in her book *Lovers and Strangers: An Immigrant History of Post-War Britain*, observes that the villages of Sylhet and Punjab were linked in an imaginary geography not to Dhaka or Delhi, but to London, Birmingham, Leicester and Bradford. For the earliest post-war migrants this was often due to their history as merchant sailors, or with the British Indian Army. The chance of economic and social advancement – at a basic level the chance of any kind of future – measured against the static nature of life on a rural smallholding, lay abroad.[7] And, as she points out, it was not the poorest who left, but those with capital to spare. 'Going to work in Britain was not the last hope of a reluctant and desperate peasantry but an investment in the future.'[8] Migration fever took hold first amongst the Jats but quickly spread to the 'status conscious' members of society.

Usually at least one family member would migrate. And nearly all who came to post-war Britain were young, single males, who sent remittances home to their extended family. They never imagined they would settle permanently in Britain for good.

Their destinations in Britain were largely confined to metropolitan areas – places like Bradford, Wolverhampton, Birmingham, Oldham, Southall and Luton – through chain migration, so there was already a network of circulation, even if it was in small numbers. These men came to fill in the gaps in the labour market – from the foundries in the West Midlands, to the woollen textile mills of West Yorkshire, and the cotton mills of Lancashire as well as the NHS. They worked the difficult shifts that no one else wanted, and it very often included hard manual work.

In Britain they were all seen as 'Asians', unlike on the Indian subcontinent where their differences – religious, regional, caste, for example – were so pronounced. They worked together in those early days, fighting for workers' rights, and in the later years against racism.

In 1951 there were 43,000 South Asians in Britain. By 1961 the number had more than doubled to 112,000.[9] The first of many restrictions began to be placed on the principles of the 1948 British Nationality Act in response to growing discomfort over the number of immigrants in the country. From 1962 the Commonwealth Immigrants Act stipulated that prospective migrants needed employment vouchers from the Ministry of Labour before being allowed into Britain. These were given to people who had specific jobs to go to in Britain, or to those with a particular skill or qualification.[10] This legislation had the unintended consequence of increasing the number of those migrating from the Indian subcontintent – people came over in a rush to beat the ban. It also meant that those who had only thought they were coming to stay for a few years chose to remain, fearing they would not be able to come back to Britain if they left. But, crucially, it also meant that wives and children began to arrive in Britain, as there was concern that they may not be allowed to join their men after the legislation was in force. These pioneers looked like a more permanent presence on the landscape, and they were laying down their roots.

20

Rootless

In November 2009, Veena Dhillon was in her late mother's apartment in Rugby, Warwickshire, sorting through her belongings. Inside a drawer, next to her mother's bed, she found a grey A4 ring binder. It belonged to Veena, and was from her days as a medical student back in the early 1980s. Her last-minute obstetrics and gynaecology revision notes were still scrawled on the inside cover. Opening out the folder she found sheets of papers with her mother's distinctive handwriting. 'She always had this funny way of writing, which I always associate with people who come from India. It's a way of writing English.'[1] There were scribbles, drawings and some sketches too. On the first page was an index for poems, short stories, and essays. Most were in English, some in Hindi. I ask if her mother left them there expecting them to be found. 'It's interesting, I've never thought of it like that … Well, maybe she did. I had never consciously thought that she might have deliberately done it for us.'

She knew her mother, Amar, had been writing some sort of autobiography, but didn't expect to discover such a treasure trove of family history. Veena took the folder home to Edinburgh, and when she felt ready, started to leaf through the loose pages. Over the next three years she typed up the writings, resisting the temptation to correct her mother's idiosyncratic English. Her mother wrote as she spoke. It felt to Veena as if her dead mother were talking to her as she transcribed; it was an emotionally draining process, but at the same time Veena felt very close to her mother. As she tapped away on the computer, a photograph of her mother was nearby, on her desk. Taken in St Andrew's in the late 1980s, Amar looks youthful and content (she had just eaten a particularly juicy mango). Veena bound her work, the collection of her mother's stories, in a printed book for her three brothers.

Veena knew very little from her parents' early life. Her father, Dharam Singh Dhillon, had always spoken of an idyllic childhood in Punjab living with his extended family. As a boy he would ride a horse bare-back, play in the nalas (canals), climb trees and pick mangoes. Veena knew her extended family lived in Nurmahal, near Jalandhar in Indian Punjab. It was where she visited with her mother for the first time in 1976, when she was eighteen. Mother and daughter had slept on the roof under the stars, and made rotis together. Veena laughs as she remembers being force-fed buffalo milk as her relatives thought she was too skinny. Veena had always assumed that this was the place they were from. The whole connection with West Punjab and Pakistan, however, had been completely removed from family life. 'This other history, this other life that existed pre-1947, it was as if it had never happened.'

Dr Veena Dhillon has just turned sixty and taken retirement from her post as a consultant rheumatologist and honorary senior lecturer at the University of Edinburgh. A delicate, thoughtful woman, with striking short grey hair, we sit together in her tasteful apartment. She talks of her retirement plans – her love of walking in the Scottish Borders, where she also has a home – and travelling. A life lived in England and Scotland, but she is only just learning of her parents' past, and is trying to piece together their life before coming to Britain.

Her father, Dharam, was very unwilling to talk about partition; he was quite traumatised by it. It was only when he developed Parkinson's disease and dementia in the final part of his life, that he started to speak of those times. Veena's mother, Amar, felt it was a subject that should not be discussed. Veena recalls an incident when they were both attending an event at the Edinburgh Book Festival, when Amar stood up to admonish an author who was presenting her autobiographical book. Amar felt the writer was being light-hearted when she spoke about partition, and told her: 'We should not share our dirty linen in public. We should all be ashamed of what happened at partition. This was a seriously traumatic episode in our history that cannot be spoken of.' She felt so strongly about it, Veena says, that she was compelled to speak her mind, in front of a sea of white faces in the audience.

And yet here she was leaving a stash of papers precisely from that time. Amar's most intimate thoughts and sharp observations. One of the joys of discovery for Veena was not only understanding her family history, but also remembering her parents as a young, passionate couple, not the crumpled figures they became later in life, crushed by the weight of their hard lives. 'They were actually in love even though they had an arranged marriage.' Her mother writes (in the third person) that on seeing a photograph of her husband who she would soon be marrying: 'It was the catalytic gaze which struck like a lightning through her whole being, and was more than enough to shatter her.'[2]

Extrapolating from the stories her mother left, Veena believes that just after partition there were riots near to where they lived in Dijkot, near Lyallpur (not far from where Mohindra Dhall was born in 1941) in Pakistan. Her parents had been married as teenagers in 1945, but, as was the custom, they had not yet lived together. Veena thinks her father must have gone to retrieve her mother from her family home not far away.

The first night they spent together, their wedding night, was on the roof of the Dhillon family home under the moonlight, 'Which is very romantic.' The following morning panic ensued, and the couple, as Sikhs, in what was now Pakistan, had to leave. Veena adds that there is an allusion to the fact that her eldest brother may have been conceived that night. She reads the title of the poem 'The Night of Flight'. Just before she starts, I sense her nervousness. 'It is quite hard for me to read without blubbing.' Veena is a woman of composure, but I can see she is finding the strength to read words which are so personal to her, words I think she may be reading out loud for the very first time.

You were young
I was young
We were young and in love
Nothing mattered
Spoil and scatter of '47
Meant nothing
We dwelt in another world
The world of love of intoxication
In a fashion
It was our first night together
The night before the flight

From ancestral home
We lay face to face
Under the blue dome
And drank from the moon
Its milky moonlight
In it we watched
Many stars twinkling in our eyes
Yours and mine
We watched and watched
All night with such a delight
Unslept the whole night
Crack of dawn the message arrived
'Be ready, we are going'
Going?
Where?
Why?
Questions ... nobody answered!
Hush on lips
Anxiety in mind
Breakfast?
Packing?
Nobody bothered 'Hurry, hurry, quick
Trucks are moving – no time
For leaving message for the left behind'
Nears and dears
Mothers, fathers
Trucks were moving, military truck
Evacuating, dwellers of stately homes,
Women and children and some men
Their guardians
Refugees![3]

There is more detail of the flight from a subsequent essay entitled 'Escape', where Amar, having woken up in the morning after her wedding night, goes to help her mother-in-law prepare breakfast before getting ready for the day:

It was still early in the morning when I went to have a bath. I heard a knock on the bathroom door, someone giving me the message to hurry up, we are leaving. The military truck is here to evacuate us. Where to? Why? Who said so? But no answer. The messenger had left hurriedly. People were so determined to hold their ground, rushed panic stricken at the first opportunity to escape leaving their cherished possessions. Such was the tension, terror and fear lived day after day for weeks and months.

I wanted to leave some message for my parents and my would-be whereabouts but there was no time. Get left behind or get into the car, I was told. I felt a hollow gripe in my stomach. Was I hungry? I had no breakfast, or was I worried, bewildered? The next moment I found myself in a red car holding my damp towel and with slippers on my feet. I had never known the capacity of a car accommodating so many passengers, young mothers with children on their laps, children standing in front of the back on the sides. It was early in the morning. The monsoons have just ended but the air was still unstuffy. The fumes rising from the sweating bodies inside the car were unbearable.

Luckily the cars started moving without much delay, sandwiched between military trucks containing soldiers with khaki uniforms, rifles in their hands, standing on alert in all directions. We picked up speed in no time as if we were being chased.

I saw Dharam amongst other young men and boys perched on top of another truck, which was full of luggage held down with nets. The convoy on the road was overtaking all the traffic in a chaotic manner. Every time they drove on the verge to evade the oncoming traffic, the lowering branches at the roadside trees tore pieces of shirts and flesh of the backs of passengers perched on top of the luggage, but the trucks were running like mad.[4]

They dodged the militia in Lahore and managed to get across the border to Amritsar in the army trucks. In Guru ka Bagh, a gurdwara, volunteers were handing out baskets of food, chapattis and boiled rice. In 'Refuge', she speaks of the Golden Temple and how the foundation stone had been placed by a Muslim, Mian Mir, a revered friend of the Guru, to emphasise respect for all religions. 'We lived amongst these peoples all our lives and for generations,' she writes in 'The Holy City'. 'We participated in each others' celebrations and bad times. How could they think of communal riots? Plundering and killing each other? It was more like the clock turned back to a primitive century. Greedy and distorted people, men had always wanted power over each other's minds, quite often religion had been the only weapon in their hands.'[5]

In her writings Amar is balanced, attributing no blame to one side or another to the horrors she witnessed.

It was the story of Veena's grandmother, however, that may have explained her father's silence about that time. The family were worried because Dharam's mother had not come across the border with them. When she finally arrived, she complained of a slight stomach ache, which developed the next day to diarrhoea and vomiting. The doctor was called and told her she had cholera and needed to be separated from the family. Veena's parents stayed with her grandmother, nursing her. Veena is reading from 'How Much Hurt Does One Feel?'. She breaks down now as she reads her mother's words, about the grandmother Veena would never meet: 'She passed away in our hands the following night. It seemed so unfair and cruel ... I've never seen anyone die before and it was so close to my eyes. It shook my faith in life. I was distracted by the grief of my husband. He had just lost his mother. Now he sat in the chair with tears streaming from his eyes.'[6]

Veena says her grandmother's swift decline from cholera was a direct consequence of coming across the border and admits that her father hadn't ever got over his mother's death: 'I just think you've lost everything and then you lose your mother ... You kind of think, what's left?' Indeed, once her father came to the UK in December 1951, he never returned to India again. 'He always used to say that India is a horrible, dirty place, full of disease. Why would anyone go back there?'

Amar wrote in 'Leaving India' that Dharam was working in a co-operative bank as an inspector, a clerical job which he found 'soul-killing with no promise or prospects. He resigned after a few months and left for England to see the world around him before settling down for good.'[7] As was the norm then, he came by himself, leaving his wife and two sons behind, the youngest being just four years old. Dharam was a graduate, but that did not count for much in Britain in 1951. He took one of the few jobs available to Indians and worked down the mines in the Coalville area of Leicestershire, which reactivated his childhood tuberculosis. He then spent four years in Groby Road Isolation Hospital in Leicester. He had an operation where half his chest wall was removed and only survived because he was lucky enough to be one of the first people to be offered the antibiotic streptomycin.

Veena's mother, back in India, was working as a head-mistress at a secondary school in Nurmahal, 'a woman before her time', Veena says. She was working full time, and raising her two boys. She was fortunate that she came from a family which believed women should be educated. In 'Leaving India' Amar wrote that her illiterate mother's belief was that 'without education a person is blind. Her [Veena's maternal grandmother's] own yearning for learning instilled an unquenchable thirst for knowledge in me which took me away from her at an early age in its pursuit.'[8]

'In Mum's time,' Veena says, 'it was considered completely wrong for a woman to be in higher education. She could only do that if she was married and Mum agreed to get married.' Her mother accepted a betrothal in order to be able to stay in education. Veena's father accompanied his wife to college and vouched for her status. It seems Veena's parents were both ahead of their time. Amar writes: 'Perhaps crossing the line of modesty, I could claim to be the first female graduate in our village, but not without hardships. After enormous impediments and the restrictions of the social and political systems, by the time I graduated from the Punjab University at the age of twenty-one in 1949. I was married and had a son of six months old.'[9]

Amar was happily working when she learned her husband was profoundly ill in England and she faced a choice:

I had settled down in my job, enjoying a respectable position in the community – job satisfaction that I was doing something worthwhile ... On the other

hand, I wanted to be by the side of my husband
through thick and thin. I relied on his decision – he
had experienced both sides of the world. He wanted
us to join him, but knew also that coming to England
with my sons would not be the bed of roses I should
expect. It would be a hard struggle, since he had lost
quite a good deal of confidence in his full recovery. He
made the fact quite clear to me. Other well-wishers in
India also discouraged me leaving home, fearing the
hardships and dangers in a strange country, but my
grandmother's words were a pillar of strength. 'You are
my granddaughter, go and join that poor boy. I know
you will make it – you and him together – that is what
I want to see,' she said.[10]

Like any young wife who has been separated from her
husband for some years, Amar admits to a natural nervousness
about seeing her husband again and whether they would still
feel the passion of their early married life:

Life plays strange tricks. Romance of a few years ago
merged into struggle, then separation and yearnings to
see each other. So far it was care and concern for each
other, will that romance revive ever again in that pure
form? I remembered the days when neither of us closed
one's eyes for a wink lest one missed the sight of the
other's eyes filled with love and [a] smile much more
sweet than that seen on the face of the *Mona Lisa*, and
burning with the desire of Parwana.[11]

One of the most moving parts of the collection of stories
is Amar writing of leaving India in the early 1950s, a young

woman on her own, with two small boys. Veena is not completely certain, but thinks the year her mother left for England was 1954. Seven years earlier she had fled Pakistan, now she was leaving India. She departed from Bombay on the P&O liner *Stratheden*:

> I stood on the deck holding the rails, I felt a lump
> rising to my throat and my eyes filled with tears.
> Parting farewells, shadows looming, the thought in my
> mind: 'Shall I ever see it again just the same?'
>   I raised my arm to wave goodbye to all. To India and
> to my past of twenty-seven years ...
>   The future unimaginable, nothing much to do except
> brooding over the past.[12]

There is one passage that stands out painfully. Amar's generation had fled religious hatred during partition, but were to encounter another hatred amongst some in the new land they sailed towards, this time because of the colour of their skin. In an auger of future indignities, Amar writes of an encounter on the ship. It is so delicately written it could be missed, and could only be detected in those who have felt that sting. In 'Strangers Aboard', Amar comes across an Englishwoman knitting a pink garment on the deck of the P&O liner. She asks how old her baby is, but there is no response as the Englishwoman carries on knitting as if she must urgently finish the garment. Holding her boys' hands Amar moves away, when one of her sons asks:

> 'What is the matter with that lady, Mummy? Why doesn't
> she speak?'

'People have many reasons, my dear. It is difficult to tell. Sometimes people don't know themselves.'

'Look, up there. How the birds are hovering – as if totally weightless,' someone was saying behind us ...[13]

To Veena this exemplifies the way her parents dealt with the considerable racism in the 1950s, '60s and '70s, some of which she witnessed growing up and still hurts her. She recounts many instances: her father denied a promotion to the position of foreman at Marwin's where he made machine tools, because the English workers went on strike saying they did not want an Indian boss. How the English neighbours of the new house they planned to buy told them they didn't want their type there. Veena's parents' response was to 'bow their heads and carry on'. Dharam did not fight for the promotion, and they decided not to buy the house.

'They were always so dignified, never responded' – though Veena, born in the UK, adds she herself was nothing like that. One time in the 1970s, she and her now husband, David, were walking down Lewisham High Street where by coincidence a National Front demonstration was going on. A skinhead attempted to give Veena a leaflet, and she started to give him a piece of her mind. David steered her away for her safety. She adds that ironically one of the first tasks she had as a clinical student in London in 1979 was to sew up a skinhead's bloody scalp after a razor attack. 'On that night I learned to stow what I felt and to be a professional, as all doctors have to do, and I think that particular skinhead learned something too judging from his manner before and after.' Different battles fought by parents and children to be accepted and respected.

Amar's drive for acceptance was to instil ambition into her children. She coached them for grammar school – telling them they had no choice but to get in, otherwise they would end up doing factory work for the rest of their lives. All of her children got a place. Three went on to read medicine at Cambridge University, the youngest elected not to sit the Oxbridge entrance exam. Amar's first-born, on gaining admission to university, appeared on the front page of the *Leicester Mercury* under the headline: 'Indian boy gets into Cambridge'. He had actually wanted to study astrophysics, but Veena's father 'made it abundantly clear that no course other than medicine was acceptable'. All four siblings became hospital consultants, two were also professors.

Veena has always strived not to be mediocre. Her mother telling her she had to succeed was probably part of it, but it was also driven by her desire not to be like her father, who was intelligent and educated yet was reduced to doing manual work.

Amar took her A-levels at around the age of fifty. She did a pharmacy course, she painted and wrote for *The Lady* magazine. She wanted to be a doctor, and her earlier essays show an interest in symptoms and treatments – whether cholera, smallpox or tending to a young girl following a road traffic accident. Amar acknowledged she was part of a generation, like so many first-generation immigrants, who sacrificed their aspirations for the benefit of the next. They achieved through their children:

Once again the age-old belief that health no. 1 and education no. 2 are the only essential ingredients for the struggle to success and prosperity and of happy living remained to prove itself. I knew both these essentials do

not come easy. If physical and mental health is God's
precious gift, which must be guarded, sound education
needed a lot of sacrifices and this time the education
of my children and health of my husband demanded
sacrifice of my personal future.[14]

Veena is sure the poems and essays she discovered were
written by her mother during the 1980s – that she found
them some twenty-five to thirty years after they had been
penned. Stories and histories which had lain dormant since
1947 would lay still for a few decades more.

Veena acknowledges she feels she knows her mother
better now. It is not lost on her, that when she was alive,
Veena was so busy forging a life, fighting her own battles
(some against her parents), that she never asked her mother
so many things.

The writings, Veena believes, were Amar's way to ensure
their family history would not be forgotten, 'because in lots
of ways I am rootless'. She thinks that her mother was trying
to give her roots. 'I've never been to the geography of the
place where probably my family and my ancestors lived for
centuries. We were geographically very stable and it's very
likely that my ancestors didn't move from that place. So
perhaps she was trying to give something to us because I don't
have a root … I suppose it's another bit of the jigsaw. It's a
little bit of a root. It's not the root I would like to have.'

She says her roots are now in Scotland as she has lived there
longer than anywhere else in her life. 'When I was a kid I used
to look in the mirror and wonder if I came from outer space,'
she adds. 'That is a sign of somebody who doesn't really know
where she belongs, is always going to be an outsider … I am
very conscious of the fact that I know who I am inside but

I know what I look like to people who don't know me, which is an ageing Indian woman. I'm an incongruous thing. I'm not one thing or another really.' She is not sure however if she feels rootless because she is the child of immigrants or because the rootlessness goes back further than that, which is the uprooting from West Punjab in 1947.

Veena is now thinking of writing a book, about her parents coming to England, their earlier life, and her and her brother's early experiences. 'We are the real *East is East*.'[15] She laughs as she recalls how, at the age of ten, she was no longer allowed to play outside (unlike her brothers), and had to help her mother cook the family meals, and on weekends wash all the clothes by hand in the kitchen sink as they did not have a washing machine. Yet at the same time she was expected to succeed. Aged eight, the first time her elder brother was dropped off at Cambridge University, she was told she too would be going there to study medicine.

The Dhillons were an unusual family. The siblings always felt quite unlike the other South Asians, more anglicised, she thinks. She and her brothers were held up as examples within the community of how all Indian children should be – studious, successful and dutiful.

I am in a rush to leave Veena, I have a plane to catch from Edinburgh. We were strangers when we met, yet after a few hours I feel as if I have asked her questions and she has given me answers that if I had known her all my life we may never have broached. She shared with me some of her most personal thoughts about her parents, growing up, her mother's personal papers. She wept as she remembered – a woman I imagine who does not cry easily in the presence of people she does not know. I cannot help but feel close to her. Yet this is all so raw, so live. Questions of our parents' history, and how losing a parent means so much more when they are the reason you are in this country and the primary tie to the land you live in.

Veena is the success story – educated in the state system, a Cambridge graduate, an accomplished doctor, homes in the city and country, and yet I am struck that she tells me she will always be an outsider. She says she went through a phase a few years back when filling in forms about her background, where she would write her ethnic group as 'other'. 'Born in Leicester, of parents who were born in India but what is now Pakistan, and married to an Englishman. What am I? Who am I?'

In retirement she is planning a month-long walk of some 350 miles, backpacking with her husband David, who was also born in Leicester. They wanted to retrace the map of their life, from their birthplace to their home in the Scottish Borders. Mostly, once she has left work, she wants to figure out who she is. The only Indian connection she feels is cooking, and how to make roti, which she learned as a ten-year-old, turning the roti with her hands on the tawa (frying pan), just like her mother and grandmother did.

We speak again around a year later. Veena tells me she has been thinking a lot about her parents' past, that she too wants to make a connection with it. She wants to go to Pakistan. 'I want to stand on the land they are from.'

Then she adds that she has been thinking about our last conversation, when she said she felt rootless. 'But when you repot a plant, you break the root, but it grows more vigorously. I have so much to be thankful for. If my parents had not come here I would never have met my soulmate, been a doctor, had the children I have. I live a wonderful life, with First World worries. Populations have always moved. They never stop.'

Veena Dhillon Wilks was born in 1958 in Leicester. She studied medicine at Girton College, Cambridge, and was a consultant rheumatologist in Edinburgh and an honorary senior lecturer at Edinburgh University. She retired to the Scottish Borders in 2018.

21

We Should Talk

When Poonam Joshi was in her early twenties, studying for her master's degree, she interviewed her mother, Nirmal, for her thesis. She recorded her partition story in one sitting, and this was its concluding paragraph: 'Partition can be summarised in great detail or in one sentence. But I still feel great distress that what happened shouldn't have happened. I think we should talk. We should talk about it very openly – we should know what happened at that time. And there is no disgrace in talking about that. It did not happen to one or two people, it happened on a large scale ... it became a part of history ... and it is no crime to be a refugee.'[1]

Poonam had already heard bits of these stories throughout her lifetime – her mother was always open about her experiences – but her daughter hadn't really been listening before. The stories were so hard to absorb while she was growing up, too painful to hear. During the formal interview, Poonam heard her mother's story from beginning to end. And this time she chose to hear it all. It made her feel closer to her mother but also very protective of her, her fear was still so palpable. The horror of what she had witnessed and went through shook Poonam, as did the knowledge that her mother had been managing the trauma for all those years, in an era before counselling. But the humanity of what Nirmal spoke of also touched her. To be honest, it must have been a relief.

Over twenty years after conducting that interview, Poonam is sitting in her Victorian home in a smart street in west London, on a late spring Sunday afternoon. The shadows of the evening sun are falling on her face. She is a warm, self-assured woman. She has just finished making some colourful cupcakes with her nine-year-old daughter, which are still cooling on an island in her kitchen. Poonam's teenage son, who is already taller than his mother, is milling around with a friend. There are musical instruments lying around the living area, just off the kitchen. This is a happy, busy, family house. The children know I am here to talk about their late grandmother, and I am not sure how much they know about her early years.[2]

Poonam was the main one in her family in whom her mother confided. The stories started when Poonam was just a child; she thinks she was younger than her daughter is now. Most parents read books to their children before they sleep. Nirmal's bedtime tales were of growing up in Lahore, the journey she made to India and the experience of being a refugee. She was not always judicious in the amount of detail she shared. Early on in her life, Poonam had a sense that something terrible had happened to her mother.

In the retelling of Nirmal's experiences, it was as if she were reliving it all again. 'It was part of our daily lives … It was the formative experience of her life and in a strange way it became the formative experience of my life because she spoke about it all the time.' Poonam does not think of it on a day-to-day basis now, but says partition defined her because it so utterly defined her mother, and shaped who she became. 'Partition is always there in the background.'

In the last years of her life, Nirmal lived in this family home, cared for by her daughter. Photos of her with her beloved grandchildren are on prominent display in the kitchen. Nirmal, or Nimmi as she was known, began her life on the outskirts of Lahore, born into a middle-class family in 1929. She spoke of her pets: the rabbits and dogs. Her family were Hindu, belonging to the Arya Samaj sect, which rejects idol worship and promotes the equality of women. Theirs was a home full of music and singing. A twenty-year age gap existed between Nirmal's parents. Her mother was married at the age of twelve, but was fortunate that her in-laws encouraged her ambitions to study. It was an unusual household, with Nirmal's mother assuming the patriarchal role. She qualified as a teacher, and worked while her husband looked after Nirmal and her sisters.

Nirmal adored her father, who in turn doted on her. Like so many of her generation, she told Poonam of how she celebrated festivals with other neighbours, irrespective of religion, though when she was much younger at school she recalled an incident of a Muslim man knifing a Hindu bookbinder, which resulted in shops being closed in their area and panic spreading. Because of this, Nirmal was taken out of the Urdu section of her school and placed in the Hindi part. From time to time incidents like this did occur in her childhood – Nirmal pointed out – amongst both Hindu and Muslim fanatics.

Nirmal observed that hopes for independence from British rule were at first about desh prem, love of your homeland. But it soon became about love of your religion. The first inkling of this came when Ashraf, a Muslim classmate seated at her desk, punched the air with her fist saying: 'We're going to get rid of all of you ... Lahore will be in Pakistan.' Nirmal dismissed it, and thought it a strange comment from the girl, but Poonam identifies this as a significant moment. 'I guess she [Nirmal] starts to see the beginning of the politicisation of parts of the Muslim community that will eventually lead to partition.'

The stories she told her daughter move on to the day before Nirmal left her home, around the time of partition. She had a Muslim neighbour who was a 'brother-friend'. He respected Nirmal's parents as his own. Every year, on the full moon in the month of Sravana in the lunar calendar, Nirmal would perform the Hindu ritual of Raksha Bandhan, or Rakhi. She would tie a thread on the wrist of her father, and male relatives – but also on this Muslim neighbour, as a sign of her sisterly affection for him. He in return would give her modest gifts promising her protection.

Poonam does not know this neighbour's name, and wishes she had asked her mother while she was alive. But this Muslim neighbour fulfilled his duty of protection to his Hindu sister, as symbolised by the ancient ritual of the tying of red thread on his wrist. He came to the family house one day and said he had just attended a secret neighbourhood meeting of Muslims. Addressing Nirmal's parents, he told them that no girl, however young, was safe – and that their daughters needed to be taken away for a couple of weeks. Nirmal was seventeen, her sister, Urmil, fourteen. Poonam adds: 'So I guess the idea would be to abduct and rape; abduct, rape and kill; or abduct, rape and keep in a relationship.'

Nirmal's father wanted to stay, but her mother insisted she was leaving with her daughters – whether he came or not. The same Muslim neighbour took the mother and daughters in a horse and cart to Lahore station; their father stayed behind. Poonam is not entirely sure what happened but Nirmal always told her of this neighbour being physically attacked at some point on the journey, and how he was injured along the way, though he still managed to get them onto the train. 'So she talked about this neighbour saving their lives and always feeling very indebted to him for doing that.'

Like Veena Dhillon's parents, Nirmal too arrived into Jalandhar, in Indian Punjab. At the train station there, she felt afraid, even though she was now in India. There was news that a caravan of Muslim refugees was moving in the opposite direction towards Pakistan. 'She talked about this sort of imminent fear of violence and fear of rape still hanging in the air,' says Poonam.

Nirmal's mother approached a Sikh man at the station asking if he would take her family in, which he did. Poonam is not sure how long they stayed with them, whether it was days or weeks, but she says, 'Once again another story of incredible kindness of this time, a stranger who took them in and protected them.'

It was clear now the family would not be away for just a few weeks. Nirmal would then go on to tell her daughter the story of the allocation of housing to the Sikh and Hindu refugees arriving into Jalandhar. She described a system of corruption where families who were already in Jalandhar were trying to seize property for themselves. As she was with her mother, they were at a disadvantage, as families with a male member would negotiate with the authorities ahead of them. Nirmal's mother had to struggle hard to secure property for her family. Eventually they were given a multi-storey house which had belonged to a Muslim police officer. Some months later, Nirmal's father joined them, and this was to be her family's home for the next forty years. Nirmal's mother eventually converted the ground floor into a primary school which she ran as the head teacher.

Before her father arrived, Nirmal lived in an unusual situation – a household of women. In their home was her younger sister and mother, but they had been joined by her newly widowed elder sister and her two children. Money was tight, so Nirmal worked to support the family. She would sing ghazals, lyrical poems often on the theme of love, and bhajans, religious songs, at the All India Radio station in Jalandhar to earn money. 'She had a beautiful singing voice,' Poonam remembers. Nirmal would go on to sing at the radio station for many years. But it meant that the neighbours cast aspersions over what kind of girl she was, because she was willing to go and sing at a radio station for money.

Poonam shows me two black-and-white photographs of her mother from that time. In one, four young women are sitting cross-legged on the floor singing into a microphone which bears the initials AIR (All India Radio). Behind them sit six men accompanying them on the tabla, flute, violin and sitar. In the other, Poonam points out her mother with two plaits. The two plaits apparently denote how modern she was. Nirmal would laugh at this, but Poonam says there was a darker side which she only learned of after her death.

At Nirmal's funeral, one of Poonam's cousins attended. He had lived as a young boy in the house, before Nirmal's father arrived. He told Poonam that the house was labelled 'the house of prostitutes' by the neighbours, something Poonam's mother hadn't revealed. Poonam thinks it must have been deeply painful to her to have known that these Hindus and Sikhs, who were supposed to be their own community, were labelling women just because they were vulnerable, and without a male figure in the household. Poonam reflects it would not have been lost on her mother that a Muslim neighbour in Lahore saved her, and yet the men who were supposed to be her Hindu and Sikh 'brothers' in Jalandhar subjected her to harassment. Poonam says Nirmal also had a real sense of injustice about double standards. She was very much of her age, but she knew that things were underpinned by inequality, and that it wasn't fair that women had a higher standard that they had to meet.

But it is Nirmal's testimony of the sexual violence, whose aftermath she bore witness to, that most deeply affected her daughter. It is no coincidence, Poonam believes, that she chose the career she did. 'I'm sure one of the reasons I work on women's rights is because of the stories she told me of what she witnessed and what she feared.'

Nirmal was explicit about what she witnessed being done to women in the name of religion. She had volunteered at a refugee camp in Jalandhar where she saw women – who had survived sexual attacks – whose rapists had carved 'Pakistan Zindabad' on their chests.[3] She spoke of one Hindu woman who was forced to abort the foetus of her rapist at the request of male family members. Poonam quotes her mother saying, referring to that woman in the camp: 'Whatever her feelings had been, she was after all a mother.' Nirmal was even-handed in attributing blame in her recollections: 'The same cases happened on both sides: that Hindus are made of gold and Muslims aren't (this isn't true). This happened everywhere.'[4]

Poonam describes how Nirmal believed this partition violence against women did not come out of nowhere. It arose from what men thought about women in peacetime as well. 'And she was very, very angry about that.' Poonam's grandmother was always described to her laughingly as a mixture of Margaret Thatcher, Golda Meir and Indira Gandhi. 'I mean she was scary. But you can see that the way that she was, was because she had to be. Reputation was everything, it was the one thing that they thought would protect them from further violence and further harassment.'

These experiences meant Nirmal was naturally very protective towards Poonam – she could not control what others did to her, but she could control where she was. 'She certainly sent me the message that you couldn't trust men, that you never knew when things could turn against you,' says Poonam.

Nirmal married in 1958 at the age of twenty-eight, and moved twenty miles away from her family to Kapurthala. Before marriage she went to law college, and after graduating became a schools inspector. Eight years after her betrothal her husband went to England to work in a factory, leaving Nirmal and their son behind. When it was clear he was not returning to India, Nirmal's mother felt her daughter should join her husband in England. Nirmal had no desire to leave India, but in the end she did. She arrived in Coventry in 1968. Her first home was a cold, damp bedsit, and she quickly caught pneumonia. Her husband was working long hours in the factory, and she was living in a country where she felt unwanted, where racism was rife and open. Poonam says twice in her mother's life she was forced to move because of decisions made by other people, decisions she felt she had no control over.

All the displacements and early life experiences affected Nirmal's mental health. She had depression and anxiety when Poonam was a young girl. She was strong in some ways, but fragile in others. The lesson Poonam took from her mother was never to think of yourself as a victim, but always to feel there are things you can determine in a situation. Poonam looked at Nirmal's two sisters, who also experienced displacement but responded to it differently. She feels there is always a question mark over what makes one person more resilient than another.

What struck Poonam about her mother's recounting of partition is its complexity. She captured the relationships people had with each other before the conflict. Nirmal didn't describe a society that was so deeply divided that you could predict the violence that was going to happen. The widespread slaughter came as a complete shock, because these were people you loved and cared about. 'If that was my mother's story,' says Poonam, 'I wonder how many other stories there were, where people transcended their identities and hate, to actually help people. And that's got lost in the retelling of partition ... Everything was simplified into Sikhs are rapists, Muslims are rapists ... And what my mother did was she always remembered the humanity of all the people who helped them along the way.'

Yet ancient prejudices prevailed too. And as with so many South Asian families, there are countervailing forces coexisting. There are the personal stories of humanity across the religious divide. But there is also suspicion and even hostility between religious communities that persists, never more so than on the delicate subject of marriage. The expectation from Poonam's parents was that she would have an arranged marriage with a Hindu, just as they and their forebears had done. From very early on it was made clear to Poonam by her family that she shouldn't ever marry a Muslim.

Poonam describes a childhood spent in gurdwaras with Sikh friends. (Arya Samaj Hindus do not attend temples, as they do not worship idols.) She recalls as a child seeing the iconography of battles between Sikhs and Muslims, of Guru Gobind Singh's youngest sons immured alive behind a wall. There were stories she was told of Muslims who decapitated Sikhs and put their heads on the steps of Sikh temples. There was a strong fear of Muslims, rooted in centuries of warfare. Partition was just the very latest episode, Poonam tells me. But race also came into it too, which obviously did not have a history going back generations, but was particular to the circumstances of South Asians living in Britain. 'So it was also don't marry anyone black – that would have been the general advice going around all Asian households.'

Poonam's father was in many ways progressive, but socially conservative. She recalls him telling a story, she has no idea whether it was true or not, of a Sikh man who found out that his daughter was going out with a Muslim. He killed both of them. 'This was the story doing the rounds in the 1980s. The message was clear,' she says.

When Poonam was in her twenties, her parents realised she was not going to accept an arranged marriage. By the age of twenty-six she was told to find a Sikh who was like a Hindu; at twenty-nine a Jewish man would do. After that anyone would do, but just not a black person or a Muslim.

At thirty-one Poonam came home with a Londoner of Egyptian origin, with a Muslim name. He was not a practising Muslim, but of course that was irrelevant. Poonam was terrified of telling her parents, so in preparation, with the help of her brother, she wrote an application on his behalf, pretty much like a job application, accompanied by a photograph, CV, and dietary practices. Poonam's brother supported her by breaking the news to their parents; she could not face it. Her father didn't speak for twenty-four hours. He then told her they had better get married soon, because if not, he would die of shame.

Poonam and Khalid did get married, and both parents came to the wedding, but her father didn't tell any of his friends. It was painful for them, what it meant for their reputation. Their friends would not have understood. Illustrating the magnitude of what she had done Poonam tells me a story from the day, in August 1997, when Princess Diana died. Poonam was with her father at a Labour Party event. A Sikh elder told them, in Punjabi: 'Well, thank God Diana died, as she was with an Egyptian.' Poonam replied that she didn't remember Diana being a Sikh Punjabi. 'But once again you get the very clear message that this is actually better, that your daughter is dead.'

Does she attribute this hostility to partition? 'I think there is something in there ... When you witness that level of violence from another community I think it's very difficult to feel trusting. I think people were able to develop friendships or able perhaps even to celebrate things together, perhaps work together, but that handing over of your daughter, be they Muslim, Hindu or Sikh, would feel very much about handing over their daughter to another family. There was a discomfort.'

But Poonam's father did, eventually, come round. When Poonam had a son, and he saw the family of three together, and how involved Khalid was, he turned to his daughter and said he understood why Poonam had chosen to marry her husband.

When Poonam was growing up in Coventry in the 1970s, during the time of the anti-racism movement, there was a shared sense, between the South Asian groups, of justice and equality. But she says then came multiculturalism, and then the shift to multifaithism. What is at stake now is a deep misunderstanding of one another within the South Asian community.

She tells me a story from the mid-1980s, after the attack on the Golden Temple (the most important pilgrimage site for Sikhs) by Indian armed forces. Her mother was teaching Hindi and Punjabi in Coventry, and one of her pupils said to her: 'You can't be Punjabi because you are a Hindu.' Her mother came home heartbroken. Nirmal said to Poonam: 'I was kicked out of Lahore for being Hindu, now I'm being told by a Sikh, who is seven years old, I'm also not Punjabi.'

Poonam says: 'One of the issues for me is, where do my son's generation get their stories from? So many of the stories I heard were countered by ones that would really fuel further mistrust and further violence. Where are the responsible stories about partition that are more complex? And why are they not part of the education system, because India is just badly covered in the curriculum? So in those Hindu, Sikh and Muslim communities now, how do they understand each other?'

Since their marriage, both Khalid and Poonam have distanced themselves from their religious backgrounds as well as the communities they grew up in. Poonam did subsequently start to re-engage with her identity by becoming involved in South Asian feminist activism. She does, however, miss the sense of community she grew up with and the immersion in Punjabi culture. I suppose she felt she had to make a choice. She plays Urdu ghazals to her children; her son shows an interest in Indian history, though does not see himself as Indian; Poonam's daughter considers herself part Indian, though neither yet know their grandmother's story in full.

During the marking of the partition anniversary, something stirred in Poonam. At an event to mark seventy years since partition she met the elderly Sikh Harchet Singh Bains, who as a young boy had travelled by foot from Montgomery district in Pakistan to Hoshiarpur, Indian Punjab. Harchet reminded Poonam of her late father. She disclosed to him that she was married to a Muslim. Poonam later wrote to me saying she was a bit worried Harchet would have been disappointed in her because of who she had married. But the meeting, 'Reminded me how much part of me loved being Indian, and how much I missed my parents and their generation.'

*

Nirmal passed away nearly ten years ago. In the final weeks of her life she left Poonam's house and was in a nursing home in Southall. She had become very frail, weighing just six stone. The view from her bed was the golden dome of the Sri Guru Singh Sabha gurdwara. It was as if she were in India.

Poonam had been told Nirmal would not survive long, but could not bring herself to talk to her mother about death or the funeral. Poonam was sitting on Nirmal's bed one day, her arms around her now shrunken mother, holding her as if she were her child. She asked her mother what her favourite song was. She answered 'Chupke, Chupke'. It was an Urdu ghazal about lost love by Gulam Ali. This seventy-nine-year-old woman, just weeks from death, then sang the song in its entirety, held by her daughter as the sun set over the gurdwara's dome.

In the last few hours of Nirmal's life, when she had already slipped into unconsciousness, Poonam played Urdu songs for her. Songs Nirmal grew up with in Lahore. The same songs Poonam would wake up to on Sunday mornings in Coventry, and hear her mother singing.

At the start of Nirmal's funeral 'Chupke, Chupke' was played. In it, the singer recalls weeping all night and the memory of a time of love.

'It was a song that I most associated with her,' says Poonam, 'and I think that's a song that reminded her of Lahore. And when she sang it, we always knew she was happy.' Poonam wanted her mother's ashes to be scattered in Lahore, where she was born, and years later fled, never to return while she was alive. 'Her happiest years of her life were those first seventeen years in Lahore. She spoke about them with such affection. That was her home. That's where she belonged. And we wanted to take her home.'

Nirmal Joshi was born in 1930 on the outskirts of Lahore and moved to Jalandhar, Indian Punjab, after partition. She studied law, and worked as a schools inspector in India. She came to the UK in 1968 and settled in Coventry. She worked at the General Electric Company factory and retrained as a primary school teacher, specialising in mother-tongue languages. She died in 2009.

Poonam Joshi was born in 1969. She studied English at Oxford University and qualified as a solicitor. She has worked on human rights issues, specialising in women's rights, for most of her career. She now runs the Funders' Initiative for Civil Society.

22

Silence

In a bijou living room, in the middle of London, is a wall full of eclectic pictures. There is a pop art poster of a blond man saying 'Namaste' to a dark-haired, thick-lipped woman. In another corner is a cover of the Smiths' 'This Charming Man'. Nestled in between these two pictures is a large sepia photo. Your eye is drawn to it. It was going to be thrown away but Tara Parashar rescued it. She had it framed and put in a place where she could see it every day, where she could feel its presence.

Scrawled on the photograph is the black ink signature of Lord Louis Mountbatten, the last Viceroy to India. It was taken outside the Viceroy's House in Delhi, and shows the household in the months before partition. Tara's grandfather is one of the few non-white faces. He is standing upright, in the second row, in his starched, white naval uniform.

Tara found this picture at the beginning of 2017 in the Delhi home of her grandfather, who she calls Dada, the Hindi for your father's father. She had been helping relatives clear his house out after he passed away. The photograph was covered in dirt and mould, the glass of the frame smashed. She cleaned it up and recognised Lord and Lady Mountbatten, but had no idea what her grandfather was doing in this photograph. There were other photographs, too, formal and informal ones of her grandfather with the Mountbattens at high-society events. None of the family members had seen these photographs. 'For years and years and years he's been living in this house, keeping all these things and just hadn't told anybody.'[1]

Next to where her grandfather slept he kept a flowery biscuit tin from Bhagwan Sweet House in New Delhi. It was the kind you get during Diwali. But Tara did not open it. She did not think it seemly to go through her grandfather's belongings before her father and uncle had. One of her uncles who lives in California took it back home with him for safe keeping.

Pran Parashar, Tara's grandfather, only really came into her life when she was sixteen in the mid-noughties. He started to spend some of the year with her family in Birmingham, another few months in California with his other son, and the rest at his home in Delhi. Everyone called him 'Captain'. Tara had no idea why. But she remembers the day her grandfather received a visitor. The guest was an elderly Englishwoman who was very particular about how her coffee should be made. Just a half teaspoon that should be stirred many times.

Tara sat with them over a decade ago, but was not really listening to their conversation. Afterwards, she asked her grandfather who the woman was. He explained he used to work for her father, and that he once held an important job, but he preferred to think about the other jobs he had in his life – being an air force commander with the Indian Navy, or his business in Hong Kong. And that was it.

It was after his death that she learned more about who her grandfather was, and about their family's history. Lieutenant

Haroon Ahmed's family fled Delhi for Karachi, Pakistan. When he was seventeen they moved to England, but his mother always felt the loss of their life in India.

A portrait of Haroon as Master of Corpus Christi College, Cambridge University. He was the first person from an ethnic minority to become a lecturer and teaching fellow in engineering at the university.

Maneck Dalal met Kay Richardson while they were both students at Cambridge University. They married in north London in 1947 and started their life together in Delhi.

As head of Air India in Delhi, Maneck, a Parsee, supervised flights taking Muslims from Delhi to safety in Pakistan after partition.

Maneck with a photo of himself, a gift for Kay when they were young. Their marriage lasted until Maneck's death in 2016 – nearly seventy years together.

Iftkahr Ahmed came to England in 1951, at first working as a gardener and butler. He met his wife Sandra in Brighton.

Iftkahr with one of his sons, Nick. It took Iftkahr decades to talk of the terrible things he experienced as he made an extraordinary journey from Delhi to Lahore in September 1947.

Khurshid Sultana aged five with her younger brother, Yusuf. The photo is the only keepsake the family took to Pakistan ten years later in 1947, and their only image of Yusuf, who died very young.

Khurshid has never been back to Delhi, the place where she grew up. She says she is still afraid to go back there and believes dividing British India was the right thing to do.

Raj Daswani taking part in a play in a refugee camp near Bombay. He lived there for years after his family fled Karachi. He and other young people put on performances for other residents.

Geeta met Raj at the refugee camp, where she taught him Hindi. Like Raj, Geeta still feels the sense of homelessness that was thrust upon them by the upheaval of partition.

Raj is strongly attached to Sindh, the province he comes from, which is now in Pakistan. When he last visited Karachi, he brought back these stones to remind him of his connection to the soil of his homeland.

Amar Dhillon as a young woman. After she died, her daughter Veena found Amar's autobiographical writings, revealing details of her life in Pakistan before partition and her escape across the border. Stories Veena knew nothing about.

Dr Veena Dhillon says that she wants to go to Pakistan: 'I want to stand on the land they [my parents] are from.'

Nirmal Joshi, centre, wore two plaits, instead of one – a sign that she was a modern young woman.

Nirmal was a gifted singer. She worked to help support her family by singing on All India Radio. This work meant her neighbours cast aspersions over what kind of girl she was.

As bedtime stories, Nirmal recounted tales of her partition experiences. Her daughter Poonam grew up feeling that partition shaped her own life, not just her mother's.

Lieutenant Pran Parashar, naval aide-de-camp to Lord Mountbatten. Mountbatten salutes at the front; Pran, in a white uniform, stands behind, to his right.

The Indian biscuit tin with Pran's photos and cuttings, found by his bed after his death.

After Pran died, Tara Parashar helped sort through her grandfather's belongings. Her family were reluctant to tell his story when he was alive, but she has been determined to try and piece it together in recent years.

Pran Parashar was the naval aide-de-camp (ADC) to Lord Mountbatten around the time of partition. He came from an educated, Brahmin Hindu family in Gujranwala, Punjab, but they were by no means wealthy. From the photographs Tara found of him in his house, you can see how close he was to Lord and Lady Mountbatten. There are pictures of the three of them together: laughing, socialising, in formal evening attire. He appears part of the social scene; it does not appear a servile relationship.

Pamela Mountbatten was the female visitor who called – the Mountbattens' youngest daughter. She wrote in her memoir, *India Remembered*, of a visit to Orissa in March 1948, when her father was governor-general of post-partition India. She wrote of how the Mountbatten family were accompanied by a naval ADC called Lieutenant Pran Parashar, and how his 'over-enthusiasm got us into serious trouble'. They were visiting a temple and the priest said they would not be allowed in. Pran, outraged on behalf of the Mountbattens, responded that he was a Brahmin, of a much higher caste than the priest, and swept them all into the forbidden area. Next morning, the headline in the local paper read: 'Temple closed for purification after being polluted by Governor-General's Visit'.[2]

No one in Tara's family spoke of this time in Pran's career. Tara's father, who was born in the years after partition, would always say, 'Why do we have to talk about this?' whenever Tara asked about Dada. It was only after the discovery of the photographs in his Delhi home that it slowly began to become acceptable to talk about that period – both her grandfather's job and their family story.

Gujranwala became part of Pakistan after partition. One of Tara's grandfather's half-brothers, the celebrated artist

S. L. Parashar, elected to stay in Lahore, where he held a prestigious job at the art school. However, he soon left with his family, though Tara does not know the details as to why. The two half-brothers never got on very well. Tara believes it was because one initially chose to stay and the other to leave.

One story that had always been told to her was that after partition, Tara's grandfather, concerned for his family, rode a motorbike across the border to try to find them and bring them to safety in India. The story of the rescue attempt always ended the same way: Pran Parashar could not find everyone. There were old photographs of unidentified family members found in Pran's Delhi home, and Tara wonders if these are the people who went missing. A *Hindustan Times* article kept in her grandfather's collection from 1998, and written by Commodore B. Krishna Dang, places Pran in Lahore in mid-September 1947. The commodore describes riding pillion with Pran on his army Royal Enfield, and driving through a bloodthirsty mob. Pran was working with the military evacuation units and Tara believes it must have been at this time that he saved some members of his family on his motorbike.

Family members corroborate the rescue mission and Pran on his motorcycle, but Tara finds it strange that no relative has ever come forward to say they were saved. 'That's a missing link for me, because I feel like that should be the case.'

Pran would not speak of his job, or partition – possibly, Tara thinks, because of the awkwardness of his position being so close to Lord Mountbatten. But what her grandfather did reflect on while he was alive was the loss of his home in Pakistan. 'That sense of sadness never really did leave him. I think it stayed with him right up to the end.' He lost not only his home, but the roots of his ancestry too. In the house that he later built in New Delhi, there is a mismatched tile.

At the bottom of a white wall a terracotta coloured tile with four cream triangles stands out. This tile was taken from their former family home in Pakistan, and Pran made it part of his home in India. She imagines it was the only object he was able to salvage from Pakistan. The Delhi house is now going to be torn down; it is too old, and will be rebuilt. The one thing the family wants to keep, though, is that tile.

Tara has lived in Britain all her life and the tile has came to represent so much. 'It says: "Yes we came from this place and this is where our father's father and mother's mother lived, and it's part of our story." Now me and my cousins are spread all over the world and it's important to all of us because it [the tile] connects us together.'

That sense of connection matters to her more as a second-generation South Asian in Britain than if she had been brought up in India. 'That's because you really don't belong anywhere when you're British Asian ... Sometimes you're too British and sometimes you're too Asian ... I think it is important you have a sense of where you belong and where you come from, and for me at least I feel it is missing.' In India she feels a foreigner, and in Britain it can feel like she is different too. For her, the tile is something that brings her back to her roots, anchors her. 'Everyone wants the tile.' She raises an eyebrow. 'We'll see, maybe there will be a family argument on that one.' This tile has assumed the significance of an ancestral home. It is the only evidence the Parashars once lived in Pakistan.

Partition to Tara is not just a historical relic. She felt the divisions were replicated amongst South Asians in Britain when she was growing up in the noughties. 'I think from the outside looking in, it looks like we're one cohesive culture, but actually it's so fragmented.' At school it was clear who was from which country on the Indian subcontinent, even though her classmates had been born here. She recalls parents of British Pakistani friends being unhappy their children were friends with her, as she was of Indian descent. 'It becomes a difficult thing that gets built into your lives,' she says. 'It does all go back to that breaking apart, to that drawing of the line between so many different people, and I certainly felt that when I was growing up.'

Tara is in her late twenties and works in marketing and social media. She lives in central London in an ex-council flat bought decades ago by her parents, but which she now shares with friends. She is gentle, articulate and thoughtful, with a dry sense of humour. Her flatmates are cooking a fragrant Thai curry as we sit in Tara's living room, the sepia photograph of Lieutenant Parashar at the Viceroy's House looking over us. She tells me how her generation has hybrid identities, religion rather than ethnicity becoming the more important part of what it is to be British South Asian. But it's not that straightforward; making her point, she says she can meet people with different religious backgrounds, be descended from different countries on the Indian subcontinent, yet feel a connection. It all depends on the context. If you're the only two people in a room and you are South Asian, you feel that connection whatever your background. If there are many British South Asians in a room then you identify with people in a different way – either in terms of religion, or region. If that same group of British South Asians goes abroad, then you are British.

Tara feels the legacy of division and partition today in the way people relate to each other; how countries are born; and how national identities get passed down through your parents. It is a live issue for her and other British South

Asians. Yet it is not one she ever learned about at school. 'It's really surprising to me that I wasn't told about [partition] because it's a massive thing,' she says. 'Millions and millions of people lost their homes … it is strange that part of my identity that is so massive would never be taught me. But I think it's an important part of British history as well to know that Britain played the role in this area of the world and that's why it looks the way it does … I think it would give people a greater understanding of South Asia as a whole if you did learn about it.'

Tara recalls conversations with racists. Her worst encounter was when she was doing an internship as a journalist during the 2015 general election. She was on an industrial estate in Teesside, Middlesbrough, asking the general public questions, when a man came up to her and said: 'When are you all going to go home?' She laughs, raising that eyebrow again, saying she has lost count of the number of times people have asked her that. But since moving to London she says she has got braver, and when drunken lads on a night out shout out to her, 'Go back home', she says, 'What, Birmingham?' These experiences make her think that if people knew the history of where her parents came from they would understand why there is a large South Asian population in Britain. That Britain was once the centre of an empire, and migration happened. That there have been people from the former colonies here for centuries, and after independence they were invited over to help rebuild the country after the war.

And yet there are still so many gaps in Tara's understanding of her own personal history. She is about to go to California, where her uncle lives. He holds the collections of her grandfather's naval logs, papers and personal diaries from the 1940s to 1970s. And then there are the unknown contents of that biscuit tin found next to his bedside table in Delhi, which her uncle now has. The Parashars are now living in different continents, America, Europe and Asia, and parts of Pran's life are split between them. But Tara, with the help of some of her relatives, is trying to piece these together. 'It's a nice thing to do being a second-generation immigrant ... to learn about your family history in this way.'

She wants to find out what Pran did, what happened on his journey to rescue his relatives, who were these saved family members, and how he felt about everything that happened to his family and country. 'I'm proud of my grandfather and I love him and I want to feel grounded within that story and I don't because it is so mysterious, and because there are so many things that we don't talk about or can't talk about.'

Tara and I do not meet for a few months, though we exchange emails about her progress. We see each other again in her flat and she has made discoveries, though I sense a change in the way she feels about the search for her grandfather's past.

She discovered what the flowery biscuit tin contained. On the inside lid, a black-and-white photograph had been stuck. It showed Pran as a boy in a white shirt, shorts and ankle socks, standing formally next to his mother, who is wearing a plain dark sari, with cream borders. Tara had never seen what her great-grandmother looked like before; she had died when Pran was young.

Inside the tin was a photograph of her grandfather on his wedding day. And a large pull-out *Times* supplement, now the colour of stained teeth, titled 'Victory Celebrations' from VE day, which had been folded four times to fit into this tin of memories. There were recipes from Pran's mother, handwritten notes from Lord Mountbatten, navy medals, photographs of relatives. Jumbled parts of a life, the most precious parts of Pran's life, stuffed into a tin, kept close to where he once slept.

Disappointingly for Tara, the diaries were illegible as they had been damaged, it appears from water stains. The diaries start to become clearer from 1974 when Pran left the Indian Navy and started life as a businessman in Hong Kong. He described this period from 1974 as 'the first chapter of a new life'. Maybe he wanted to start the story again Tara thinks. And knowingly, or unknowingly, that is what the family did. Their collective family story always begins with Pran in Hong Kong, just like the diaries.

Tara did, however, learn more about the rescue attempt. Pran saved many members of his family. What was surprising, was that Tara had known these rescued relatives all her life, but she had no idea they were the ones who had been taken to safety by her grandfather. She does not think the withholding of this piece of information by them was intentional, but an extension of the silence the whole family kept over the experience of partition. 'Because partition was so hard to talk about no one ever acknowledges it. And when you don't acknowledge a thing for a very long time, then you forget about it, not in a sense that you forget it ever happened – you don't consciously think that you're not going to talk about it.'

Maybe, she ponders, it was too hard for her grandfather to talk about, and that is why it is so hard for the rest of the family to discuss it too. 'The silence about partition started with him. And I think that silence has come to the rest of our family,' says Tara. 'It's difficult to talk to my uncle about it. It's difficult to talk to my dad about it. I have that whole bunch of relatives who never mentioned it, even though he saved that part of the family, and it is a tricky subject to bring up. Maybe if he had been more open, told more stories ... we would find it easier to talk about, and I wonder if that would have made a difference to our family.'

Even after her grandfather had died, the subject of who was saved in the rescue mission didn't arise. Relatives began talking only once Tara asked. The answer to the question of who Pran saved was easier to answer than the question of which family members were left behind. The only thing her uncle told her was that it was a very sad thing some relatives weren't found in time. She still doesn't know who they were and what eventually happened to them.

Tara thought her search would bring her family from around the world together. But now she thinks that, because they hadn't ever spoken of partition, they never responded to the story, and it didn't become part of the fabric of her family, or the story they told about themselves. 'There is a part of me that thinks maybe I was kind of naive when I went out to California.'

So there are still big questions left for Tara. Though her grandfather kept artefacts from that time, newspaper clippings, photographs, there is no evidence of his thoughts. How far, she wonders, do you push the story if he would not have wanted you to, how far can you push your relatives to reveal the past? Partition obviously meant a lot to him, even if he never spoke of it, as he kept all the memorabilia from that time until the day he died. Yet should she stop? Before she started searching, she thought partition was a big part of her identity, but now, on reflection, she believes perhaps she was misguided. The story does not belong to her but the people who lived through it. Maybe it should not be a core part of who she is, because if her grandfather had wanted that, then surely, she thinks, he would have told her about it.

How she feels partition affects her today is the story of difference: how it can be created between people who have lived together side by side for centuries. It's pertinent to her, being of South Asian descent, living in Britain, who feels different and looks different from the indigenous population. 'One thing that is missing from this whole story is that surely my grandfather and my family would have had friends who were Muslims, but that is all absent.'

I think maybe that is it: Tara has given up looking for answers.

A few weeks later I receive an email headed 'I've just found out something new'.

'Apparently my grandfather went back to Pakistan in 2000,' she tells me. 'I found this so interesting and exciting and wanted to let you know! I think having had so many conversations about it, my dad has begun to open up a little bit and share more stories.'

Pran returned to Quetta and met an old school friend that he had been keeping in touch with the whole time since partition. 'Considering he moved around the world so much, and was at sea for much of the time I'm really surprised to hear this,' says Tara. 'Also surprised that despite all of my questioning this has never, ever come up. For my own benefit I'm trying to figure out who went with him as he would have been eighty? Who was the friend? Where are they now? So many questions!'

We meet up again later in the year. Apparently her father knew about this meeting but didn't think it was important to mention. She knows little more at the moment. But she has been mulling over her family's past the last few months and changed her mind about pursuing her family history. And it's all because of the New Delhi biscuit tin and the clues it left. 'If he hadn't wanted us to know about that part of his life, then he wouldn't have kept that tin with all the photos with the Mountbattens and articles. He must have known we would have found it.' She is resolutely carrying on her search into her past.

Her family are beginning to finally open up following the seventieth anniversary and the response to Pran's story from friends and family. She has now learned that the tile in her grandfather's house was not taken by him, but by her uncle when he went on a squash tour to Pakistan in the 1970s. That yearning for a hold on the past clearly existed with the second generation too, even if they didn't speak of it. The family has agreed that it will be re-set into her grandfather's old house, which is currently being renovated, and where her aunt and cousin now live.

It was the reaction from Tara's old school friends to her story, however, that she found most revelatory. These were friends of South Asian origin: Muslim, Sikh and Hindu. At school in Birmingham they didn't discuss issues of race with each other, in the way Tara says younger people do now. But her friends identified very strongly with what Tara felt. These people that she had sat next to day in, day out, had always felt the same as her, but they had never had the conversation about 'How you do feel a bit out of place, or how you feel sometimes too Asian or too British or not enough of either.' She also learned that they had been having similarly difficult conversations within their own families about partition, 'and they had all had the same process of discovery that had come out of their own initiative, because it is not part of the national curriculum … It had not been part of their immigrant story. And I thought we could have had all these conversations when our grandparents were still with us. And we just didn't.'

Tara Parashar was born in Birmingham in 1991. Her parents, both doctors, arrived in the UK in the 1970s. Tara works as a social media editor in London.

23

My Father

It took almost seventy years for my dad to talk about what had happened to him during the months around partition. Now I realise, having spoken to so many people who lived through that time, that this was not at all unusual. For so long when I tried to broach the subject I was told there was nothing to say. But in the months around the seventieth anniversary, and what would become the months before he died, he revealed in a series of interviews what happened to him, and what he saw. And I am not surprised he chose silence.

In the days after his death I wore his cashmere jumper, which still had the faint scent of his cologne, and carried his handkerchief in my pocket. I avoided listening to the interview tapes for months. I couldn't quite bear to hear his voice. But when I returned from Haridwar, after we had scattered his ashes, I did play them. I could hear now how weak he had become, how his breathing was already failing him. I do wonder if his faltering health gave him the strength to finally speak, so that he too could put on record what he lived through.

He was slightly bemused by the interest, on television and in the newspapers, around the seventieth anniversary. 'Has everyone just realised that partition happened?' he would ask with a smile.[1] Well, actually, in many ways. yes. He watched every programme about that time assiduously. During one, *Dangerous Borders* on BBC Two, I sat side by side with him as the second-generation British Pakistani reporter walked through the bazaars of Lahore – and I realised my dad had no idea what modern-day Lahore looked like. It was frozen in time for him.

Officially, my father was born in Lahore on 4 July 1935. He was actually born on 27 July, but birthdays were rarely registered at the time, and, when they were, officials put down memorable dates, like American Independence Day. His father, Ramji Das Puri, worked on the railways. The North Western Railways headquarters were based in Lahore and the city was linked to Delhi, Karachi and Calcutta. The family – his mother, Maya Devi, and his four siblings – lived at Road Number 31, in Lahore Cantonment. Established in 1850 by General Sir Charles Napier, it was a well-planned cantonment, with wide roads, parks and carefully laid-out living spaces. For their part, they were a Hindu family living amongst a predominantly Muslim population. Their temple was just opposite the house. It was a peaceful and safe childhood that he remembers. His primary school was a mixed one of Muslims, Sikhs and Hindus. His paternal uncle, a police inspector, would patrol around the cantonment with his stick, so the family felt well protected. His maternal uncle, who was a senior officer in the army, would take him at weekends to one of the city's many parks or museums. It was the Lahore one reads of: cosmopolitan, culturally diverse, the heart of Punjab.

At the start of 1947, however, things deteriorated very rapidly. My father says once the question of partition came up, people began to differentiate on the basis of religion. It became too dangerous to go out at night. There would be processions and shouting of nationalist slogans in the street. As children, they could hear all this from the house. They were terrified. One night, there was a particularly large procession near their home. My dad, defying his parents' orders, watched it from the balcony. The next morning, the family's good friends and neighbours, all Muslims, came to their home, saying they worried for their safety, and how it would be difficult for them to protect them against the hooligans, and that they should consider moving for now.

That day, a few months before partition, members of the RSS, the Hindu right-wing national volunteer organisation, helped remove their essential belongings, and they moved to the home of close friends nearby – jewellers who were living in a Hindu district. They stayed with them for some weeks. My dad was now in high school but his attendance was sporadic, as the school would close whenever there was trouble. His classmates were mainly Hindus. By this time my father, on the cusp of being a teenager, had joined the RSS, and was taking part in demonstrations, shouting: 'Hindustan Zindabad, Musalman Murdabad! Long live India, death to Muslims.' A Muslim family friend and neighbour, a hakim, a herbal physician, from their old cantonment (in fact he had been one of the people urging my family to move for safety) saw my father shouting these slogans at one protest and warned him not to get involved with the RSS, that he was endangering himself. My dad ignored him: 'I was young and easily excited ... the RSS is very strong and can convert you and your ideas and emotions.'

It was only when the random communal killings that were now commonplace in the city touched someone he knew, that things changed. A Muslim fruit-seller in the bazaar, a kind man whom he was acquainted with, was walking home one night after he had closed up shop, when he was stabbed to death by a Hindu. Things were now so precarious, anyone could have been killed just for being in the wrong place. My father says he became 'wiser with events' and stopped his association with the RSS. He was so scared at night, he had taken to sleeping next to his father.

The main preoccupation for my grandparents was the safety of their elder daughter, who was fifteen. My father overheard them talking of their concern that as a young woman she was particularly vulnerable. For her safety they decided that my father, his siblings and mother would leave for Moga, near Ferozepur, to live with the maternal grandparents. They left, my father believes, around June 1947. They were lucky enough to have time to take whatever valuables they could, mostly jewellery and some clothes. Some of that jewellery, which was given to my grandmother for her wedding and which I now have, went with them on that journey. The family were followed days later by their cow, which travelled by train in a wagon car all to itself. The family loved their cow, and were concerned that if it stayed, as a religious symbol of Hindus, it could be slaughtered at the hands of Muslims.

My father was never a man to covet things. 'Possessions!' he would jokingly exclaim when the grandchildren would ask for the latest plastic toy. They are not much use when you need to leave in a hurry. Maybe that is how he categorised things. Unlike those who have a brick, stones, dust, a tile, some physical connection to the place they left, my father had no tangible evidence that he had once lived in Lahore. Not even a photograph – imagine that. As an adult in Britain he became an avid photographer. He snapped his bachelor days, the early years of his marriage, his friends, trips abroad, and later his children. When we were younger, he would show us photographic slide shows in our living room. Perhaps he wanted to document his life as much as he could, to make up for his early years.

The family all felt safer once they were in Moga. They were surrounded by Hindus mostly. My father started going to school regularly again. The five siblings living with the grandparents all slept on the floor in one bedroom, but no one minded. My dad's father had remained in Lahore as his job was still based there. One night, weeks before partition, he was cycling home from work when a Muslim man stopped him, shouting: 'Babu where are you going?' My grandfather answered that he was on his way home. But the Muslim bystander said to him: 'Do you know there are killings going on in the city?' My grandfather replied in Urdu: 'Allah is with me.' Thinking he was a Muslim, the man said: 'Go home quickly.' But my grandfather never went home again. He headed straight to the train station and left that day for Moga.

In the days while they were waiting to hear which country Moga would go to, there was still concern among the family about my father's eldest sister. My dad overheard the adults discussing how they would protect the young women if the Muslims entered their home – be it people from Moga or the Balochistan army, who controlled the curfew.

Two days after independence they learned by word of mouth that Moga had become part of India. The family had made preparatory arrangements that if it were awarded to Pakistan they would move immediately towards Indian territory. They thanked God that they did not have to leave, and were spared the prospect of a refugee camp. Lahore and their former home was now in Pakistan and was within a tangible ten miles or so from the border. Would my father's family have survived if Moga had gone to Pakistan? It's difficult to say, he says, probably not.

The bloodletting against Muslims then began. My father recalls that the Muslim family and their beautiful daughters at the end of the road were slaughtered by Sikhs. He implied the girls were raped first, but did not want to talk about it further. He remembers his family and many of their Hindu neighbours feeling sad at their death, but says they could not have stopped the killing. 'Hindus could not protect them, they would have killed the Hindus. The whole thing was so high, they, the Sikhs, would not care who they were killing and who they were not.'

The things he witnessed subsequently in Moga had been too hard to speak of in the decades to come. He saw 'poor innocent babies snatched from their mother's lap and they were killed in front of them'. The mob then proceeded to kill the newly bereaved mothers. Another time he saw a Muslim wrestler, a strong man, ordered by a fifteen-year-old to put his head down. He was then stabbed. While he was on the ground, the wrestler asked a passing woman for some water. She brought it to him, but the boy killed him before his thirst could be quenched.

After seeing these things my father was so disturbed he stayed inside the house. Seeing this bloodshed, he acknowledged, left him a changed person. Knowing what others had witnessed, and knowing my father had evaded my gentle questioning about partition for so long, I had always imagined he must have seen terrible things. Why else would he not want to talk about it? And I am sure there was more that he wanted to spare me from hearing. Yet when he finally told me about those times, the thing that surprised me most was the cow. The fact that the family had felt so much for it they had hired a train wagon – just so it could be with them. This simple act of love (my father's word, 'love') was touching, and mildly ridiculous, given the backdrop of what else was going on in the city.

My father had his demons. Whether they started because of his experiences during partition is hard to know. It is difficult to pinpoint where the source begins: is it at birth, living through hard times, or coping with the trauma after the event? I cannot ask him any more. Though he probably would not have been able to answer the question. What I do know is that it was only in our final recorded conversation, two months before his death, that he fully described the murders he witnessed, and in the eighty-second year of his life, he remembered every detail as if he were that twelve-year-old boy watching from the roof of his grandmother's house. The image of the mothers seeing their children being killed had never left him, even though he hadn't spoken of it.

And why did he not speak of these things, even when I had been asking for the longest time? Why burden the children, he would say, there is nothing pleasant to tell. Better for the next generation to grow up happy and learn how to live together. I later learned that he didn't even tell his dearest friends or his wider family. All his siblings who lived through partition have now died, so I have no idea if they ever discussed it together. His closest brother-cousin, who was with him in Delhi from 1950, was surprised when I recently told him of what my father had witnessed during partition. He said he had never once mentioned it.

My father was phlegmatic; like those of his generation he was also resilient. He didn't forget what it was like to be a refugee, and always felt empathy for those in a similar predica-ment. But having seen his parents start life again; relying on the goodwill of relatives; sleeping on the floor of other people's homes, all this only acted as a spur for him. There was no time to dwell. 'Circumstances make you accept everything, hardship also, and then you learn how to work hard.' Work hard he did. He completed high school, did his BA in Delhi, after his father had been transferred there, and then became a representative for Pfizer pharmaceuticals, travelling across northern India. In 1959 he heard through his cousin, who was already in the UK, of a graduate traineeship in Middlesbrough at Dorman Long – the engineering company that made the Sydney Harbour Bridge and London's Lambeth Bridge. He wanted a challenge, and was ambitious and applied.

I often wondered how he could have made that journey, on his own to Britain, when a brief call to his family was so expensive it could only happen every few months. The only way to communicate with his parents was on the weekly blue aerogramme letters. In his first letter home from England, he was so shocked by the November cold and grey, he wrote: 'I see the sun never rises on the British Empire.' In those early days, struck down by flu and struggling to understand the Middlesbrough accent, he even thought of returning home for good. Occasionally he would receive tape cassettes from his family in India. A medley of voices, they would be giving family news, local gossip and requests for presents, but it would always end the same way. *Come back.* But he never did. There were too many opportunities in Britain, he said. He acknowledged that he had sacrificed the love of his family in India to make a life for himself in England. And it was a good life. He went on to get his MA, then a Ph.D., and to become a prize-winning structural engineer specialising in tall buildings. Achievements he felt he may not have gained in India. Education was his bulletproof vest against the vagaries of life. For him, it was all worth it.

Yet it was only understanding what he and his generation went through during partition that something else quite revelatory occurred to me. When the worst had already happened to him back in 1947, and his family had lost everything and been forced to leave their home – moving to England, even by yourself, could never be so much of a wrench. The concept of what is home and where you belong changes for ever after that terrible initial upheaval. Moga, then Jalandhar, and Delhi where the family all moved to, didn't really feel like home. So why not move again?

*

My father had one last request, which he had shared with us and close family friends in the final weeks of his life. At his funeral he insisted on other religions being reflected. The man who had chanted Hindu nationalist slogans in his youth, had to leave Lahore for being a Hindu, and who saw children and their mothers murdered in cold blood just for having a different faith, chose inclusion not hate. That is how he lived his adult life, and raised us too.

At his funeral service, his dear Sikh friend read the 'Mul Mantar', the same prayer that Harchet Singh Bains had uttered on his journey to India. One of my father's oldest friends from his time in Britain, Hafeez Sheikh, a British Pakistani who studied with him in the 1960s at Southampton University where they both did their doctorates together, recited the Muslim prayer on dying:

O Allah, ease upon him his matters,
And make light for him whatever comes hereafter,
And honour him with your meeting,

And make that which he has gone to better than that
which he came out from.

My father's first boss, Vincent Thompson, a wonderful
man and second father to him, was a devout Methodist, and
took my dad along to many services. We always had a Bible
in the house. In his memory, and to mark the influence on
my father's life, my sister-in-law read the moving Methodist
funeral prayer:

Bring us Lord, Our God,
at our last awakening,
into the house and gate of heaven,
to enter into that gate,
and dwell in that house,
where there shall be no darkness or dazzling,
but one equal light;
no noise nor silence,
but one equal music;
no fears nor hopes,
but one equal possession;
no ends nor beginnings,
but one equal eternity;
in the habitation of your glory and dominion,
world without end.

My father-in-law, wearing a yarmulke, spoke the ancient
Aramaic words of the Kaddish, the Jewish prayer of death.
In that moment, on 30 November 2017, friends and relatives
told me, they noticed it had begun to snow outside.

I suppose it was an unusual service. The pandit, the Hindu
priest, thankfully appreciated the inclusion of the other faiths.

Afterwards we all gathered at a favourite Indian restaurant of my father's. There were so many people there weren't enough chairs. Knowing of my interest in partition, people came up to me and quietly started to tell me their stories of living through that time, as if they were giving confession.

One uncle pulled up his trouser leg and shirt sleeve to reveal two deep scars – sword wounds. In his back, he told me, a bullet is still lodged. His father, a prominent Hindu, was targeted and, as they left Peshawar to catch a train to escape, a mob caught up with them and he watched as his mother was killed before him and his six-month-old brother thrown into the river. I have known this man all my life. He is the husband of one of my father's cousins. Our families would spend many Sundays together; he and my father would snooze on the carpet after lunch as if they were schoolboys. And yet I had no idea.

Another family friend started telling me her father's story, a gentle man I have known for years, who drove me with all my bags to university when my parents were travelling. That generation went through so much she said, and we have benefited from them.

These stories were everywhere. I had just spent a year of my life trying to find people to speak to about partition, and they were all here, right under my nose.

*

I watched my father take his last breath. His final intake of air was in England. The first in Lahore. He was laid to rest with his ashes scattered in the River Ganges in India. For him home could be many things. He didn't feel he had to choose. My father lived in Lahore for twelve years, India fourteen and

England for fifty-eight. He always wanted to return to the city of his childhood, but never did.

His concept of home was where his children and grand-children were. But it was also Lahore, the place of his birth. So too was it India – it was in his blood and soul he would say. That generation will always be in the no-man's land of where they belong. It is not always a bad thing. I think my father saw it as liberating: he could reinvent himself.

I too feel a profound connection to Lahore. Whenever I meet anyone from there, or read about it, I have an almost physical reaction. I shall always feel tied to India too, where my father's family moved to, and where I scattered my father's ashes. In Haridwar there was something soothing in laying him to rest in the way his forebears had been. I had always felt an observer in India, but with the act of placing his ashes in the Ganges, I felt my place in the line of my ancestors who had done the same for their parents. I am anchored to India. But Britain is my home. I was born and raised here. End of Empire saw my father leave Pakistan for India, but it also brought him to Britain where he put down roots, raised a family. I am here because of him. Born a subject of the British Raj, my father died a British citizen. We are all, everyone of us, post-colonial citizens.

Ravi Datt Puri was born in Lahore, British India, in 1935. After completing his degree in Delhi he worked as a representative for Pfizer in Northern India. In November 1959 he came to Middlesbrough, England, on a graduate traineeship for Dorman Long, the engineering company. He did his Ph.D. in structural engineering at Southampton University, and was a senior uni-versity lecturer. He went on to work for Selhurst Trust, part of BP (then Rio Tinto) on construction projects around the world. He later started his own company. He died on 20 November 2017.

Epilogue

In Bengali there are two separate words for home. Bari has the connotation of permanence; it does not matter where you live now, it is your desh, the home of your ancestors, it is where you belong; even if you have never seen that place, it is where your ancestry can be traced. Basha is where you lodge at the moment.

Dr Anindya Raychaudhuri's grandparents moved permanently from East Pakistan to West Bengal. He speaks of what it means to lose your sense of bari. 'Once you've become an immigrant refugee family, you never really get that back, but it is because you never get that back that it comes to symbolise so much.'[1]

It is accentuated when you are a refugee first (through no choice of your own) and then choose to become a migrant, as many of the partition generation who came to Britain did. Being born into a refugee family you understand transience and fragility, that things can change quickly, and you understand what it is to be rootless – there is often no place to go back to that belongs to you. Being the child of migrants you understand rootlessness too, but also the impermanence of your place in the country of your birth. They are not the same, but they are connected.

Of course not all families who lived through partition and went on to migrate to Britain were refugees when India became divided, but many were. This double displacement and the consequences, are passed down through the generations, both knowingly and unknowingly. The obsession with owning property, getting the best marks at school, becoming a doctor, can all be traced back to that feeling of insecurity, whether you came from a family who were once refugees, or migrants, or both. I was raised knowing that the one thing that could not be taken away from me is my education.

Of those from the second and third generation who I have been in contact with, many say they do not know their own history, they want to find out about their family, and that it helps them navigate the choppy waters of who they are.

What is bari when it no longer exists in the same way? Is Britain now our bari?

Understanding who you are and your place in Britain depends on many things, not least, wider political events. Anindya bought a house in Edinburgh with his wife around the time of the referendum to leave the European Union. After the decision by the majority to 'Brexit', and the reports of an increase in racist incidents, it became more important to him to have the security of his own home. 'Macro-political large-scale events, whether it's something like partition or whether it is Brexit, or whatever, have a role to play in how you feel about where you live and where you feel safe.'[2] He says he felt 'explicitly uncertain' about his position in Britain in racial terms after the Brexit vote.

There is an inherent fragility to being born of a refugee family. You know how quickly things can turn. If it happened in your parents' or grandparents' generation, it could happen again to you. There is also a fragility to being from an immigrant family – are you ever accepted?

The first, second and possibly third generation have a heightened sense of vigilance too, a sixth sense for the changing of the wind. It was there during Brexit, and I felt it again more recently in the Windrush scandal, when Caribbean migrants to post-war Britain were told they were illegal and some were deported, and it's there too in the anti-Semitism row in the Labour Party.

When the 'other' is demonised or singled out in this way, we are all the 'other', we are all vulnerable, fragile. It makes us question who we are, where our allegiances lie. It reminds us of what our parents and our grandparents went through, what we went through as kids in the 1970s and '80s; the singling out of otherness never leaves you.

How many generations does it take for refugee immigrant families to lose this feeling of impermanence? Will my children still feel it? Will they ever think, if we have to leave quickly, what would I take? The imaginary suitcase above the wardrobe. I want the attachment to India and Pakistan to remain with them and their children, it is part of who they are, but I hope the sense of fragility leaves them.

The first generation are the reason we are here in Britain. When they pass they take their stories with them. We have no ancestral home, or past, in this country beyond them. They had a choice to return home if they wanted to; we who were born in Britain do not. This is our home. History matters in this absence. For descendants of South Asians, it explains who we are, why we are here and how we relate to one another. British people need to understand why Britain looks the way it does, who their compatriots are and the way our histories are connected. Yet it is baffling that given the number of South Asians in Britain, the history of Empire, how it ended, and why migration to Britain from the Indian subcontinent happened is barely taught in schools.

What I had not appreciated before I started speaking to the partition survivors was that so few people in Britain knew of partition and Empire, and how delicate a subject it is to broach for those who were once colonised and the colonisers.

Three vicars – Reverend Canon Michael Roden from Hitchin (now Canon Chancellor of Bristol Cathedral), Reverend Canon Chancellor Edward Probart of Salisbury Cathedral, and Martin Henwood, a vicar from Dartford – are spearheading a campaign called the 'Partition History Project'. Working with the Runnymede Trust, they are pushing to get partition history written into the national curriculum. This trio of vicars said that they knew so little about partition, and could not understand why, in their interfaith work, different communities from South Asia refused to speak to each other. They felt they were stumbling onto a huge trauma that was well beyond their understanding. So together they went to the Indian subcontinent to try and understand, and then began to hear stories of partition. Michael Roden thinks the trauma of partition hasn't ever been addressed. He believes that if partition is the hardest part about teaching South Asian history and Empire, then let's start with that.

Roden is not your usual priest. He plays in a rock band and drives a black cab. In his picturesque fourteenth-century church in Hitchin, Hertfordshire by the pews, over seventy years after the British left India, stands a modest memorial. It shows a map of British India with a red line marking the 1947 division. A single A4 typed sheet of paper on a music stand explains that, in the absence of a national memorial, this makeshift one will act as a surrogate to commemorate the millions who died and were displaced. Around the sign, candles are lit in remembrance. At the end the statement reads: 'We have screened off the most beautiful part of this church to symbolise terrible loss of life, loss of mutual trust and loss of access to holy sites at the time of partition.'

It is achingly moving to see, in this corner of England, a 'do-it-yourself' memorial where no official one exists anywhere else – in Britain, India, Pakistan or Bangladesh.[3] I do wonder what Canon Roden's congregation, so representative of Middle England, thinks of his almost obsessive mission to have partition recognised in a memorial and in schools.

Michael Roden has roots in India too. His great-grandfather worked for the Public Works Department and built bridges, including the one in Chappar Rift, Balochistan. His grandfather, Hugh, was born in Jhansi, and his first memory was of running along the beach in Karachi, something Canon Roden hopes to do one day too.

Why should partition matter to Canon Roden and his parishioners? 'People don't know the South Asian story, so quite often don't know why they have South Asian neighbours. Therefore teaching South Asian history is vital for people to understand each other. So it's a story of Britain.'[4] He believes that part of the reason it is not taught in schools is because of Britain's national shame: the country has not addressed its role in partition and Empire, and it has become a taboo subject. There are so many partitions today, says Roden. It needs to be taught compassionately so students understand Britain's former relationship with its colonies, community cohesion, religious pluralism and migration. It is also a way to talk of loss, displacement and how our histories are tied together.

Empire, how it ended, and migration from the Indian subcontinent is a story of Britain. Its legacy is all around us: in the food we eat, our language, the people of this country. It is who we are as a modern nation. We – the British and those of South Asian heritage – have a shared history, as do the different groups within the South Asian community.

*

Of the many people I talked to, what was revelatory was the connection that people had with the land that was left behind, the land that is currently 'enemy territory'; the land so many still think of as home – even if that concept of home has been modified, encompassing both the country they moved to on the Indian subcontinent as refugees, and the place they eventually migrated to. Bari is where they wish to return to one last time: to see the tree they climbed as a child, to visit their mother's grave, to have their ashes scattered. This has endured, despite the years.

The partition generation recalls a time which was not always perfect, but when people lived alongside one another, celebrated each other's festivals, were part of one another's happiness and sorrows. They shared culture, food, language and traditions. A time before division, borders, partition. That is what they choose to speak of, too, after seventy long years.

If there is a purpose to all the testimonies gathered it is to remember the time before separation, so future generations understand that there were Hindus in Lahore, and Muslims in Amritsar. Hindus who tied rakhis (a thread promising protection from a 'brother' to his 'sister') on the wrist of their Muslim brothers, and Muslims who brought ladoos to their Hindu friends to celebrate Diwali. Friends and strangers who transcended hatred to commit acts of kindness and humanity during the worst of times.

It cannot be just the stories of violence and hate which are passed down. Even though every story told to me was shattering, I felt hopeful. Hopeful that people wanted these stories of compassion to be recognised, and that the visceral pull of the place of your birth, and that of your ancestors – the love of your land – remains so strong. Hopeful that these are the stories that will survive too.

CODA

I didn't expect to be writing any more about partition, at least not so soon. I could not have imagined the afterlife of putting *Partition Voices* out into the world, and how events would change the way the testimonies are received and interpreted.

Since recording these interviews, there has been an awakening – both a quiet, private one, within families, and a public, convulsive one, triggered by the Black Lives Matter protests in the summer of 2020. Within families it has raised questions about who they are, where their roots begin, and why the decision was made to leave their homelands for Britain. Within our country it has become about who we are, what really is our history, and who gets to tell and hear it. Stories of partition, born of Empire, and resulting in migration to Britain, have become part of a wider, urgent conversation.

Soon after I began documenting experiences of partition, I found that these stories were all around me, including from people I'd known for years. Outside the school gates a mother approached to tell me that her Pakistani grandfather, a supporter of the Congress Party before partition, had been imprisoned for wanting an undivided

India. Another mum caught up with me to relay the story of her family's migration from Pakistan to India. On sports day, as we watched our children in the sack race, a father told me of his dad who had served with the British Indian Army during partition: towards the end of his life, he had broken down, talking of seeing trains full of corpses. It was the first time the man had seen his father, a reserved Englishman, cry.

After a book-signing and talk I gave in Gloucester, I noticed four people hanging back from the crowd. When everyone left, they approached: two sisters of South Asian heritage accompanied by their husbands. They showed me an original copy of a letter, written by their father, that had been read along with his last will and testament. The paper was faded and yellowed, the words written with a typewriter. Their dad, who had died in the 1990s, had one request which had been underlined in thick red felt-tip pen. He wanted his ashes to be divided into three and scattered in the Pakistani village in Punjab where he'd been born; in the River Ganges at Haridwar in India; and by the Severn Bridge in England. These three places made up his life: displacement by partition from Pakistan to India, and then migration to Britain. He felt he belonged in each of those three places, wanting some part of him to remain, in death as in life.

In the past few years, as partition stories have begun pouring out across Britain, people around the country have shared details of their private family histories with me, not just at the school gates, but by email, letter, on social media and at events. I started keeping a note of all the stories I was told, until my notebook filled up. People wanted to recount family testimonies, or fragments of them, as if saying them out loud or writing them memorialised them. The writer Elif

Shafak notes that it is the third generation descended from immigrants who dig into memory: they have 'older memories even than their parents. Their mothers and fathers tell them: "This is your home, forget about all that."'[1] But for them identity matters.

Many of those who contacted me after this book was published were from the third generation. Their responses were often one of two things: how do I question my relative about their past if the subject has never been broached before? Or, simply: I wish I had asked. The latter group must reconcile with the silence that will never now be stirred from the partition generation and find other means of attempting to piece together a family history. For those who can ask, there is still time, and they can receive the most precious gift of knowing about their past – something they too can pass on.

Maz Halima, a blogger and journalist, got in touch via Instagram during the Covid-19 lockdown of early 2021. She had first heard the term 'partition' during the seventieth anniversary coverage: she'd watched everything she could on the subject and cried while reading the testimonies in this book. At the age of thirty-one, Maz was now looking into her own family's partition history; she'd started asking questions about where her grandparents came from, why they'd moved to the UK, and how that had affected the childhoods of her parents.

I met Maz at her home near Croydon. I asked if her maternal grandparents, who lived close by could come along to our meeting. I was curious to hear what they thought about their granddaughter asking about their past. But they declined.

Initially, when Maz started asking her grandparents questions, they tried to fob her off. 'It took a lot of coaxing,' she says. 'Maybe they've been in England for so long, it's something they'd just rather not remember.'[2] But they were also moved that their granddaughter wanted to see photos of their parents, to know their names.

Over the course of five interviews Maz learnt that her mother's parents were born in the late 1930s (they are not sure exactly when; there are no birth certificates) and were children at the time of partition. Maz's maternal grandmother was living in Kasur in Punjab, not far from Lahore. She remembers weapons – guns, a sword, an axe – and her father patrolling the family home. There were joyous childhood memories, too, before that time: she talked of playing with the children of her Hindu and Sikh neighbours. Not just focusing on the trauma was important, Maz felt, when recording their memories. Before partition was announced, the family moved briefly to their ancestral village in Multan, fearing Kasur may be made part of India. However, it remained in Pakistan, and the family returned home. In the time they'd been away, all the Hindu and Sikh families had left.

Maz's paternal grandparents are now dead, and her father is the only source for information on that side of the family. He had always said they were from Amritsar (which Maz imagined wasn't far from the Taj Mahal), but she never tried asking him anything more. Now she questioned him further and, though he remained reticent, found out his family were actually from Gurdaspur. Her grandmother had made the eighty-mile journey from Gurdaspur to Lahore – much of it alone, and heavily pregnant with her first child – when it was announced that it was to be part of Pakistan. Her husband, who'd served with the British Indian Army, had been imprisoned en route for being a Muslim. She received no word of him for months so assumed she was a widow, until one day, on a Tannoy, she heard her husband's name being called out, asking if anyone knew him. That is how they were reunited. Maz's father was born nine months later.

Maz will never know what the journey was like for her grandmother: to leave her home, carrying a child inside her, alone. In a blog post Maz remembers her grandmother as a woman 'who pottered around in her salwar kameez pouring pools of butter in the middle of steaming hot rice before she ate it, smiling sweetly'. She 'never gave even a clue that she'd ever experienced hardship. I wish I'd known; I wish I'd asked her things; I wish I'd been able to speak Urdu because if I'm honest we had no way of communicating.'[3] The story of that part of her family, Maz believes, is now unreachable.

'I was born here,' Maz continues, 'but prior to that, I have nothing outside of a small history in Croydon … European people can trace their family trees back and it's a blur for me.'[4] She is, however, realistic as to how much more she can discover; she doesn't want to keep bothering her elderly grandparents, draining memories they would rather leave fallow.

Maz took a DNA test to learn more about her identity. 'I think after exploring the story of partition, I wanted to define who I was,' she explains. The test revealed strong evidence that 89.1 per cent of her genetic make-up is from the regions of northern India (Delhi, Maharashtra, Uttar Pradesh, Gujarat) and from Indian and Pakistani Punjab. She'd been curious about Afghan blood she'd been told existed on her paternal side, and the test confirmed that 10 per cent of her DNA was from Kabul.

The DNA results have changed Maz's view of who she is. 'I feel really proud to have Indian heritage,' she says. 'Once upon a time it was just India, there was nothing else. Pakistan is a name, it's a creation, but it's not a physical thing that represents me anymore. I also realised nationalism can be really dangerous. And I bond a lot more with my Indian friends over it now, like we know that we're all one, we know that we were once upon a time unified.'[5]

Maz's father, born after partition and proudly nationalistic, takes a different view. He wonders why she wanted to do the research at all. 'You should be so proud [of Pakistan],' he tells her, 'because people laid down their lives and look at the sacrifice that was made. Just embrace that. Why would you want to explore outside of that?'[6]

For Maz it feels unfinished. She wants to return to Multan, the Pakistani village her maternal grandmother comes from. Unlike her dad, she wants to visit India and find the place in Gurdaspur his parents left.

*

On a sunny Sunday afternoon in June 2021, I meet up with Sparsh Ahuja, a filmmaker and co-founder of Project Dastaan, a charity which helps partition survivors reconnect with the land of their birth. We meet at his home, in a modern apartment block in Brick Lane, east London. There are few furnishings, but I notice a Dishoom cookbook on the dining table. The windows are open; someone drives by Bengali music playing loudly from their car. It breaks the silence. 'There's always Bengali or Punjabi music playing around here in Brick Lane,' he says. 'It's why I wanted to live here, the sounds, the smells. I feel I belong.'[7]

Sparsh was born in India twenty-five years ago. He grew up in Melbourne, came to England to study and has remained in the UK ever since. From his accent it would be hard to pin down where he's from. He could pass as Indian (he has good spoken Hindi), Australian or British. But it's his Pakistani side that in the past few years has become his obsession.

In 2018 Sparsh set up Project Dastaan with some university friends. The project uses twenty-first century technology, virtual reality (VR), to enable partition survivors to glimpse the homes they left behind in the middle of the last century, but without the logistical and emotional challenges of physically returning. Survivors are interviewed and, using the information, project volunteers return to their village to find the refugees' ancestral homes, and sometimes their friends, neighbours, and descendants. Wearing a headset these now elderly men and women can see their childhood homes, even if they can't or won't travel there. As Sparsh and I chat about the project, I think of my Dad and how I wish he had had that chance.

There is a seriousness about Sparsh that is beyond his twenty-five years. I recognise the heaviness in him that comes from recording traumatic testimonies. He admits hearing those difficult stories leaves its mark. He has interviewed dozens of survivors. The person he interviewed first, and who inspired Project Dastaan, was his own grandfather, Ishar Das Arora.

During the seventieth anniversary of partition, Sparsh was in Delhi spending time with Ishar. He knew his grandfather originated from Pakistan, but little more. He'd noticed that he would write down small things, like phone numbers, in Urdu. Sparsh asked him if he could record his partition story. Ishar was hesitant at first – partition was not spoken about by him or anyone in the family – but gradually he warmed to the idea, happy that someone was showing an interest.

On the day of the interview, Sparsh's grandfather turned up in a smart white shirt, wanting to look his best, knowing his grandson was also going to film him. Sparsh was nervous, but once his grandfather started speaking this all changed: it was 'the first time I got to know him properly', he says.[8]

Ishar was born in Bela in 1940, a Muslim majority village near Jand in Punjab. His parents ran a small shop on the side of the road which sold peanuts and lentils. He describes a peaceful time in undivided British India. But around the time of partition, when Ishar was seven, there were raids from tribesmen near the Afghan border. The family were taken to the house of the numberdar (the chief of the village) – a Muslim man known as Sher Khan – who hid them. When a mob brandishing pistols came knocking on the door looking for Hindus, Sher Khan refused to allow them in. Ishar's overriding memory of this time was fear. He does not remember their subsequent migration to Delhi.

Sparsh's reaction on hearing this story was immediate: he wanted to go to Bela. 'I just knew straight away that I had to go back to that village. I didn't feel like our family story could be complete unless one of us saw the place again.' Sparsh's grandfather still refers to Bela as home, but the trauma from events nearly seventy-five years ago never left him. He was afraid for his grandson to return there.

In March 2021, Sparsh journeyed to Pakistan in search of his grandfather's first home, accompanied by Project Dastaan co-founder Sam Dalrymple. Travelling by taxi towards Jand via Attock (formerly Campbellpur), they stopped off on the way to buy mithai for the villagers. Sparsh had no expectation he'd meet anyone in Bela who knew his family, he says, but at least he could bring the villagers sweets as a gesture of goodwill. Sitting in the back, he clutched a piece of paper on which his grandfather had sketched the area of his first home, and its geographical landmarks – including an echoing hill where people would go and scream their name and the sound would reverberate back. As the landscape became more mountainous, and the earth red clay, the taxi began to struggle with the terrain. The driver berated them for taking him to such a remote area. Sparsh started to notice people selling peanuts at the side of the road, just as his great-grandparents had once done. He knew they must be close.

They drove on, through a valley and then into a small village. There were fruit trees, cows roaming around, mud huts. An Urdu sign announced this was Bela. In these parts, Sparsh learnt, the population is counted by how many 'stove tops' there are. Here there were between thirty or forty, so around 150–200 people lived in the village.

Sparsh located the village head, a man in his eighties. In his best Punjabi, Sparsh explained that he was looking for a man called Sher Khan: he wanted to know if he or any of his relatives were still alive so he could thank the family for saving his grandfather's life. The numberdar went quiet. He then said that he was the son of Sher Khan; his father was no longer alive, but he himself remembered Sparsh's family.

The man took Sparsh back home to meet his son and grandson. They gave Sparsh some tea: he listened to a familiar story – how his family had been protected during partition but told from the perspective of those whose ancestors had saved them. Sher Khan's son then announced that he knew where Sparsh's grandfather had lived and would take him there. He did so – accompanied by three generations of the Khan family.

Ishar's original home is no longer there. However, the plot of land is – next to the mosque, just as his grandfather's map showed. The whole journey was filmed by Sam. On the walk towards the house Sparsh bends down and puts some of the earth into his pocket. When he sees his family's land, Sparsh instinctively falls to his knees, prostrate, both palms touching the dusty cracked earth. Kneeling, he then puts his hands together in a namaste, kissing them, and raising them to his forehead. When he stands up, Sher Khan's grandson is there: he opens his arms to him in an embrace, and Sparsh weeps on his shoulder. Seventy-four years on, Sparsh stood for the first time where his grandfather last stood as a scared seven-year-old. 'It was just the weight of that moment. I felt like I finally made it here. It's not something I ever expected would be possible in my lifetime.'

The night of the visit, Sparsh sent the video to his grandfather. 'I am proud of you, my son,' Ishar replied from Delhi. 'You have touched my motherland with your hand and mouth, which I could not explain in words.'

Before this visit, says Sparsh, the mere thought of partition had made him angry – but 'a lot of that fire died down after that day. I felt like I could let it go. I was always thinking about partition a lot before. I feel like I was able to let go a little bit of that intergenerational trauma. If you have grown up being told this is where we came from and yet we were never able to go back. That's not the story I will tell my children, if I ever have children. The story will be: we lost this land, but then we went back. So, it's like that loop is now complete. It's not just hanging.'[9]

It took three generations for this traumatic story of partition to be rewritten. The two families are now connected on WhatsApp and are regularly in touch. They greet each other on their respective festivals, just as they used to when their ancestors were in the village together. Sparsh's grandfather now hopes one day to return too. However, there are those on both sides with harder attitudes. Some in Sparsh's family support the Hindu nationalist Bharatiya Janata Party (BJP), and there are those from the Khan family who saw the Taliban takeover of Afghanistan in 2021 as a victory for Islam. But there is a conversation at least.

*

Ciaran Thapar was sitting on a park bench in Kennington, south London, reading *Partition Voices* in the autumn of 2020, when something in him jumpstarted. As he read the stories, he began to feel closer to his paternal grandparents – Punjabi Hindus who lived in Southall and had come to Britain in the 1960s. He suddenly felt he was able to understand their experiences, he explained later. It was like having a dialogue with his now deceased grandparents.

I met up with Ciaran, a youth worker and writer, at the flat he shares with his fiancée Yasmin Macé. Ciaran met Yasmin at Bristol University, where they bonded over being some of the only non-white students in their halls of residence. Even though growing up Ciaran had spent many weekends with his paternal grandparents, he'd never known about partition, and hadn't asked them anything of their histories. His father had not asked his parents either. Ciaran has some awareness now of what his grandparents lived through or must have seen. 'On one level,' he says, 'I am grateful for the protection of silence handed down by my elders. I understand it. But I can't shake the feeling that, decades on, the ledger of reasons for why I exist has been removed from view. There is something missing.'[10]

Ciaran has easy access to the family history on his English mother's side, going back 300 years, but his 'Indian history stops with my dad'. He has started learning Punjabi and plans to travel more to the Punjab to fully immerse himself and write about his experiences. He is trying to find out about his family history, but it's not straightforward given family politics in London. Ciaran's not sure where the journey will take him: 'I don't know what the end goal will be,' he says. 'I want to try and understand the relationship between both sides of my heritage. I just feel so restless to understand that. I definitely want my children to have a really strong sense of pride and understanding about where they're from.'[11]

Yasmin's mother's family are from Pakistan, and her father is French. 'I don't think my [maternal] grandmother ever talked about partition that much,' she says, 'but it's very embedded in my understanding of our history.' She knows that they fled across the border from India and that her grandmother was in a horse and cart, hiding at night, and that she saw people who worked for her family burnt alive. 'There's a lot of trauma associated with it. But that's where it stops. So, I know that's the history, but I don't really know much more.'[12]

Ciaran says it was only when he read *Partition Voices* that he had an epiphany: 'Learning about partition over the last six months has been the first time I can honestly say I've realised that Yasmin and I are ethnically the same, even if our families are divided by religion and politics. I've never really thought about that. I've always thought about there just being an absolute difference. But there really isn't an absolute difference. And that difference was carved up quite arbitrarily, actually.'[13]

'Our English and French lives almost feel more different,' adds Yasmin. 'It feels like we have more in common [through our Punjabi side] than we do through our white sides. So, it's interesting. I feel like we're not religious, so that takes away that difference. And when you strip that back. The history, the land, the food, the language, there's a lot in common.'[14]

Three generations on, the grandchildren of the partition generation, from different sides of the Radcliffe line, are together as a couple. Ciaran has turned detective. He is just at the start of his journey to find out about his family's past. Who knows where he will get to? However, these two do not need a DNA test to prove that half of them comes from the same place. Both their families have passed down tales of helping people of the other religion during partition. Though they remain largely in the dark about their family histories, Ciaran and Yasmin have inherited these tales of kindness.

My head is swimming at thoughts of this couple – clearly so in love, their roots on either side of a border created almost seventy-five years ago – and how they have found each other and see only what they have in common. I wonder what their grandparents would have made of their union. 'Maybe the grandparents even met,' Yasmin laughs. She tells me that when her grandmother was annoyed, she would say the colloquialism: '*I am going to Ludhiana—*'

'Which is where my grandparents are from,' says Ciaran, picking up.

They will never know if they met, I suppose. But such intimate connections all these years on are important to this young couple today. Ciaran and Yasmin got married in Morocco in April 2022. In his wedding speech, Ciaran wanted to honour their shared history. He gave guests a quick lesson on partition to explain the couple's Punjabi connection, and how their grandparents lived only an hour away from each other in undivided India. 'Hindus and Muslims were separated by the line. Generations on, our union is one of religions too.' For their honeymoon they wanted to travel to India and Pakistan, but they say it's too complicated given their names, and getting the visas. How is it that history is stopping each of them visiting the 'other' place, even today, Ciaran muses?

*

To delve into your history is a luxury most first-generation immigrants to Britain did not have. They were struggling to survive and looking to the future, wanting to protect their children from past sorrows. Those of the second generation often existed between two different and competing worlds. The third generation – people like Maz, Sparsh and Ciaran – want to explore their roots, and do so with a stronger sense of their place in Britain than their grandparents possessed.

This searching throws up not only personal questions about family history but more broadly about what history is taught, or rather not taught, in British schools. Ciaran says he feels his history was hidden from him at school. Maybe if he'd learnt about Empire and partition, he says, he could have asked his grandparents about it while they were alive. 'History matters and feels relevant.' Maz says she feels a censorship of her history has taken place: 'It is a huge thing. There's a lot of British Asians here [in this country]. Why are we here? Why was that not explained?'

Britain's difficult history came to the fore during the summer of 2020. A wave of global anti-racist protests erupted following the murder of George Floyd by a police officer in the United States. In Bristol, the statue of slave trader Edward Colston was toppled into the city's harbour. History has become a hugely politicised part of the so-called culture wars: an existential struggle between a history that is preoccupied with tradition, patriotism, and a glorification of Britishness, and one that seeks to better understand Britain's violent, exploitative colonial past and its relationship with racism and inequality in the contemporary world. How and what history is taught in schools has been in the spotlight. The historian William Dalrymple says it as a 'real problem' that 'in Britain the study of empire is still largely absent from the history curriculum. Now more than ever, we badly need to understand what is common knowledge elsewhere: that for much of history we were an aggressively racist and expansionist force responsible for violence, injustice and war crimes on every continent.'[15]

'Decolonising the curriculum' has become part of the battleground – and one of the teachers on the frontline is Shalina Patel. Shalina teaches history at Claremont High School Academy in Harrow, north-west London, where over 90 per cent of children come from ethnic minority backgrounds. Shalina's roots are from Gujarat: her grandfather came to Britain in the 1960s, and all three generations still live near each other.

Shalina recorded one of her lessons on partition to show me, as Covid rules meant I could not come along in person. It is for Year 8 – children aged between twelve and thirteen. Her passion for history is infectious and she is brimming with new ideas for engaging her students. Before this lesson on partition, Shalina delivered ones on the history of the Indian subcontinent. 'It's really key that the students see India without the lens of the British Empire,' she says. Her students who don't have South Asian heritage are surprised to learn that Britain once ruled India. After the Mughals, and the East India Company, Shalina teaches about the rule of the Raj, the fight for independence, and the role of the Second World War. All this needs to be understood, she says, before tackling a complex subject like partition.

Testimonies from *Partition Voices* – those of Nirmal Joshi, Iftkhar Ahmed and Karam Singh Hamdard – are used in her teaching. These three people, who thought their stories were unexceptional, not even worthy to mention to their own families in any detail, are now being discussed with great seriousness by school children in Britain. One student points out that on the day that Karam's father was killed by a Muslim mob, Karam's sister was saved by their Muslim neighbours. These young students talk of colonial India, the complexity of the time of partition and the effect of partition and intergenerational trauma with ease and fluency. It makes me wonder why some politicians fear an open discussion of Empire.

There is currently no statutory obligation to teach the history of Empire in schools in England. In June 2021, in response to a petition signed by 268,772 people,[16] Parliament debated whether there should be compulsory teaching of Britain's colonial past. Strong arguments were made in its favour but the motion was rejected, the government stating: 'Within the history curriculum there is already a statutory theme at Key Stage 3 titled "Ideas, political power, industry and empire: Britain, 1745–1901", as such we do not believe there is a need to take this action as the option to teach this topic exists within this compulsory theme.'[17] There is no data collected on how many schools teach 'Empire', or how this is approached. It is at the discretion of schools what to teach within this broad period.[18]

Change is happening, however. The devolved Welsh government has announced that Black, Asian and minority ethnic histories will be mandatory parts of the new curriculum due to be introduced in September 2022. Shalina says teachers who are in contact with her, and those she meets at conferences, want to teach Empire and its end but lack the confidence to do so. They, like her, weren't taught it at school, and there is some anxiety around it as it has become such a political minefield. It would help the teachers who do want to teach it, she says, if resources could be shared, as has been done successfully with Holocaust teaching.[19]

In lockdown Shalina started 'The History Corridor' on Instagram, which includes posts on forgotten people or events in history. It now has over 20,000 followers. In the absence of diverse history being taught in schools, or there being open discussion in families, young people can learn about their history online, through accounts such as Shalina's and others like 'Brown History' and the 'South Asian History Project'. Looking at her students and the people who contact her via social media, Shalina observes that the third and fourth generation have a confidence that their parents (and grandparents) may not have had in asking questions about their history. They feel British but they also want to know the other story too – *how* they got to be in Britain. 'If we don't ask no one else will,' says Shalina.[20]

For young British people descended from immigrant families, whose ties to this land can feel fragile and may be one, two or three generations old, they want to know their story in all its complexity and how it started long before their family came to these shores.

I wonder if for these young British South Asians, who are not subjected to the nationalism on the Indian subcontinent, it is easier to feel a connection to the place that was left long ago. In Britain there is certainly less of a demand to feel an allegiance to India, Pakistan, or Bangladesh. British South Asians can feel many things: British; an allegiance to a place here, say, Bradford, Wolverhampton, or Birmingham; South Asian; a tie to a region on the Indian subcontinent, or to a language that crosses borders. And that's just for starters. We are used to feeling these multiple identities and having them coexist.[21]

There is a curiosity for that 'other' place, where the journey may have begun with partition. And once they discover their family story, a place that was left behind, there can be an ache – or as Edward Said described it, a homesickness for a place that exists in nostalgia, through inheritance that has been passed on.[22]

Aanchal Malhotra is an oral historian based in Delhi and author of the seminal book *Remnants of a Separation* based on interviews with the partition generation. Her interest in the subject began a decade ago, sparked by her own family history. All four of her grandparents are from what became Pakistan. As those eyewitnesses are now dwindling, she has begun interviewing later generations about the legacy of partition. This is an evolving field where we are only just beginning to grapple with what has been passed on, knowingly or unknowingly, through nostalgia and trauma. In her forthcoming book, *The Language of Remembering* (2022), she looks at this inheritance – what she describes as the 'second-hand sadness, second-hand loss, second-hand pain', and asks: 'Can all these emotions still be felt in their second-handedness?'[23] For subsequent generations, she argues, there has been 'no word for the memory of partition survivors'.[24]

Compared to the Indian subcontinent, Britain is behind in this respect: we are only just discovering nationally and within families what partition was and what it meant. However, like India, Pakistan, and Bangladesh, we in Britain are only just beginning to articulate the vocabulary to describe the many complex emotions it evokes through the generations.

For Binita Kane part of this process is bringing the history of partition and Empire to the mainstream in Britain and starting a conversation. She works full-time as a respiratory consultant in Manchester, is a mum of two, and looks after her father; but whether talking about medicine or her ambitions for changing how South Asian history and culture is understood and absorbed into British life today, she is fiercely single-minded.

The seventieth anniversary of partition changed her irreversibly, says Binita. Before that time, she felt as if she had been walking through life with her eyes 'closed in a blind stupor'.[25] As part of the TV documentary, *My Family, Partition and Me*, aired on the BBC in the summer of 2017, she travelled alone to her father's village in Bangladesh. Binita was the first member of her family to return to the place from which her dad had fled in 1947. Her eighty-one-year-old father, Bim Bhowmick, a specialist in the care of the elderly who worked for the NHS for forty-nine years, felt the journey would be too traumatic. Muslim friends from the village had helped his Hindu family escape Bangladesh by boat, and Bim's father died several weeks later from starvation.

Binita describes the trip as 'the most intense emotional experience of her life', and one which triggered a huge identity crisis. It was the first time she ever felt she belonged. She had grown up in Wales, but when she was in Bangladesh she felt welcomed as their daughter: 'no one in Wales would say that of me'. After Binita returned and shared her experiences with her father, it uncovered deep emotions. She felt closer to him. He went through a period of grieving, decades on, for his lost family members and lost childhood. At times he would see visions of his father. He still cries about what happened.[26]

Binita too feels 'cheated' that she learnt nothing of partition history during her schooling. She has made it her mission not only to educate herself but others too. She is a co-founder of South Asian Heritage Month, which, since it was established in the summer of 2020, has seen more and more people – not just British South Asians – joining events across the country and participating on social media. Manchester Museum and the British Museum have been involved, and companies including PricewaterhouseCoopers, Viacom CBS and ITV have used the month to hold events to educate their staff and celebrate British South Asian culture. Binita believes that stories of our histories connect us and help with social cohesion both within different groups of South Asian heritage and within British society.[27]

*

On Binita's fireplace, in her home in Manchester, is a jar. It contains soil from the land her father was born and escaped. She collected it when she visited Bangladesh in 2017. I think of Raj Daswani and the stones from Karachi he keeps in his London study; and of Mohindra Dhall and his brick from Faisalabad in his Edinburgh living room. How many houses are there in Britain with remnants from lost homelands? I'd always thought of those physical reminders – stones, dust, bricks, soil – as being the equivalent of an ancestral home. There is a visceral need for physical evidence, something to look at, to touch. It's almost like saying: this is proof we existed there too.

And I think of Sparsh, who keeps on his bedside table three smooth, grey pebbles which he brought back to London from the family's plot of land in Bela. He is considering getting them engraved and made into jewellery, maybe a necklace or a ring: one is for his grandfather; the others are for any future children. Why do these physical objects matter to him, I ask?

'It's sentimental,' he says 'against all the odds, my family managed to keep this bit because everyone came with nothing and going back was just out of the question. Even before I learned about the partition… [if] something about Pakistan came up, it was just like a hush in the family. That country you can never visit, that is off bounds. So, that's why I think it matters so much that we managed to do it.'[28]

'As a South Asian, it's just like the whole idea of dharti, your soil and watan, your homeland, is not something you can separate from yourself,' he continues. 'That pebble is not just a rock for me. Those [pebbles] are my ancestors, like their literal bodies are broken down and it's that continuity. So, it's the same thing. It feels like that's a bit of my past that I can keep. I can't look up my family's histories and archives, but I've got that pebble. So, it'll have to do for now. And that is why I want to hand these pebbles on. I want to make sure the future generation, at least in my family, have that.'[29]

I felt both the beauty of what Sparsh was saying, but also a great sadness. The pebbles were the only proof of his family's life in Pakistan. As he says: against the odds.

Not everyone can go back, and other objects hold a different significance. Earlier this year, Maz Halima's grandmother gave her a gift of two saris for her wedding. Maz takes them out to show me. They are carefully folded in white muslin. It's the only thing Maz has from India, she tells me. They are in pristine condition: one is emerald green with a gold Aztec print, the other sapphire blue with gold thread. Maz has coveted them for years, but her grandmother was always very protective of them: they were given to her by her husband when they were newlyweds in the 1950s. They are the only thing her grandmother has from India.

Maz smothers her face in the saris, taking in the aroma. 'I'm amazed that they're nearly seventy years old,' she says. 'They still have that smell … cinnamon, cardamom.' They are 'all the Asian spices. It smells of back home.'[30]

I know exactly the smell she means.

When Maz's grandmother dressed her in one of the saris, it felt alien and strange, like she had been transported back in time. She had wrapped the sari around her granddaughter like a pro, which surprised Maz. How on earth did she know how to do it? Maz asked. She'd learnt from her Hindu and Sikh friends before partition, her grandmother said. She had always admired the fashion and so practised until she got it right.

Maz realises that the act of putting the sari on her was, for her grandmother, a reminder of that time: 'It's a part of her identity that she has almost washed away.' She explains that as Pakistanis, a sari was often associated with India. And as a religious woman, she never saw her grandmother expose her midriff: 'That was far too sexy,' Maz smiles. 'It's definitely not something she'd wear now, and not something I would associate with my culture at all.'[31]

The saris are a connection to another world, another time. Her grandmother's gift is a reminder to her that 'we were all once just Indian, and it was that simple'. She adds, 'our cultures were mashed together; our clothing was similar. And I don't know if that reminder has actually sunk in for me.'[32]

If Maz has children, she says, she will hand them down, along with her grandmother's gold jewellery. 'I want to raise my children in a way where they value their heritage.' Just like the aroma of those saris, indistinguishable from India or Pakistan, a borderless smell: 'They are a reminder of unity, of what India once was.'[33]

*

Every 15 August, the anniversary of partition, I think of my interviewees and those who have died. I remember each and every one of them – how they told their stories with courage, speaking as if it were yesterday. It felt present to them; it had just lain dormant for all those years.

The bureaucrats who drew the boundary line nearly seventy-five years ago could not erase their history, memories, emotions. The partition generation, with their unique stories, know a truth: even with a manmade border, on each side the sky remains the same, the birds sing no differently, the earth smells the same after the rains. There was division, but some things real or remembered cannot be divided. It was a British border drawn to divide British India as the British Empire started to be dismantled. Subjects of the Raj came to Britain and are its citizens, and multiple generations live in these isles in their millions. Partition and the end of Empire could not be a more British story.

The author and artist Edmund de Waal says of the descendants of Holocaust survivors that they grow up 'aware of the silences, you're completely aware of what you're not being told, of those protected spaces of anxiety. What do you do with that? You can either just move on or you can go into them. And the moment you go into them, you have to go through to the end. You are in freefall.'[34] The same could be said for the children and grandchildren of partition. They have a choice. Once they know about the historical event, they face a decision. If they choose to enter the protected spaces of anxiety, as Maz, Ciaran, Sparsh and Binita have, they are all in freefall. Irreversibly. How can they not be?

Britain, too, faces a choice about its past. Understanding, learning, teaching partition and Empire is not a threat; it is British history. It is part of the long story of Britain. 'We are here because you were there,' as the scholar and activist Ambalavaner Sivanandan, who died in 2018, famously said.

What I have only understood in the last few years is that acceptance of British South Asians is also an acceptance of their long history, including the story of colonialism. Ultimately it is acceptance it is British history – that we too are just as British, that our stories need to be heard, told, and represented, and not just for a designated month.

I think of the children, grandchildren, and great-grandchildren across Britain today, unpicking the complexity of that era, wanting to understand their past, to understand themselves. And all I can think of are the silences, the wasted years where no one asked or spoke. How even the very word 'partition', representing one of the most seismic historical events of the twentieth century, was not widely known.

These inheritors of partition and Empire – whether they have South Asian heritage or not – will determine what they pass on of this shared history; what is remembered and what is forgotten. The legacy will live on in ways we do not yet know. It happened long ago but, somehow, I feel we are only at the beginning of understanding it – within families, and in Britain.

My feelings for Lahore have never subsided. I asked my friend who was travelling there, where they had been struggling to get copies of my book from India, to leave one under a park bench, just so it could touch its earth. I wanted to know it was in Pakistan somewhere in the place my dad grew up and then fled. He wanted to go back but never did. In a tiny way the book was a return, and I will go there, for him, for me. And when I do, I will be there with his grandchildren, my children, walking by my side. They know their history. They are its keepers for now.

April 2022

Notes

INTRODUCTION

1 Ceri Peach, 'South Asian migration and settlement in Great Britain, 1951–2001', *Contemporary South Asia*, 15:2 (June 2006), pp. 133–46.
2 Author telephone interview with Professor Joya Chatterji, 14 February 2018.
3 Author interview with Dr Anindya Raychaudhuri, London, 1 March 2017.
4 Author interview with Nick Yearwood, Brighton, 9 January 2017.
5 Urvashi Butalia, *The Other Side of Silence*, Penguin Books, 2017, p. 13.
6 Author interview with Dr Raychaudhuri.
7 The British Library Sound and Moving Image Catalogue, reference C1790.

I END OF EMPIRE

1 Cited in Yasmin Khan, *The Great Partition: The Making of India and Pakistan*, Yale University Press, 2008, p. 17.
2 The 1945 Labour Party's Election Manifesto *Let Us Face the Future* described its aim as 'the advancement of India to responsible self-government' (see http://www.labour-party.org.uk/manifestos/1945/1945-labour-manifesto.shtml). Historian Andrew Roberts describes the independence of India as a 'national humiliation' for Britain, but that it was necessitated by urgent financial, administrative, strategic and political needs (Roberts, *Eminent Churchillians*, Phoenix, 1994, p. 78).

3 See Nisjid Hajara, *Midnight's Furies: The Deadly Legacy of India's Partition*, Amberley Books, 2015, p. 7, which continues: 'During the war His Majesty's Government had racked up huge debts to India – more than $6 billion – for the soldiers it had sent to the deserts of North Africa, the boots and parachutes produced in its factories, the care and feeding of British troops battling the Japanese in Burma.'

4 In her memoir (*Halfway to Freedom*, Simon and Schuster, 1949. p. 20) the photographer Margaret Bourke-White writes: 'When peace returned to Calcutta on the fifth day, the street were a rubble of broken bricks and bottles, bloated remains of cows, and charred wrecks of automobiles and victorias [horse-drawn carriages] rising above the strewn figures of the dead. The human toll had reached six thousand according to the official count, and sixteen thousand according to unofficial sources … vast areas were dark with ruin and black with the wings of vultures that hovered impartially over the Hindu and Muslim dead.' Nisjid Hajara (in *Midnight's Furies*, p. 19) quotes Ian Stephens, editor of *The Statesman*: 'On plots of waste ground, you could see mounds of decomposing, liquefying bodies, heaped as high as the second floors of the nearby houses because of lack of space elsewhere.'

5 Khan, *The Great Partition*, p. 83.

6 See Ian Talbot and Gurharpal Singh, *The Partition of India*, Cambridge University Press, 2014, p. 7.

7 http://www.nationalarchives.gov.uk/education/resources/the-road-to-partition/mountbatten-radio-broadcast/

8 Pankaj Mishra, 'Exit Wounds: The Legacy of Indian Partition', *New Yorker*, 13 August 2007.

9 Alex von Tunzelmann, *Indian Summer: The Secret History of the End of an Empire*, Simon & Schuster, 2007, p. 202. Khan quotes Shahid Hamid, private secretary to the British general, Sir Claude Auchinleck, and later a major general with the Pakistan Army, who was shocked at the new date for partition (though in favour of partition itself): 'It was a bombshell! I wondered what brought this last-minute change? Does he [Mountbatten] realise its consequences? Why this hurry? Why this shock treatment? Why is he bulldozing everything and leaving no time for an organised handover?' (*The Great Partition*, p. 92).

10 According to Von Tunzelmann: 'A Sunni Muslim from the Punjab may have more in common with a Sikh than he did with

a Shia Muslim from Bengal; a Shia might regard a Sufi Muslim as a heretic; a Brahmin might feel more at ease with a European than he would with another Hindu who was an outcaste' (*Indian Summer*, p. 229).

2 THE DAYS OF THE RAJ

1 Recollections in this chapter are based on author interview with Pamela Justine Dowley-Wise, Surrey, 3 March 2017, and subsequent telephone interviews, January and July 2018, as well as Justine Dowley-Wise, *In Those Days: A Scrapbook of Growing Up in India in the Days of the Raj*, iUniverse, 2005.

2 Ian Melville Stephens's memoir *Monsoon Morning* cited in Janam Mukherjee, *Hungry Bengal: War, Famine and the End of Empire*, Oxford University Press, 2015, p. 132.

3 Nitish Sengupta, *Land of Two Rivers: A History of Bengal from the Mahabharata to Mujib*, Penguin, 2011, p. 424. Mukherjee, *Hungry Bengal*, is also excellent on the causes of the Bengal famine; see also the BBC Radio 4 programme: 'Things We Forgot to Remember' (https://www.bbc.co.uk/programmes/b008m7cb).

4 Sengupta, *Land of Two Rivers*, p. 420.

3 HURT THE BRITISH!

1 Recollections in this chapter are based on producer interview with Ramen Bannerjee, East London, 27 April 2017, and author interview on 6 March 2018, and subsequent telephone interviews, 2018.

2 Sengupta, *Land of Two Rivers*, p. 411.

3 A. G. Noorani, 'Vande Mataram: A Historical Lesson', *Economic and Political Weekly*, Vol. 8, Issue No. 23, 9 June 1973.

4 Quoted in 'The History of the Origins of Vande Mataram', *Indian Express*, 27 July 2017.

5 Even as late as 1939, records from Bengal show that only one in four Muslim boys and 6 per cent of girls stayed through to higher education (Alan Peshkin, 'Education, the Muslim Elite, and the Creation of Pakistan', *Comparative Education Review*, Vol. 6, No. 2, October 1962, pp. 152–9. See also Talbot and Singh, *The Partition of India*, p. 28).

6 Joya Chatterji, *The Spoils of Partition*, Cambridge University Press, 2007, pp. 108–9, which continues: 'significant numbers [of East Bengal's Hindus] were landlords settled in the countryside; others worked as teachers or accountants on zamindari estates. In the district towns, there were many Hindus among the professional and administrative men employed in the courts and schools. Traditionally these people were at the apex of a predominantly Muslim society.'

7 See also Talbot and Singh, *The Partition of India*, p. 28.

8 The division of the province of Bengal in 1905, which included Bihar and Orissa, was officially said to be for administrative reasons. A Muslim majority province of East Bengal and Assam was created, and another province – West Bengal, Orissa and Bihar – formed. Many Hindus complained the division was done because of the burgeoning nationalist movement in Bengal. There were mass protests before and after the partition, including the boycott of British-made goods. The partition was annulled in 1911.

4 I BECAME CONVINCED OF THE MUSLIM LEAGUE

1 Recollections in this chapter are based on producer interview with Bashir Maan, Glasgow, 18 January 2017, and subsequent author telephone interviews, 2018.

2 Bashir Maan, *The New Scots: The Story of Asians in Scotland*, John Donald Publishers Ltd, 1992, p. 161.

3 Khan, *The Great Partition*, p. 20.

4 Talbot and Singh, *The Partition of India*, p. 32.

5 Ibid, p. 36.

6 Ibid.

7 Jat: a person from a traditionally agricultural community from (what is today) Northern India and the provinces of Punjab and Sindh in Pakistan.

8 Maan, *The New Scots*, p. 160. Maan goes on to say that in 1950 there were around 600 South Asians in Scotland, rising to approximately 1,300 by 1955. The majority were Pakistani, from Punjab (*New Scots*, p. 55).

5 FISHING WITH DEAD BODIES

1 Recollections in this chapter are based on author interview with Kenneth Miln, Dundee, 16 January 2017; and telephone interviews in late 2017 and early 2018.

6 IT WAS MAGIC

1 Recollections in this chapter are based on author interview with Denys Wild, Dorset, 1 March 2017, and telephone interviews, early 2018.

2 www.nam.ac.uk/explore/independence-and-partition-1947

3 In *Gandhi: The Years That Changed the World 1914–1948* (Allen Lane, 2018, p. 836) Ramachandra Guha says that in late July 1947, Gandhi travelled via Amritsar to Rawalpindi by train en route to Srinagar. The train would have almost certainly have passed through Lahore station as it was the main hub of the North Western Railway.

4 Ian Talbot and Tahir Kamran, *Colonial Lahore: A History of the City and Beyond*, Hurst, 2016, p. 16.

5 William Dalrymple, 'The Great Divide – the Violent Legacy of Indian Partition', *New Yorker*, 29 June 2015: 'From the vantage point of the retreating colonizers, however, it was in one way fairly successful. Whereas British rule in India had long been marked by violent revolts and brutal suppressions, the British Army was able to march out of the country with barely a shot fired and only seven casualties.'

6 Khan, *The Great Partition*, p. 129.

7 Khanduri, *Thimayya: An Amazing Life*, p. 394.

8 Khan, *The Great Partition*, pp. 128–9, which continues: 'Mountbatten confidentially stated that British Army units had no operational functions whatsoever, could not be used for internal security purposes and would not be used on the frontier or in the states. There was only one exception: they could be used in an emergency to save British lives.' See further in Chandra B. Khanduri, *Thimayya: An Amazing Life*, Knowledge World, 2006, p.105.

9 The last unit to leave India was the 1st Battalion, Somerset Light Infantry (Prince Albert's), which embarked at Bombay on 28 February 1948: thank you to the National Army Museum, London, for this information.

7 PARTITION

1 Von Tunzelmann, *Indian Summer*, p. 248.

2 See Bourke-White, *Halfway to Freedom*, p. 99, and Khan, *The Great Partition*, p. 126.

3 www.nationalarchives.gov.uk/education/resources/the-road-to-partition/jinnah-partition

4 Khan, *The Great Partition*, p. 158.

5 Anchal Malhotra, *Remnants of a Separation: A History of the Partition Through Material Memory*, Harper Collins, 2017, p. 12. In June 1947 the *Times of India* published an article where Viceroy Mountbatten was asked if he foresaw the mass transfer of population. 'Personally, I don't see it,' he responded. 'There are many physical and practical difficulties involved. Some measures of transfer will come about in a natural way ... perhaps governments will transfer populations.'

6 Talbot and Singh, *The Partition of India*, p. 61.

7 Figures range from the low estimate of 200,000 by the British civil servant Penderel Moon, up to 2 million by some South Asian scholars (see Talbot and Singh, *The Partition of India*, p. 62, quoting Moon, *Divide and Quit*, Oxford University Press, 1998, p. 293).

8 Von Tunzelmann, *Indian Summer*, p. 265, continues: 'The figure of 1 million has now been repeated so often that it is accepted as historical fact.'

9 Talbot and Singh, *The Partition of India*, p. 66. Some historians (including Talbot and Singh and Joya Chatterji) claim the violence after partition 'assumed genocidal proportions in the Punjab and in parts of India' (see Chatterji ' "Dispersal" and the Failure of Rehabilitation: Refugee Camp-dwellers and Squatters in Bengal', *Modern Asian Studies*, Vol. 41, No. 5, 2007).

10 Talbot and Singh, *The Partition of India*, p. 89.

11 Researchers at the South Asia Institute, Harvard University, are currently studying these figures. Initial estimates of both deaths and population movements in Punjab based on detailed census returns and sophisticated population modelling, suggest higher numbers than previously thought.

12 Joya Chatterji, 'From imperial subjects to national citizens: South Asians and the international migration regime since 1947', *Routledge Handbook of the South Asian Diaspora*, Routledge, 2013,

p.187. By the end of 1947 the MEOs had evacuated 5 million refugees across the border between India and Pakistan.

13 Khan, *The Great Partition*, p. 9.

14 'Freedom and Fragmentation: Images of Independence, Decolonisation and Partition', 2017 exhibition at the Centre of South Asian Studies Archive, University of Cambridge. See further, Sanjena Sathian, '70 Years Later, They're Still Homeless', 31 May 2016 for Ozy.com.

15 Uditi Sen, *Citizen Refugee: Forging the Indian Nation After Partition*, Cambridge University Press, 2018, p. 7, says: 'Official estimates of East Bengali migrants who sought refuge in India between 1946 and 1970 vary between 5.8 million and 4.1 million.'

16 Indian census https://www.census2011.co.in/religion.php; Pakistan census: http://www.pbs.gov.pk/sites/default/files// tables/POPULATION%20BY%20RELIGION.pdf
Bangladesh census: p. 11; http://203.112.218.65:8008/ WebTestApplication/userfiles/Image/National%20Reports/ Population%20%20Housing%20Census%202011.pdf

8 MY FAITH IN HUMANITY IS SHAKEN

1 Recollections in this chapter are based on author interview with Gurbakhsh Garcha, Lewisham, London, 10 May 2017 and telephone interviews, early 2018.

9 DESH

1 Recollections in this chapter are based on producer interview with Harchet Singh Bains, Hitchin, 19 May 2017 and author interview 14 November 2017.

2 In her memoir, Bourke-White describes the caravans as having an 'Old Testament quality about them; and the massive suffering that was Old Testament too' (see text accompanying 'The Great Migration' collection of photographs, *Halfway to Freedom*).

10 MY MIND IS STILL CONFUSED

1 Recollections in this chapter are based on author interview with Karam Singh Hamdard, London, 4 May 2017, and subsequent telephone interviews, 2018.

2 Yasmin Khan, 'Why India and Pakistan remain in denial 70 years on from partition', *Guardian*, 6 August 2017.
3 Andrew Whitehead, 'Partition 70 years On – the Turmoil, Trauma and Legacy', BBC News Online, 27 July 2017.
4 Khan, 'Why India and Pakistan remain in denial'.

11 I HAVE SEEN THIS

1 Recollections in this chapter are based on producer interview with Swaran Singh Rayit, Hayes, 21 April 2017, and author interviews on 10 August 2017 and 14 March 2018.

12 SHE TOOK A STAND

1 For further reading see Rita Menon and Kamla Bhasin's *Borders & Boundaries: Women in India's Partition*, Rutgers University Press, 1998.
2 Author interview with Urvashi Butalia, London, 15 May 2017.
3 Butalia, *Other Side of Silence*, p. 138.
4 Ibid, p. 139.
5 Ibid.
6 Appeal in the *Hindustan Times*, 17 January 1948, quoted in Butalia, *Other Side of Silence*, p. 160.
7 Butalia, *Other Side of Silence*, p. 161.
8 Ibid, p. 164.
9 Andrew Whitehead, *India: A People Partitioned*, Episode 3, BBC World Service.
10 Butalia, *Other Side of Silence*, p. 227.
11 *The Day India Burned*, BBC Two documentary, 17 August 2007.
12 Butalia, *Other Side of Silence*, p. 241.
13 Recollections of Khurshid Begum, producer interview, Cardiff, 8 May 2017 and author interview with Khurshid Begum's son in early 2018.

13 THE GOOD OLD DAYS

1 Recollections in this chapter are based on author interview with Mohindra Dhall, Edinburgh, 17 January 2017, and subsequent telephone interviews, early 2018.

14 YOU HAD TO CHOOSE

1 Recollections in this chapter are based on producer interview with Haroon Ahmed, Cambridge, 19 December 2016 and author interview, 27 October 2017.

2 Gyanendra Pandey, *Remembering Partition: Violence, Nationalism and History in India*, Cambridge University Press, 2001, p. 122, quoted in Von Tunzelmann, *Indian Summer*, p. 282.

15 HORRIBLE DAYS

1 Recollections in this chapter are based on author interview with Maneck Dalal, Hampton, 25 January 2017 and Maneck Dalal's *An Indian in Britain*, draft of memoir, to be published in 2019 by Bharatiya Vidya Bhavan.

2 *Hindustan Times*, 25 July 2016.

3 *Cambridge Evening News*, 5 March 2017.

16 INDIA WAS MINE AS WELL

1 Recollections in this chapter are based on author interviews with Iftkahr Ahmed and Nick Yearwood, Brighton, 9 January and 15 June 2017 and subsequent exchanges in late 2017 and early 2018.

2 Sukeshi Kamra, *Bearing Witness: Partition, Independence, End of the Raj*, University of Calgary Press, 2002, p. 174. In Larry Collins and Dominque Lapierre, *Freedom at Midnight*, Harper Collins, 1997, they say: 'initially the Purana Qila had two water taps for 25,000 people. One visitor noted its inmates defecating and vomiting in the same pool of water in which women were washing their pots'.

17 THEY BECOME LIKE ANIMALS

1 Recollections in this chapter are based on author interview with Khurshid Sultana and Sarah Mohammed, Hertfordshire, 24 March 2017, and subsequent exchanges, 2018.

2 Talbot and Singh, *The Partition of India*, p. 121.

3 Ibid., p. 145.

4 Talbot and Singh, *The Partition of India*, pp. 145–6: a good explanation of tensions between the local population and the

Muhajirs, and how the latter became a political force with the formation of the Muhajir Qaumi Mahaz (MQM) party in 1984.

18 MOTHER, I HAVE COME HOME

1 Recollections in this chapter are based on author interview with Raj and Geeta Daswani, London, 11 February and 16 June 2017, and subsequent telephone interviews in 2018.
2 Uttara Shahani, 'Sindh and the Partition of India', Ph.D. thesis, University of Cambridge, September 2018, p. 176. Refugees themselves wanted to name the camp 'Sindhunagar' after Sind and some continue to refer to it as such.
3 Shahani, 'Sindh and the Partition of India', p. 176.
4 Sarah Ansari, *Life After Partition: Migration, Community and Strife in Sindh 1947–1962*, Oxford University Press, 2005, p. 56. Many came then because of a rare outbreak of communal violence in January 1948 in Karachi, when departing Sikh refugees were targeted by newly arrived refugees from India. This intensified the rate of non-Muslim departure from Sindh.
5 Shahani, 'Sindh and the Partition of India', p. 175.
6 Talbot and Singh, *The Partition of India*, p. 121. The 1941 Census shows of a population of over 386,000 around 180,000 were Hindu and 162,000 Muslims. https://archive.org/details/in.ernet. dli.2015.116051/page/n106.

19 LEGACY

1 www.ons.gov.uk/peoplepopulationandcommunity/cultural-identity/ethnicity/articles/2011censusanalysisethnicityandreligiono fthenonukbornpopulationinenglandandwales/2015-06-18
2 Susheila Nasta with Florian Stadler, *Asian Britain: A Photographic History*, The Westbourne Press, 2013, pp. 13–14. For a detailed and scholarly look at the long history of South Asians in Britain: Rozina Visram, *Asians in Britain: 400 Years of History*, Pluto Press, 2002.
3 Visram, *Asians in Britain*, p. 254.
4 See Peach, 'South Asian migration', pp. 133–46.
5 Claire Alexander, Joya Chatterji and Annu Jalais, *The Bengal Diaspora: Rethinking Muslim migration*, Routledge, 2016, p. 73. After partition, workers from Sylhet (now part of East Pakistan)

were abruptly cut off from Assam's tea gardens, as they were part of India. From 1948 the government of Assam put pressure on 'outsiders', particularly Muslims, to leave the state, and Sylhetis were among the thousands who were forced to return to East Pakistan. Partition also cut Sylhet off from Calcutta. India made it clear that Pakistanis were no longer welcome in the merchant marine. Two traditional streams of labour were disrupted.

6 Yunus Samad, 'The Pakistani Diaspora: USA and UK', *Routledge Handbook of the South Asian Diaspora, Routledge*, 2013, p. 195. Samad adds the connection to Mirpur and Britain, 'Mirpuris were sailors in the merchant navy, often working in the engine rooms, prior to the Second World War. With the outbreak of hostilities many came to work in the munitions factories in South Shields and established a bridgehead, which facilitated the arrivals of fellow countrymen.'

7 Clair Wills, *Lovers and Strangers*, Penguin, 2017, p. 61.

8 Ibid., p. 202. See also Roger Ballard (ed.), 'The Emergence of Desh Pardesh', *The South Asian Presence in Britain*, Hurst and Co., 1994, pp. 9–11.

9 Peach, 'South Asian migration', pp. 133–46. There was no official breakdown at that time of which regions on the Indian subcontinent people came from.

10 Joya Chatterji, *Routledge Handbook of the South Asian Diaspora*, Routledge, 2013, p. 192.

20 ROOTLESS

1 Recollections in this chapter are based on author interview with Veena Dhillon Wilks, Edinburgh, 17 January 2017, and subsequent telephone interview 7 May 2018.

2 Umbi Amar Dhillon, private papers, the Dhillon family.

3 'The Night of Flight', Dhillon papers.

4 'Escape', Dhillon papers.

5 'The Holy City', Dhillon papers.

6 'How Much Does One Feel?', Dhillon papers.

7 'Leaving India', Dhillon papers.

8 Ibid.

9 Ibid.

10 Ibid.

11 Ibid.

12 Ibid.
13 'Strangers Abroad', Dhillon papers.
14 'Leaving India', Dhillon papers.
15 The 1999 comedy drama film set in Salford centres on a Pakistani-born father, his English wife, and their mixed-heritage children.

21 WE SHOULD TALK

1 Poonam Joshi, *Arms to Fight, Arms to Protect: Women Speak Out About Conflict*, Panos Publications Ltd, 1995, p. 118.
2 Recollections in this chapter are based on an author interview with Poonam Joshi, London, 11 February 2017, and subsequent conversations during 2018.
3 Joshi, *Arms to Fight*, p. 115.
4 Ibid.

22 SILENCE

1 Recollections in this chapter are based on author interview with Tara Parashar, London, 29 April 2017, and subsequent conversations during 2017 and 2018.
2 Lady Pamela Hicks, *India Remembered: A Personal Account of the Mountbattens During the Transfer of Power*, Pavilion Books, 2007, p. 207.

23 MY FATHER

1 Recollections in this chapter are based on author interview with Ravi Datt Puri, Kent, December 2016, and subsequent conversations during 2017, as well as author interviews in 2014 and 2015 for the Radio 4 series *Three Pounds in My Pocket*.

EPILOGUE

1 Author interview with Dr Raychaudhuri.
2 Ibid.
3 Later that year in August 2017, the Partition Museum opened in Amritsar, India, founded by Lady Kishwar Desai.
4 Author interview with Canon Michael Roden, 26 April 2017, Hitchin.

CODA

1   Elif Shafak speaking to the *Guardian*, 18 July 2021.

2   Author interview with Maz Halima, 6 July 2021.

3   https://mazhalima.com/2017/08/14/partition-70-years-on/.

4   Ibid.

5   Author interview with Maz Halima.

6   Cited in ibid.

7   Author interview with Sparsh Ahuja, 27 June 2021.

8   Ibid.

9   Ibid.

10 Ciaran Thapar, 'It's time to smash down the wall on partition and imperialism', 23 August 2021, *GQ* magazine (https://www.gq-magazine.co.uk/article/india-partition-1947-representation).

11 Author interview with Ciaran Thapar, 8 June 2021.

12 Author interview with Yasmin Macé, 8 June 2021.

13 Author interview with Ciaran Thapar.

14 Author interview with Yasmin Macé.

15 William Dalrymple, 'Robert Clive was a vicious asset-stripper. His statue has no place on Whitehall', *Guardian*, 11 June 2020.

16 https://petition.parliament.uk/petitions/324092.

17 https://hansard.parliament.uk/Commons/2021-06-28/debates/21062855000001/BlackHistoryAndCulturalDiversity InTheCurriculum. It continues: 'The history curriculum gives teachers and schools the freedom and flexibility to use specific examples from history to teach pupils about the history of Britain and the wider world at all stages. It is for schools and teachers themselves to determine which examples, topics and resources to use to stimulate and challenge pupils and reflect key points in history.'

18 The Runnymede Trust says: 'At Key Stage 4, three GSCE modules on migration and empire already exist which schools can OPT to teach, but many fail to do so,' (https://www.runnymedetrust.org/blog/teachracemigrationempire-7-simple-actions-to-change-the-history-curriculum).

19 In their seven actions to change the history curriculum the Runnymede Trust says: 'The issue is not just what we teach, but how we support our teachers to deliver this content. To

accompany curriculum reform, we need a research-led national teacher training programme on empire, colonialism and migration that equips teachers with the confidence and subject knowledge to teach these important topics, and to help create anti-racist classrooms. The work of UCL's Centre for Holocaust Education provides an important blueprint for an effective research-led teacher education programme.' Groups like the Partition Education Group, British Library Sound Archive, for example, are currently working to provide resources.

20 Author interview with Shalina Patel, 25 August 2021.

21 See series 1-4 of *Three Pounds in my Pocket* on BBC Radio 4 that discusses this complex sense of belonging among the British South Asian diaspora

22 James Woods in his excellent essay 'On Not Going Home', (*London Review of Books*, Vol. 36, No 4, 20 February 2014), quotes Edward Said's essay 'Reflections on Exile': 'Exile is strangely compelling to think about but terrible to experience. It is the unhealable rift forced between a human being and a native place, between the self and its true home: it's essential sadness can never be surmounted ... The achievements of exile are permanently undermined by the loss of something left behind for ever.' Similarly, the Welsh word *hiraeth*, to which my friend Hannah MacInnes introduced me, means: 'A homesickness for a home to which you cannot return, a home which maybe never was; the nostalgia, the yearning, the grief for the lost places of the past.'

23 Aanchal Malhotra, in *The Language of Remembering* (Simon and Schuster, 2022), citing Marianne Hirsch on postmemory: 'She describes the term postmemory as a "relationship that the 'generation after' bears to the personal, collective and cultural trauma of those who came before" and how these experiences can be 'transmitted to them so deeply and affectively as to seem to constitute memories in their own right', *The Generation of Postmemory: Writing and Visual Culture after the Holocaust*, (Columbia University Press, 2012), p. 4.

24 Ibid.

25 Author interview with Binita Kane, 16 May 2021.

26 Ibid.

27 The Partition Education Group is closely affiliated with South Asian Heritage Month. It campaigns to include partition, South Asian and British colonial history into the UK national curriculum: https://partitioneducationgroup.wordpress.com.

28 Author interview with Sparsh Ahuja.

29 Ibid.

30 Author interview with Maz Halima.

31 Ibid.

32 Ibid.

33 Ibid.

34 Louise Carpenter interview with Edmund de Waal, *The Times*, 17 April 2021.

Acknowledgements

This book would never have happened without the con‑
tributors who trusted me to listen to and then tell their
stories. For so many, these experiences were not easy to speak
of, dredging up memories of difficult times.

It has been a privilege and an honour to have heard the
testimonies, but also to meet the interviewees and their fam‑
ilies. I am grateful to the contributors and family members
for reading, correcting and double-checking facts and details
of their chapters; and also to those who shared their personal
archives – photographs, letters, and personal documents. My
heartfelt thanks to all. Some contributors have died since
being interviewed, a reminder of how fortunate we were to
have heard their experiences.

The book is based upon interviews conducted for the Radio
4 series *Partition Voices*, commissioned by Mohit Bakaya. He
understood immediately the importance of documenting
these stories, ceaselessly supported me, and championed the
programmes. Hugh Levinson, the series editor, and one of the
kindest and cleverest colleagues I know, kept a firm, guiding
hand and ensured the series was as good as it could be. I was
blessed to have had Michael Gallagher as the series producer.
My researchers and producers, Ant Adeane and Tim Smith,

travelled round the country with me – from Dundee to Dorset. They showed unfailing respect and thoughtfulness to the contributors and cared about the project as much as I did. So much of this book is down to their hard work. James Harding, then head of BBC News and Current Affairs, backed the 'Partition Voices' project becoming a wider endeavour, and supported me in ensuring the anniversary was covered in a significant way. I am also thankful to James Montgomery, Marianne Bell, Jon Zilkha and Gavin Allen for funding the digital project. Ravin Sampat, Katie Lloyd and Sarah Lambley gave me endless encouragement. I am grateful to Jo Carr, Jim Gray and Neal Dalgleish in BBC TV Current Affairs for giving me the space from my day job to pursue this labour of love.

Mary Stewart, Rob Perks and David Govier at the British Library Sound Archive worked to make sure the testimonies will be kept for future generations. The transcripts of the original interviews can be viewed on the Sound Archive's website and the oral recordings accessed at the Sound Archive.

There were very many people and organisations who helped in the quest for contributors. Desi Radio, BBC Asian Network and BBC local radio did call-outs. And special thanks to: Reverend Canon Michael Roden, Kamaldeep Sandhu from the 1947 Partition Archive, Professor Radhika Mohanram, Sonali Campion, Marya Burgess, Susheila Nasta, Rav Sanghera, Sej Asar, Arshia Riaz, Bobby Tiwana, Trishna Singh, Koi Hai Association of Tea Planters, Ronen Dam, Dr Lakhu Luhana, Malcolm Deboo, Kensington and Chelsea Bangladesh Centre, Hamara Ghar Retirement Home, Derby Sikh Community Centre, Christian Missionary Society, Beera Mahli, Alyas Karmani, and Paul Sabapathy.

For their advice and knowledge thank you to: Jasdeep Singh of the National Army Museum, London; Lady Kishwar Desai, founder of the Partition Museum, Amritsar; Urvashi Butalia; Kevin Greenbank from the Centre of South Asian Studies, University of Cambridge; Sajid Iqbal and Hania Quazi for their help with translations. Uttara Shahani kindly gave me an advanced copy of her Ph.D. thesis on Sindh, which proved an excellent source. Particular thanks to Sue Dalal for a draft of the memoir about her charming father, Maneck Dalal, 'An Indian in Britain' (to be published by Bharatiya Vidya Bhavan, 2019) which was invaluable in the writing of his chapter.

Dr Anindya Raychaudhuri of St Andrews University generously assisted in finding contributors, and sent me an early draft of his book: *Narrating South Asian Partition: Oral History, Literature, Cinema* (Oxford University Press, 2019). Professor Sarah Ansari of Royal Holloway, University of London, kindly read some chapters and gave me important insights. Professor Joya Chatterji of the University of Cambridge has been a constant support and extremely gracious with her time and expert knowledge, from the radio programmes to the writing of this book, and I will for ever be grateful for all her red-pen comments on chapters. My former BBC colleague Andrew Whitehead, author and honorary professor at Nottingham University, was from the very beginning an avid cheerleader of the project. I drew on his excellent BBC World Service series *India: A People Partitioned*, which was broadcast to mark the fiftieth anniversary. He helped in finding interviewees and read a full draft of the book. I am sincerely appreciative of his assiduous notes.

My thanks too to my literary agents Louise Lamont and Danielle Zigner at LBA Books. My editor at Bloomsbury, Michael Fishwick, grasped what I wanted to do with this book, and its significance, from the very start. His advice to me was to write the book I wanted to write. I did, but very much with his expert help. The hard-working team at Bloomsbury kept me on track and made this book a reality. Thank you Kate Quarry, Kate Johnson, Ruth Killick and Lilidh Kendrick.

This book became much more personal than I ever intended. To my parents I owe so much. Their unconditional love, hard work and sacrifice have allowed me to be the person I am today. My parents-in-law are pillars of integrity and kindness, and have always supported me and the family. How lucky I am to have wonderful friends who have been with me through the ups and downs of life, and listened to me bang on about this book. My husband, Guy Leschziner, also shares a complex family history. He understood why this book mattered to me and read much of the manuscript, making many improvements. More importantly, he sustained me, as he always has, with love and belief along the way. My beloved girls have, mostly patiently, lived with my obsession for the past few years. This book is for them, when they are older, so they may understand a part of their history.

May 2019

Image Credits

Harchet Singh Bains: Tim Smith. Reproduced by arrangement with the BBC.
Khurshid Begum: Tim Smith. Reproduced by arrangement with the BBC.
Mohindra Dhall: Ant Adeane. Reproduced by arrangement with the BBC.

Young Haroon Ahmed: From a private collection.
Haroon Ahmed (b. 1936), Master (2000–2004), Professor of Microelectronics (1992–2004): © Louise Riley-Smith.
Kay and Maneck Dalal's wedding: From a private collection.
Young Maneck: From a private collection.
Older Maneck: Ant Adeane. Reproduced by arrangement with the BBC.
Iftkahr Ahmed with Sandra: From a private collection.
Iftkahr with son Nick: Ant Adeane. Reproduced by arrangement with the BBC.
Khurshid Sultana as a child: From a private collection.
Older Khurshid: Tim Smith. Reproduced by arrangement with the BBC.
Raj Daswani in a play: From a private collection.
Raj with Geeta: Tim Smith. Reproduced by arrangement with the BBC.
Raj with stones: Tim Smith. Reproduced by arrangement with the BBC.
Amar Dhillon: From a private collection
Veena Dhillon: Ant Adeane. Reproduced by arrangement with the BBC.
Nirmal Joshi with plaits: From a private collection.
Nirmal singing: From a private collection.
Poonam Joshi: Tim Smith. Reproduced by arrangement with the BBC.
Pran Parashar with Lord Mountbatten: From a private collection.
Pran's box: From a private collection.
Tara Parashar: Tim Smith. Reproduced by arrangement with the BBC.

Index

A Note on the Type

The text of this book is set Adobe Garamond. It is one of several versions of Garamond based on the designs of Claude Garamond. It is thought that Garamond based his font on Bembo, cut in 1495 by Francesco Griffo in collaboration with the Italian printer Aldus Manutius. Garamond types were first used in books printed in Paris around 1532. Many of the present-day versions of this type are based on the Typi Academiae of Jean Jannon cut in Sedan in 1615.

Claude Garamond was born in Paris in 1480. He learned how to cut type from his father and by the age of fifteen he was able to fashion steel punches the size of a pica with great precision. At the age of sixty he was commissioned by King Francis I to design a Greek alphabet, and for this he was given the honourable title of royal type founder. He died in 1561.